WORKERS ON THE MOVE

Cambridge studies in sociology

1 *The affluent worker: industrial attitudes and behaviour* by John H. Goldthorpe, David Lockwood, Frank Bechhofer and Jennifer Platt

2 *The affluent worker: political attitudes and behaviour* by John H. Goldthorpe, David Lockwood, Frank Bechhofer and Jennifer Platt

3 *The affluent worker in the class structure* by John H. Goldthorpe, David Lockwood, Frank Bechhofer and Jennifer Platt

4 *Men in mid-career: a study of British managers and technical specialists* by Cyril Sofer

5 *Family structure in nineteenth-century Lancashire* by Michael Anderson

Cambridge papers in sociology

1 *Size of Industrial Organisation and Worker Behaviour* by Geoffrey K. Ingham

2 *Workers' Attitudes and Technology* by D. Wedderburn and R. Crompton

3 *Perceptions of Work: Variations within a Factory* by H. Beynon and R. M. Blackburn

Workers on the move:
the sociology of relocation

MICHAEL MANN
Lecturer in Sociology, University of Essex

CAMBRIDGE
at the University Press 1973

CAMBRIDGE UNIVERSITY PRESS
Cambridge, New York, Melbourne, Madrid, Cape Town, Singapore,
São Paulo, Delhi, Dubai, Tokyo

Cambridge University Press
The Edinburgh Building, Cambridge CB2 8RU, UK

Published in the United States of America by Cambridge University Press, New York

www.cambridge.org
Information on this title: www.cambridge.org/9780521097871

First published 1973
Re-issued in this digitally printed version 2010

A catalogue record for this publication is available from the British Library

Library of Congress Catalogue Card Number: 72-88613

ISBN 978-0-521-08701-8 Hardback
ISBN 978-0-521-09787-1 Paperback

Contents

page vii Preface

1
1 Industrial relocation and the conurbations

2
9 Public attitudes to migration and relocation

3
40 The worker's dependence upon employment

4
68 The case-study company

5
105 The relocation

6
129 Movers and non-movers: relocation decisions

7
165 The movers in Banbury

8
203 The experience of the non-movers

9
213 Conclusions

242 Methodological Appendix
250 Questionnaires used
255 Bibliography
263 Index

v

To my Father and Mother

Preface

This book tells of the relocation of a factory: the complete move in 1965–6 of Alfred Bird and Sons Ltd (now General Foods Ltd) from central Birmingham to Banbury, in which a large proportion of the existing labour force was successfully transferred. My focus was the relocation decisions made by individual employees, each of whom was faced with the alternative of moving with the company to Banbury or of staying in the Birmingham area and finding other employment. By studying these decisions I have been able to submit to a critical test current sociological theories in a wide variety of fields, namely urban and regional planning, family and community sociology, and industrial sociology.

The first of the problem areas is a practical one. Industrial relocation plays an important part in urban and regional planning policies in this country, especially those geared to the relief of congestion and the poor living and working environment of Britain's six major city regions or conurbations. Ever since the last war central and local government plans to solve these problems have taken the form of 'overspill' of population from the conurbation to new developments, either on the fringes of the conurbation or further away in new and expanded towns. The volume of planned overspill has steadily increased and now, in 1972, the government is more or less committed to the overspill of over two and a half million people from the conurbations before the end of the century. Central to most overspill schemes is the relocation of jobs as well as the population; and thus the more that is known about industrial relocation, the easier it will be to fulfil the overspill programme.

At the moment, however, there are grave doubts as to the practicability and the desirability of the overspill programme which can only be resolved, one way or the other, by this kind of research. The programme may be wholly impracticable because of industry's refusal to relocate, and without a quota of factory and office jobs the new and expanded towns cannot function successfully. And the programme may be undesirable, because large sections of the population to be overspilled may not want to move. These two problems are linked, and one of the reasons for industry's reluctance to relocate is its belief that its employees are also reluctant.

Case studies usually offer only limited assistance in solving complex

problems because of the narrow area they cover. If, for example, I confined myself to describing how many employees of the case-study company relocated, and with what degrees of willingness, my results would
have little predictive power for relocations from other places, and none
at all for cases of overspill which did not include job movement. Any
general conclusions as to popular references for or against overspill must
be grounded on a general sociological theory of the nature of people's
relative commitment to family, community and employment. For example, if we want to know how many employees and of what type will accept
the offer of job transfer in an overspill scheme, we must analyse the
nature of their commitment to their present employment. But if we use
the term work commitment, and similar terms such as work dependence
and job satisfaction, we must first master the debates in recent industrial
sociology about the 'meaning' of work for the worker. Consideration of
these debates will help us to clear up what we mean by 'commitment to
employment' as well as providing us with a theoretical framework for predicting employee reactions to industrial relocation. The various policy
alternatives available to the conurbation planners involve varying degrees
of disturbance to family, community and employment. Hence any conclusions as to their respective merit must be based on knowledge of
people's ties to these aspects of life. This is the very general sociological
task that I will attempt in this book.

I have strayed far into industrial sociology in order to be of use to the
practical town planner. Yet I also hope that this case-study of industrial
relocation will illuminate the industrial sociology debates themselves
because of its two great methodological advantages. First, the relocation
decisions of employees, in a situation where they can either accept
transfer with their company and move house, or refuse transfer and lose
their job, provide useful evidence for the relative commitments they have
to work and non-work aspects of life. Obviously the reasons for their
relocation decisions must be considered carefully before we can arrive at
such conclusions. Second, the internal structure of the case-study firm
offers a convenient test of current theories of 'technological determinism'
in industrial sociology, as it employs large groups of workers in different
technological environments. By linking these themes together, I can use-
fully illuminate the relationship between technology, type of job, and
commitment to work.

The framework of a study must be judged by its results. The success of
the Birds relocation, its ability to show that the practical problems can be
overcome, owes nothing to me. I have, of course, acted as a publicist of
the company in explaining how the relocation succeeded. Yet the importance of my findings derives from the general sociological concepts with

which I have interpreted the case-study. I show in the course of this book that *employment dependence* is the critical determinant of relocation propensity, that modern technology is increasing employment dependence through the operation of the internal labour market, that working-class communities are a declining feature of contemporary Britain. These and other findings are of general sociological interest: they are also of use in the practical and political debates surrounding regional and urban planning.

The plan of the book is as follows. In Chapter 1 I describe the problems of the conurbations to which industrial relocation is so relevant. In Chapter 2 I look at existing data on individual and industrial mobility. In Chapter 3 I pursue the question of work dependence into the literature on industrial sociology. These chapters constitute the general background to the problem. Chapters 4–8 chronicle this case-study of relocation. Chapter 6 is the centre-piece, investigating with the aid of an interview survey of employees why such a large proportion of the male labour force accepted the relocation offer and which kinds of employee were more likely to do so than others. The reader interested in the methodology of my 'before and after' relocation surveys should turn to the Appendix before reading these chapters. In Chapter 9 I integrate the various strands of the argument and present my conclusions.

If this case study of relocation can be of general practical and theoretical use, many people besides myself will owe a debt to General Foods Ltd for co-operating so wholeheartedly with the study. The investigation and presentation of oneself, warts and all, is often tiresome at the very least, and I wish to thank all the employees of the company who gave so much of both their official and private time to assist me. Thanks are similarly due to officials of central and local government and of trade unions. For their criticisms of the Oxford D. Phil thesis on which this book is based I wish to thank Robert Blackburn, Alan Fox, John Goldthorpe and Jill Mann. As this has been a case of sponsored research, I ought to state more forcefully than is conventional among authors that the views expressed here are my own.

University of Essex   M. M.
   August 1972

1
Industrial relocation and the conurbations

I do not intend to give a detailed account in this book of 'the problem of the conurbations' or of the various policies that have been advocated as solutions to the problem. Excellent, if slightly dated, books are already available,[1] while the current and very recent situation would need a separate analysis of statistics such as the 1971 Census, combined with an 'insider's' view of the growing conflicts between the responsible planning authorities. Here I will merely summarise those problems and policies for which industrial relocation has a special relevance.

Since the Second World War the mobility of industry and its workers has been crucial to the major issues of conurban and regional planning. This has been most evident in the case of the prosperous conurbations of Greater London and the West Midlands, whose health has long been viewed as demanding a policy of industrial dispersal. In the last years this policy has been under severe, if sometimes covert, attack from several of the planning authorities concerned, and at the present time the conflict amounts to a real crisis in planning policy. The crisis turns critically upon the question of whether industry and commerce is willing to relocate, and this in turn is dependent upon whether employees are willing to relocate. These are the issues I will explore further in this chapter.

Central and regional government planning has been based since the war on a clear-cut diagnosis of the problem of the conurbations – they were congested. The overall solution seemed equally clear – either people or jobs or both must be dispersed outside present conurbation boundaries. This overall strategy has never been, and is still not, seriously questioned by any responsible planning authority. The dimensions of the public over-spill programme might be affected by the decline in the conurbations populations in the 1960s, by an increase in private overspill, by acceptable schemes of high-density redevelopment of the conurbations themselves, or by national economic stagnation. Yet it is agreed that *some* planned overspill is necessary if living standards and space are to meet modern expectations and if industry is to have room to expand. The second point on which there is broad (though not total) agreement is that the relief of the prosperous conurbations and the depressed areas should be linked.

---

[1] P. Self, *Cities in Flood* (Faber and Faber, 1961); P. Hall, *London 2000* (Faber and Faber, 1963).

1

Industry and offices should be hindered from expansion in the conurbations and encouraged to move to the Development Districts.

Two main alternatives for overspill present themselves. Either development could proceed at the fringes of the existing conurbations, or new and existing towns could be developed some distance away from the conurbation. The planners have generally convinced themselves that ideally the latter would be the better policy. On environmental grounds, and influenced by 'Garden City' ideals, they have generally deplored 'urban sprawl' and fought to secure a Green Belt for each of the conurbations. Fringe development is also probably more expensive because of land and conurban transport costs (particularly commuting costs). For these reasons, a main plank of the overspill programme was the development of New and Expanded Towns at some distance away from the conurbations. Of course, there remains the question as to how much of this kind of overspill should be planned, and debate has largely centred on the relative weight to be accorded to, (*a*) high-density redevelopment of the conurbation, (*b*) fringe development, and (*c*) New and Expanded towns. These are the main policy alternatives.

Since the war the advocates of the third policy have predominated. It was adopted by the post-war Labour government and continued by the Conservative governments of the 1950s. Its first prong was the New Towns policy, its second, since 1953, the Expanded Towns policy. While at first applied solely to London's problems, it was extended throughout the 1950s and 1960s to include schemes for New and Expanded Towns to alleviate congestion in all the conurbations. These schemes can be divided into four groups: the eight original New Towns in the South East, all established 1964–9 and virtually finished now; the large number of South-Eastern Expanded Towns, set up in the 1950s and 1960s and still operating on a small scale; the heterogenous New and Expanded Towns of the other regions, set up in the 1950s and 1960s and still very much in operation; and finally, the latest set of government proposals for large-scale development of existing towns and regions (South Hampshire, Peterborough, Northampton, Milton Keynes, Swindon–Newbury, Ashford, Chorley–Leyland, and the West Midlands 'corridor'). All those schemes together currently involve the relocation of about two and a half million people.

Nearly all these long-distance overspill projects combine housing overspill with industrial overspill. The normal New Town scheme, as officially stated, starts by attempting to attract employing organisations to the town, normally from within the conurbation to which the scheme is linked. These organisations can bring their entire labour force with them, and the Development Corporation of the town will provide transferred

2

employees with housing to buy or rent. People moved with their firms will have a variety of reasons for making the move but we can assume that many will do so primarily to retain their jobs. If, however, the incoming firm brings only a few 'key' workers or is a new firm, it will have to recruit new employees, and this it should do mainly from the housing-list of the conurbation local authorities, through the Industrial Selection Scheme (there is very little labour supply available from the existing population of the New or Expanded Towns outside of the Development Districts). Those recruited in this way can be expected to move largely for housing reasons. Thus, when we come to analyse popular preferences about policies, we will have to separate very carefully housing and industrial overspill, for different types of person will support the two main types of scheme. Most Expanded Towns follow the same dual pattern, but as the proportion of newcomers to existing inhabitants is so much smaller, existing industry will absorb many of the newcomers, and reduce the over-all importance of industrial relocation.[2]

Most New and Expanded Town schemes depend critically, therefore, on their ability to attract industry and commerce from the conurbations together with a substantial proportion of their employees. After twenty years of relative success, a crisis has now been reached – many signs indicate that industry is reluctant to move and some planners consider the reluctance to be justified. The consequences might well be to increase the relative weight accorded to high-density redevelopment and fringe over-spill.

The crux of the problem is that there is not enough mobile industry to carry out all government policies. At a national level the shortfall is now large. Present government policy for the designated New and Expanded Towns alone involves the future relocation of well over one million people.[3] For all projects outside the development areas, the need is for the transfer of 836,000 people by 1981, which implies an annual demand of around 16,000 jobs in manufacturing industry up to 1974 and 13,000 thereafter. Inter-regional movement of manufacturing jobs is currently at about 44,000 per year, of which the large majority goes (and will go in future as well) to the declining areas. It is probable that present trends will not allow sufficient industry to move into the New and Expanded Towns to fulfil all the current projects. The shortfall could only be made up by stronger government direction of industry to these schemes.

The problem is most acute in the Birmingham conurbation. Under the

---

[2] Except in the case of towns like Swindon where incoming industry has taken on labour from local declining industries.
[3] See two articles entitled 'New Town and Town Expansion Schemes' Part I by D.A. Bull in the *Town Planning Review*, 38 (1967) and Part II by D. Field, in 39 (1968) of the same journal.

West Midlands Economic Planning Council's 1967 estimates, 330,000 people are expected to move from the conurbation to overspill reception areas by 1981. For this 98,000 jobs in manufacturing industry must be moved with them, which amounts to thirteen per cent of the conurbation's manufacturing jobs. Previous experience offers little encouragement: in the period 1954–65 80,000 jobs left the conurbation but about three-quarters of them were transferred to development areas, leaving Birmingham's overspill estates as largely dormitory settlement.[4] In fact the area's local planning authorities themselves have estimated that only between 24,000 and 43,000 manufacturing jobs can be expected to move by 1981 under present policies.[5] It is obvious that something must be done – either the overspill programme, or the powers to encourage or force industry to move, must be changed. And it is obvious that a crisis has been reached when the two major planning organisations for the area are suggesting that the choice be made differently. While the West Midlands Economic Planning Council set up by the government is proposing new incentives to industry,[6] the local planning authorities advocate more wholesale peripheral development of the conurbation. The former involves the easing of I.D.C. restrictions on expansion in the region, the latter involves acceptance of industrial immobility, increased commuting, and erosion of the Green Belt (though talking grandly of the integration of urban and rural environments). However, even the former involves a reduction in contribution of the New and Expanded Towns programme from two-thirds to one-half of the total overspill, and the support for fringe development varies only in degree. What has caused this reversal of attitudes toward industrial mobility, a reversal also shared by the G.L.C. in London?

THE WILLINGNESS OF INDUSTRY TO RELOCATE

This is not the place, nor am I the person, to give a detailed cost–benefit analysis of alternative locations for industry. Yet on the face of it, industry's immobility might seem surprising. The costs that are easily quantifiable, like site and transport costs either show no marked differences between conurbation and 'outer ring' locations or, as in the case of rents, favour relocation.[7] Moreover, it is clear that many factories and offices in the conurbations are very congested. For example, in the Birmingham

---

[4] B. M. D. Smith, 'Industrial overspill in theory and practice: the case of the West Midlands', *Urban Studies*, 7 (1970).
[5] West Midland Planning Authorities, *A Developing Strategy for the West Midlands* (West Midlands Regional Study, 1971), p. 27.
[6] *The West Midlands: an Economic Appraisal* (H.M.S.O., 1971).
[7] For a review see, Hall, *London 2000*, pp. 57–66.

redevelopment plan we read that 'many factory owners have asked for alternative sites three to five times the area of those they at present occupy'.[8] This would probably apply to all the conurbations, even London where so much factory suburbanisation has already taken place. But London bears the brunt of the other major disadvantage of congestion: the suburbanisation of the labour force which increases recruiting difficulties, particularly of lower-level office staff.[9] Yet all these factors seem to be outweighed by industry's desire to be 'at the centre of things', to stay in touch with what is called the 'contacts market'. Different writers take with differing degrees of seriousness the claim by industrialists that they must stay in such close contact with their customers, their labour supply, and their competitors,[10] and the 'linkage' problem remains far from solved.

There is, of course, one special reason to be found within government policy itself for industry's reluctance to relocate, and this has emerged through the well-publicised conflicts between the former Ministries of Housing and Local Government and the Board of Trade. While the former has been committed to a policy of relocating industry to New and Expanded Towns, the latter has attempted to steer industry to the Development Districts. In the South and the Midlands these policies have been directly contradictory, with the Board of Trade having the whip-hand through its control over the granting of Industrial Development Certificates. In the early years of the South-Eastern New and Expanded Towns this did not greatly matter because there was then sufficient mobile industry to go round, but this is no longer so even in the South East. The imposition of I.D.C.s and O.D.P.s may have prevented industry from undertaking needed expansion anywhere, because of the belief that permission will only be granted in the distant and unattractive Development Areas. This seems more plausible in the case of factories rather than offices, where permission has very readily been granted to expand in overspill areas, but certainly the imposition of both I.D.C.s and O.D.P.s has resulted in a sharp fall in demand for extra floor-space within Greater

---

[8] *City of Birmingham Development Plan*, Approved Statement (1960) p. 24.
[9] Economist Intelligence Unit, *A Survey of Factors Governing the Location of Offices in the London Area* (Location of Office Bureau, 1964) p. 128.
[10] For a very sceptical view, see D. E. C. Eversley, 'Social and Psychological Determinants of Industrial Location' in T. Wilson (ed.) *Papers on Regional Development* (Blackwell, 1965); for the opposite view, on London, see J. H. Westergaard, 'The Structure of Greater London', in Centre for Urban Studies (eds.) *London: Aspects of Change* (MacGibbon and Kee, 1964); for a moderate view admitting imperfect knowledge, see Hall, *London 2000*. A recent advance in the problem of quantifying 'contact' and 'linkages' have been made in a research report by the Location of Offices Bureau, *Offices in a Regional Centre: Follow-up Studies on Infrastructure and Linkages* (L.O.B., October 1969).

London.[11] And all the bodies that complained to the Hunt Committee laid part of the blame on the Board of Trade's reluctance to grant I.D.C.s outside the Development Districts. The complaint was repeated so often to the Committee that it undertook some research on this point in the West Midlands and the South East.

It found, first, that whereas about half of all mobile jobs in the South East in the period 1945–65 stayed within the region, only a small minority of those in the West Midlands did so, with most of the remainder going to Development Districts. The Committee saw that the only way to decide if this constituted an obstacle to industrial relocation of any kind, was to go out and ask industry. It therefore commissioned surveys of industrialists in the two areas. Unfortunately, it obtained an extremely low response rate (only 25 per cent in Birmingham, 32 per cent in the South East), but for what it is worth it found only a minority of firms conscious of Board of Trade policy as an obstacle: for example, 13 per cent of Birmingham and 5 percent of London respondents claimed to have been deterred from even applying for I.D.C.s because of the Board's policy.[12] Moreover, the Committee recommended to the government that policy should be changed so that any firm in a conurbation should be allowed to expand in designated overspill areas if it wished.[13] If this is acted upon – and there will be pressures against this from the Development Districts – one obstacle will be removed to the fulfilment of the current overspill programme.

Yet, as Eversley has argued, it seems that there is at least an element of straightforward conservatism in industry's attitude, if only in the fact that most organisations do not consider relocation at all until it is literally thrust under their noses by severe shortage of space.[14] Thus, mere publicity of the advantages of relocation can increase the rate of actual relocation, as the experience of the Location of Offices Bureau has shown.[15] In Birmingham, moreover, suspicion exists that the planning authorities have done little to encourage the industrialists. Their general refusal to aid financially the overspill areas (claiming this to be a central government matter) and Birmingham's long series of applications to build dormitory estates on the edge of the city, have conveyed to some writers the impres-

[11] Greater London Development Plan, *Report of Studies* (G.L.C., 1968) p. 60.
[12] The Hunt Committee, *The Intermediate Areas* (H.M.S.O., 1969), pp. 104–6.
[13] *Ibid.* p. 145.
[14] Economist Intelligence Unit, *A Survey of Factors Governing the Location of Offices*, pp. 48, 91; the Annual Reports of the *Location of Offices Bureau*, e.g. that for 1967–8, Table 5, that for 1966–7, Table 5, p. 41, that for 1966–7, Table 5, p. 35; J. V. Aucott, 'Dispersal of Offices from London', *Town Planning Review*, 31 (1960) p. 44; and D. I. Trotman-Dickens, 'The Scottish Industrial Estates', *Scottish Journal of Political Economy*, 8 (1961) p. 50.
[15] *L.O.B., Annual Reports*, e.g. that for 1967–8, p. 5.

sion that the will to implement the principle of dispersal has long been lacking.[16] This is now openly acknowledged by London as well as Birmingham planners for both are arguing that their conurbations need economic expansion if actual stagnation is to be avoided.[17]

The economics of this argument are outside of my competence. But where the will is lacking, the rationalisations begin. Even though accurate information on linkage is not available, it is seized upon as a major argument for immobility. Similarly, there has arisen a general belief that employees will not relocate with their firms, even though accurate information is again lacking. The Regional Planning Council boldly stated 'the difficulty which many conurbation firms face over a move to the new towns is the reluctance of the people in the business on whom they depend to move with them.'[18] This is a view shared generally by businessmen. For example, a Location of Offices Bureau study found that office firms considering decentralising from London thought that staff difficulties were the major obstacle, and 36 of the 85 responses indicate that the firm anticipated losing much of their staff on relocation.[19] This view is also prevalent in Birmingham according to a Department of Trade and Industry official whom I interviewed:

> the overall impression I have is that taking your employees
> with you is not often considered seriously. I don't know
> whether they are correct or not, but they seem to believe that
> a lot of people are wedded to their own backyards.

But where does this view come from? One argument often advanced in support of fringe housing development is that 'this is the way in which housing needs would be met if there were no controls and so it may correspond most closely to what people want'.[20] But this is to confuse demand with choice – the controls imposed upon individuals then would be those of the housing market, and we have no way of knowing whether they would actually prefer this 'choice' to that presented by, for example, a New Town scheme. One would hope that the view was better supported than this, by actual studies of preferences. But this is rarely done, for the evidence is generally lacking. As the 'East Anglian Study' points out:

[16] Smith, 'Industrial overspill in theory and practice. . .'; D. Hall 'Underspill in the West Midlands', *Town and Country Planning* (May 1971).

[17] For a criticism of London's position see Town and Country Planning Association, *London under Stress* (London, 1970), and *The West Midlands: an Economic Appraisal*, West Midlands Planning Authorities.

[18] *Ibid.* p. 70, See also a similar statement, without supporting evidence by B. Loasby, 'The Experience of West Midlands Industrial Dispersal Projects', *Town and Country Planning*, 29 (1961) p. 312.

[19] Economic Intelligence Unit, *A Survey of Factors Governing the Location of Office*, p. 51.

[20] *The West Midlands: an Economic Appraisal*, p. 69.

7

'There is a serious lack of published research on the operation of planned migration schemes.'[21] Some studies do exist, but in view of their paucity and brevity it is necessary to combine them with other kinds of evidence. We can derive evidence for public opinion on overspill from four main sources:

(a) studies of voluntary migration – the numbers and types of migrants, and the distances they move;

(b) studies of local authority housing overspill schemes, that is where the relocation is based on rehousing over short distances;

(c) studies of the overall operation of New and Expanded Town schemes, that is where the total relocation is composed of mixed housing and industrial relocation;

(d) studies, usually case-studies, of industrial relocation.

In all these studies we have to consider not only the types of people making a choice of whether to move or not, but also the various aspects of the overall choice regarded as cost and benefit by them, together with the overall level of willingness with which they make their decisions. Furthermore, we cannot end our analysis at the time of the move but must also consider its after-effects. We must attempt to predict what kinds of people will be satisfied or dissatisfied after they have made their decision.

This is a very complex task. It can be only undertaken by building up a clear notion of the relationship between work and non-work for different groups in contemporary Britain. If we have a choice between offering carrots and sticks in the job sphere and in the housing sphere we need to know the relative importance for the people affected of work and non-work. This is the sociological task I will begin in the next chapert.

---

[21] East Anglia Economic Planning Council, *East Anglia: A Study* (H.M.S.O., 1968) p. 26.

2
Public attitudes to migration and relocation

Voluntary migration in Britain is certainly not infrequent. Every year around ten per cent of the population move house.[1] But the vast majority of moves cover only short distances. The 1961 Census revealed that half of those who had moved in the previous year had stayed within the boundaries of one local authority, while another quarter had moved 14 miles or less over a boundary. Furthermore, mobility and particularly long-distance mobility is significantly correlated with two factors, the occupation and the age of the household head: the younger, and the higher the occupational level, the more likely to move, and the more likely to move far.[2] Manual workers and men over the age of about 35 are relatively unlikely to move voluntarily over long distances.[3]

The age differences are easy to explain: they are the product of the family life-cycle. The Rowntree Trust study states this very clearly:

> there appears to be a cycle of movement, beginning with young new households who split off from existing households, rising to a peak of mobility among the small families with younger children, and declining through the later stages of family development to a relatively immobile old age.[4]

What of the other bias, the occupational differences? Why are working-

---

[1] In the 1961 Census, 11.3 per cent of the population of England and Wales are estimated to have moved house at least once in the period 23 April 1960 to 23 April 1961; in the Rowntree Trust Study, 15 per cent of people in England and Wales had moved between January 1960 and March or April 1962, an annual rate of about 7 per cent. The discrepancy is probably due to the fact that the Census counted all household members separately, and larger households were more mobile than smaller ones. Sources: Census 1961. England and Wales. *Migration Tables* (H.M.S.O., 1966), Table 12; V. B. Cullingworth, *English Housing Trends: a Report on the Rowntree Trust Housing Study*, Occasional Papers on Social Administration, No. 13 (G. Bell, 1965) p. 58.

[2] 1961 Census, Tables 2 and 16; see also Cullingworth, *English Housing Trends*, p. 60 and C. Jansen, *Social Aspects of Internal Migration* (Bath University Press, 1968), pp. 9–13.

[3] The 'bulge' among migrants from central cities to suburbs and from London to the Outer Metropolitan Area occurs slightly later, among household heads aged between 35 and 44. See Jansen, *Internal Migration*, p. 11; and the Sample Census 1966, England and Wales, *Migration Summary Tables*, Part II, Tables 12A and 12B.

[4] Cullingworth, *English Housing Trends*, p. 65. The principal American study also places the life-cycle at the centre of mobility processes: P. Rossi, *Why Families Move* (The Free Press, 1955) especially p. 9.

class people less likely to move? One plausible answer is that they might actually wish to find larger accomodation during the earlier stages of marriage but are unable to afford it. This problem is rendered more acute in contemporary Britain because of the decline of the privately-rented sector of the housing market. The working-class man is often unable to start buying a house, and has to remain immobile in order to qualify for a council house. Once in that house he is immobilised again because of the lack of alternative housing.[5] Among working-class households, financial factors probably hinder the life-cycle from making its full impact upon mobility. By contrast, work and financial factors reinforce the effects of the life-cycle among middle-class families. So let us now analyse this in some detail.

PATTERNS OF MIDDLE-CLASS MOBILITY

The careers of middle-class men have two main aspects, one familiar, the other perhaps unfamiliar. The former is the 'work-career' of the household head. The latter is the 'housing-career' of the family. The importance of the work-career of the middle-class family is obvious. As Watson puts it, most non-manual men,

> enter into life-careers of an almost identical pattern, whatever the nature of their work and the considerable variation in salaries. This pattern is a progress upon the ladder of promotion through competition for higher posts with greater responsibility and with higher salaries and prestige.[6]

But I think it is useful to differentiate these two career aspects because of the way that the housing market has increasingly cut across the labour market as a determinant of economic life-chances in Britain. Such idiosyncratic factors as the fluctuating availability of mortgages, employment in an organisation which offers mortgage assistance and guarantees, the state of the local housing market, the division of housing into several largely non-competing sectors (owner-occupation, council tenancy, controlled and decontrolled private tenancies, tied houses) – all these factors cut across simple wage and occupational levels in determining how much economic progress a person has made. Moreover, the influence of housing has been increased by specific government policies of housing

---

[5] Cullingworth, *English Housing Trends*, pp. 101–4.
[6] W. Watson, 'Social class and social mobility in industrial communities' in M. Gluckman (ed.) *Closed Systems and Open Minds* (Manchester University Press, 1964) pp. 144–5. For a discussion see C. R. Bell, *Middle Class Families* (Routledge and Kegan Paul, 1968).

subsidisation in the form both of council housing, and of tax relief on mortgage interest payments. The latter has a peculiarly progressive effect of course – it is 'sound economic sense' to be morgaged up to the hilt, and thus the incentive to move to a bigger house when one's income rises is increased. At this stage in the family life-cycle, moreover, the need increases with the number of children. Thus for those people, mostly in non-manual occupations, whose incomes are progressive, housing, family and work-cycles reinforce one another as determinants of standard of living. As the quality and price of housing in most cities and conurbations increases with the distance it lies from the city centre (with the outstanding exception of west central London), we can plot the fairly short distance moves of the middle-class family head with a fair degree of accuracy. As his salary increases he moves further from the city centre and hence, as we noted above, migrants from cities to suburbs tend to be older than other migrants. Their moves will also be normally to owner-occupied property, as can be seen readily from the character of the suburbs and the Green Belt communities, though the first move may be from privately rented accommodation which is heavily concentrated in inner city areas.

What now of middle-class migration over greater distances? Although long distance movers are disproportionately middle class (except in the case of international migration), we must remember that they are still a small minority of the middle class. Most middle-class people, though they may make more than one housing move in their lifetime, tend to stay within the same locality. The exceptions, those who move over long distances, are generally termed 'spiralists', and this returns us to the question of middle-class careers, this time to work-careers. Though most middle-class people do enjoy progressive work-careers, the character of this progress differs radically between *spiralists* and *locals*.

Spiralist is a very apt label for a man who moves around geographically in order to move up socially: his movement spirals outwards and upwards at the same time. The ideal-type of the spiralist is to be found in William H. Whyte's American 'Organisation Man',[7] a manager in a large corporation who moves around the country either at the corporation's bidding or while changing corporations. He is prepared to go anywhere to further his career. If, on the other hand, the middle-class man achieves his career progression while staying within one particular locality, he is termed a local. A specialised type of local is the 'burgess', the man who develops strong roots in an area and is predominant in its social and political life.[8]

[7] Whyte, *The Organisation Man* (Penguin edition, 1960).
[8] For a general discussion of these types see Watson in *Closed Systems and Open Minds* and Bell, *Middle Class Families.*

These types will obviously have differing mobility experiences. Can we then identify the groups which approximate to the ideal-types and make predictions about their attitudes to various kinds of migration?

The first point is that the spiralist is more likely to work for large and progressive industrial organisations, like I.C.I. or Unilever, who expect their managers to gain experience in a variety of their geographically scattered activities.[9] Moreover, the type of manager found in these organisations will be relatively willing, if changing jobs, to change districts as well. This is partly due to educational experience: university and some other forms of higher education may have already given him experience of living away from his area of upbringing, while his qualifications are recognisable to employers anywhere. Thus the government's 1963 survey on labour mobility found that educational qualifications were highly correlated with distance of migration, number of moves, and moves for work reasons: those with higher qualifications were much more likely to have moved long distances, several times and for work reasons.[10] Note however that not every geographical move will necessarily mean a change of employer for the spiralist in the large organisation. Thus the most recent large survey found that frequency of changing employment was not correlated with educational experience,[11] while a recent study by Sofer of a leading chemical company showed that the unusually highly educated managers there had rarely worked for another company and were heavily dependent upon their present employer.[12]

The greater frequency of migration by spiralists gives us another way of recognising them, by the district they live in. Recent movers are more likely to live in new houses. Thus, a new private housing estate will contain a larger proportion of recent movers who have already changed locality and are also contemplating changing again. Contrast, for example, the two most thorough studies of middle-class suburbs, by Willmott and Young in Woodford, Essex and by Bell in Swansea. In Woodford, a long-established outer suburb dominated by inter-war housing, though only 12 per cent of residents were born there 65 per cent of the middle-class (and 75 per cent of the few working-class) residents had lived there for 10 years or more. Moreover, only 23 per cent of the sample were born outside Woodford and the London area – the vast majority had moved out from London as they moved up in their careers.[13] On a new suburban estate

[9] Watson in *Closed Systems and Open Minds*, pp. 151–2.
[10] Government Social Survey, *Labour Mobility in Great Britain, 1953–1963* (H.M.S.O., March 1966). The statement about the distance of the move is only a plausible deduction from the other explicit findings on the pp. 11, 17 and 19.
[11] D. G. Clarke, *The Industrial Manager: His Background and Career Pattern* (Business Publications, 1966) pp. 88–9.
[12] C. Sofer, *Men in Mid-Career* (Cambridge University Press, 1970), chaps 9–10.
[13] P. Willmott and M. Young, *Family and Class in a London Suburb* (Routledge and Kegan Paul, 1960) pp. 3, 30.

12

in Swansea, however, the population was much more diverse in its mobility experience: of the 108 established households, 38 had previously lived in Swansea, but 47 had come from outside Wales altogether. Moreover, less than half the households expected to be living there in five years time, and all but 2 of the 44 households who expected to leave the Swansea locality had come from outside Swansea anyway. As Bell concludes, the division between spiralists and locals is a real one, and the estate divided into two main groups who, by and large, conformed to the ideal-types I have already presented.[14]

Finally, we must consider the age of the careerist. As we have already seen, age is a crucial variable in determining geographic mobility, and it obviously interacts with career progress in determining migration. Clearly a man who has in the past been a spiralist, but who is now at the top of his work career is relatively unlikely to move again in the future. Thus most of the people on the Swansea estates who did not expect to move at all in the next few years had not previously had purely local careers – what united nearly all of them was that they had reached the peak of their work careers (Bell terms them 'spent spiralists'). By and large, these were older men.[15]

Now we can generalise about the attitudes of middle-class people to migration. Compared to the studies, reported on later, of working-class people we have seen very little deep attachment to a local community. In the case of the spiralist in mid-career this is obvious: his work comes first, and his commitment to any local community will be minimal. But for the local or the 'spent spiralist' this may be almost as true. Willmott and Young compare the nature of community contacts in the settled suburb of Woodford with that of the contacts in working-class Bethnal Green. They argue that the level of psychological investment in the Woodford community is not as high as in Bethnal Green.[16] Thus, though the level of community participation of spiralists and locals alike may be high, their psychological dependence upon it is not.

This leaves the true 'burgesses', born and bred in the same area, though having moved house within it, and leading the social and political life of the community. These are men who clearly have deep roots in their community. Yet even with them, it is not a question of non-work life taking precedence over work life, for most of them are also tied by work to their locality. For the most part they are small businessmen and self-employed professionals, men whose whole lives, economic and non-economic, are bound up with the locality through interlocking ties with families, clients and committee colleagues.

[14] Bell, *Middle Class Families*, pp. 34–8, 159.
[15] *Ibid.* pp. 38–42.
[16] Willmott and Young, *Family and Class*, p. 129.

13

THE MIDDLE CLASS AND OVERSPILL POLICIES

It seems clear, then, that most middle-class people are not strongly opposed to geographical movement. Nearly all move house within a district, and many move between districts as well. Only 'burgesses' have deep roots within a particular community; while many others are active in their local communities, they are relatively willing to transfer their activity to other communities if their work and housing careers so dictate. As the policy alternatives for the conurbations are based principally on the manipulation of the housing and the labour markets it should be relatively easy to solve conurbation problems to the satisfaction of the middle class. This may even be so of long-distance overspill.

Long-distance movement is less normal among the middle class, being largely confined to 'spiralists', yet the heavy dependence of most middle-class people upon their work careers raises interesting possibilities for long-distance industrial overspill. If they are dependent upon their present employer they may well feel compelled to relocate with him if asked. Nor would there necessarily be marked differences between locals and spiralists in this respect. Whereas the spiralist may be more disposed to regard geographical mobility as part of his normal career pattern, the local may be more dependent upon his present employer. Moreover, as very few British managers do appear to change their employer after they reach the age of thirty or so, the dependence of nearly all, local or spiralist, on their employer might be fairly high. After all, the typical spiralist is possibly no more likely to change employers than the local. His career pattern typically consists of relocation-type situations in which he accepts geographical transfers within the same corporation in order to move up its hierarchy. And as neither group typically possesses deep roots within a local community, they might be very willing to relocate.

Obviously, these suppositions must be tested in actual cases of relocation. A study which can give us a little guidance was conducted by the Location of Offices Bureau on samples of office workers in Liverpool and central and outer London. In this study the office workers were asked whether they would move to various locations with their firms if they were compensated financially for the move. Among the men about two-thirds would move to fairly desirable locations (e.g. the South East outside London for the central Londoners) and a third to the most undesirable (Liverpool for the Southern samples). This represents quite a high degree of attachment to their employment, and one which was spread fairly evenly between age-groups and occupational levels. The age/sex/occupation breakdowns are not given in enough detail for us to be able to construct groups such as locals and spiralists, but it seems that the two

14

factors of age and the local – spiralist dimension might be cancelling each other out in this situation. For example, while younger men mention as a reason for accepting transfer their desire for a progressive career older men mention security and pension rights.[17] This, too, is evidence for the argument that most middle-class people in the conurbations would move out of the conurbations if certain housing incentives and job threats were part of public policy.

This is not the same as saying that middle-class people want to leave the conurbations, however. There is no evidence at present which would directly support such a statement. Certainly, more of them are leaving the conurbations than ever before; certainly, many others settle down in suburbs within the conurbation only because they have reached the peak of their work career and cannot afford to buy themselves more living-space. But at the moment we do not know how widespread these attitudes are. One indirect and rather unreliable guide might be the Government Social Survey study of labour mobility in which people were asked 'what sort of things would persuade them to move right away from their area of residence for work'. About half of the men, despite the bias of the question asked, replied that nothing would induce them to move. Though a breakdown of replies is not given by occupation, the better educated (and loosely 'middle-class') men were slightly more willing to consider moving. Those willing to move overwhelmingly pick out non-industrial areas as their preferred destinations.[18] The conurbations might seem rather unpopular, but whether this feeling is shared by their own population, middle or working class, remains unclear.

INTERMEDIATE GROUPS

In dealing with middle-class people I have made several assumptions about them which over-simplified reality for the sake of clarity of argument. I assumed that most non-manual workers have progressive careers; that after the first few years of marriage they will live in owner-occupied property; and that privately owned housing areas contained only non-manual workers. As later in this section I will be tending to make converse assumptions about manual workers, i.e. that they do not have progressive work careers and do not live in owner-occupied property, I ought now to deal with the intermediate groups that confuse this simple

---

[17] Location of Offices Bureau, *White Collar Commuters – A Second Survey* (L.O.B., June 1967) Part VII.
[18] Government Social Survey, *Labour Mobility*, pp. 23–31. We should not place much reliance, however, on results based on such a hypothetical question.

picture. The distribution of types of household tenure by occupational groups is given in Table 1. These figures are drawn from the 1966 Sample Census for England and Wales. To classify occupations I have compressed the Registrar General's Socio-Economic Groups, excluding those not relevant for my purposes here. Remember that these groups are not representative of the country as a whole. Excluded are all the agricultural groups, members of the armed forces, the unclassifiables and those not in employment. My intention is to show housing trends within the relatively urbanised employed population.

Table 1: *Housing tenure by occupation of household head England and Wales, 1966 (% of households)[a]*

Occupational groups, with Registrar-General's reference No.	Housing tenure		
	Owner-occupied %	Rented from council %	Other %
Higher non-manual (Groups 1–5)	71	8	21
Lower non-manual, and small self-employed (Groups 6–8)	51	21	28
Skilled manual (Group 9)	41	34	24
Semi-skilled and unskilled manual (Groups 10–11)	30	40	30
All these groups	48	27	26

[a] Sample Census 1966. England and Wales. *Housing Tables Part I* (H.M.S.O., 1968) Table 8*A*.

From this table we can see that several of the assumptions made so far have been over-simple. Though the higher non-manual groups are overwhelmingly owner-occupiers (and those that are not will be mostly young adults), only 51 per cent of the lower non-manual group are buying their own houses. In this group are most clerical and sales workers, foremen and supervisors, and self-employed people with very small businesses. They are certainly not 'spiralists', and few will have had very progressive careers: either they will have already achieved what little progress they can and tend to be council tenants, or they will tend to be younger men with possible future promotions, in which case they are likely to swell the proportion with 'Other' tenancies in Table 1. When dealing with local authority overspill schemes in the next section of this chapter, we must bear in mind that a significant minority of households involved will be 'lower middle class'.

A larger 'deviant' group is composed of manual workers buying their own houses. We can see that no less than 41 per cent of the skilled and 30 per cent of the less skilled manual workers are owner-occupiers. However, it is probable that the majority of these will not be residing in the type of residential area like Woodford or the Swansea estates we have already examined. More likely areas are those new housing estates which offer the lowest-cost private houses and the older, cheaper terraces in inner urban areas. There is little statistical evidence available to re-inforce this commonsense observation, but some support may be found in the occupancy rates given in the 1966 Census. Whether in owner-occupied, council rented, private rented, or other accommodation, manual workers' households have a higher occupancy rate and a higher pro-portion are overcrowded than among the non-manual groups. Moreover, if we consider the conurbations alone, working-class housing emerges as slightly more distinctive. All the conurbations except South-East Lan-cashire and (marginally) West Yorkshire have a lower proportion of owner-occupiers among manual workers than in England and Wales as a whole. Furthermore, the owner-occupier manual workers in the con-urbations are disproportionately likely to live in worse housing.[19]

Thus the overlap between manual and non-manual households in the conurbations is rather less than appeared at first sight. Working-class persons are less likely to be owners, more likely the renters of their dwellings, and whatever the tenures are more likely to live in crowded, sub-standard housing. Perhaps this point should be brought out more in the case of council property, for one can be misled by the appearance of suburban council estates and new tower-blocks into thinking that these are the typical council dwellings of the conurbations today. In fact, a great deal of the sub-standard property in the conurbations is under local authority ownership, though this varies greatly between the con-urbations. London's council property has a much higher occupancy rate than its owner-occupied sector, and though very few of its council pro-perties now lack basic sanitation facilities those which do lack them are overwhelmingly concentrated in the working-class 'housing stress areas' of inner London.[20]

So when dealing with the housing preferences of the conurban working class we cannot assume that poor housing conditions are to be found only among those at present in privately-rented or 'other' accommodation. There will be many other manual workers either already in council pro-

[19] Sample Census 1966, England and Wales, *Housing Tables Part 1* (H.M.S.O., 1968).
[20] G. L. C., *Report of Studies*, pp. 21–8.

17

perty or buying their own houses who will be rather overcrowded and lacking normal sanitation facilities. Thus it is that we find people wanting to move out of their present accommodation in all types of tenure. This is probably most marked in Glasgow, but it is for Glasgow that we have the best source of information, Cullingworth's *A Profile of Glasgow Housing*.[21]

Cullingworth centres his findings on the concept of family life-cycle and so distinguished between new households (mostly at marriage) and continuing households (where an existing household moves on). Because very few newly marrieds are eligible for council housing, they are forced onto the private housing market, and where older, dilapidated houses are available for purchase in large numbers, this is where they will often start their married life. Of those new households formed since 1961 in his sample, 40 per cent moved into owner-occupied property, for which the average price was only £1,000, and (predictably) 45 per cent moved into privately rented accommodation. But as their family grows, they start to want larger better dwellings. Cullingworth found that 18 per cent of households were intending to move when interviewed, in the sense that they had actually started to make moving arrangements. Almost all of the intending movers had applied to Glasgow Corporation for rehousing in council property, whether they were buying or renting their present accommodation, and owner-occupiers were only slightly less likely to be intending movers to council property than were renters. Thus the sample showed fairly uniform housing preferences whatever their present tenure, and the dominating reason for wanting to move among all groups was a desire to increase housing size to cope with a growing family. This is, of course, very similar to the preferences of younger middle-class people as well. Indeed, the London Housing Survey found that the desire to increase the size and improve the quality of housing was easily the most important reason for moving given by existing households.[22]

MANUAL WORKERS AND HOUSING OVERSPILL SCHEMES

With working-class people, however, we can move beyond studies of voluntary mobility and of hypothetical housing preferences, for we can examine the actual workings of local authority housing schemes. Luckily

---

[21] J. B. Cullingworth, *A Profile of Glasgow Housing*, University of Glasgow Social and Economics Studies, Occasional Paper No. 8 (Oliver & Boyd, 1968) especially chap. 5.

[22] G.L.C., *Report of Studies*, p. 16. Note that both the Glasgow and London surveys found that, at the other end of the family cycle, the converse held: the most important reason for the movement of elderly households was to *decrease* the size of the accommodation.

for our purposes, both high-density and housing overspill types have been extensively studied by sociologists. Moreover, the group of early studies inspired by the Institute of Community Studies in Bethnal Green has exerted a considerable influence on the beliefs, though not the policies, of town planners. The belief can be summarised thus: working-class people in the conurbations welcome the housing improvement offered by over-spill, but deplore its consequences on their social lives. If this is indeed true, perhaps high-density rebuilding, involving least disturbance to social relations, is the policy most preferred by the working class itself. I will now turn to the studies on which this belief was based, and then examine the criticisms it has drawn before returning to the implications of the debate upon policy alternatives.

The early 'orthodoxy' of the Institute of Community Studies has (perhaps unkindly) drawn upon itself the description: 'The more we are together, the happier we shall be.' Certainly, the essential finding of this group of studies (and, indeed, of other studies too) is that the majority of residents in traditional working-class areas in Britain's towns are deeply attached to their local communities and do not want to leave them. This has been claimed for Bethnal Green in London by Willmott and Young and by Townsend; for the Gorbals in Glasgow by Brennan; for 'Crown Street' in Liverpool by a team of Liverpool University sociologists; and for Swansea by Rosser and Harris.[23]

Yet the preferences revealed in these studies are by no means straight-forward. They contain many elements, some of which are not always present in central areas or absent in peripheral estates or new towns. The following are the most important advantages of the central areas sur-veyed: their abundance of facilities, the long residence of their inhabitants, their provision of jobs, and their low cost of living.

Willmott and Young base their argument on the second point. Fifty-three per cent of their general sample were born in Bethnal Green. This means that they were surrounded by their families and had frequent contact with them. They found that each member of the extended family served as a go-between with other people in the district, and by this in-direct link a sense of community was built up. The extended family provides services and significant social gatherings: grandmothers look after grandchildren while the mothers are at work, the old and sick are cared for by their children, social life is composed of family gatherings,

---

[23] M. Young and P. Willmott, *Family and Kinship in East London* (Penguin Books, 1962 edition). P. Townsend, *The Family Life of Old People* (Routledge and Kegan Paul, 1957). T. Brennan, 'Gorbals: A study in redevelopment', *The Scottish Journal of Political Economy*, 4 (1957) pp. 114–26. University of Liver-pool, Department of Social Science, *Urban Redevelopment and Social Change* (Liverpool University Press, 1961) p. 93; C. Rosser and C. Harris, *The Family and Social Change* (Routledge and Kegan Paul, 1965) p. 58.

and the family circle is the main source of help in a variety of problems.

With such attachments to their community, they argue, there is one factor alone which persuades families to accept housing overspill, and that is the housing improvement offered. And indeed this has been shown in all the studies of overspill based on rehousing to be the major inducement to move, even by those writers critical of the above argument.[24] If the move is for housing alone, adjustment to the other changes brought about by the move may prove difficult. And indeed the argument proceeds to describe all the difficulties experienced by overspill families in their new estates. They are unable to cope with community life. They have never joined formal associations which do not have a family basis, and they are separated from their kin. They have ill-developed skills in making new friends, born out of lack of practice in handling formal invitations and introductions. They will thus be unhappy on the new estate. Indeed, Young and Willmott bring forward impressionistic evidence which appears to support all this with respect to an overspill estate, Greenleigh in Essex.[25]

Let us pause here for a moment and assume that this argument is valid. What then would be the implications for policy? One question would immediately arise: if such families want an improvement in housing but do not want to leave their present communities, would they accept high-density living in the central areas? If they would, this constitutes an argument against overspill of any sort.

Traditionally, evidence on the houses v flats debate has been brought to bear at this point. However, recent research has concluded not only that high flats have no social advantages but that they are not even efficient means of building at high densities.[26] Increasingly, high density rebuilding of the conurbations means either renovating existing property or building new, low-rise, terraced dwellings. This can more easily preserve existing communities, and if Young and Willmott are correct we should expect this to be a popular policy.

However, the detailed findings of Young and Willmott have been subsequently challenged. In the first place, it is held, no attempt has been made to separate the effects of Willmott and Young's crucial variable, the effects of long residence, from those of the other elements mentioned above. Bethnal Green, an unusually settled community, may not be a

[24] For example J. B. Cullingworth, 'The Swindon Social Survey: Second Report on the Social Implications of Overspill', *Sociological Review*, 9 (1961).
[25] Young and Willmott, *Family and Kinship in East London*, pp. 97–166.
[26] This unequivocal conclusion has been reached by P. Jephcott, *Homes in High Flats* (Oliver and Boyd, 1971).

good base for predicting the preferences of residents of other working-class areas, while, in any case, if long-residence is the determinant of a sense of real community, then the overspill estates might eventually become communities. Secondly, Willmott and Young admit that major complaints at Greenleigh are that there are no jobs and few public and commercial facilities provided locally, but they do not assess the contribution of these complaints to the general malaise they find. In two articles, Cullingworth has done this on overspill estates in Worsley in Lancashire and Swindon in Wiltshire.[27] At Worsley he also found complaints about the lack of local work available, a lack which forced 70 per cent of his sample to spend at least 90 minutes and 2s 6d per day on commuting. He also noted that rents in Worsley were three times as high as they had been in Salford. The result was a fair amount of dissatisfaction: 10 per cent of families had already returned to Salford and another 17 per cent said they wanted to return. But discontent with the stretching of extended family ties played very little part in this.[28] Twenty-two per cent of families had actually brought a 'Mum' with them; most of the other 'Mums' were well able to look after themselves and many were working. Indeed, relief was sometimes expressed by young married couples that they had got away from the 'interfering . . . !', who had previously attempted to dominate their lives. Cullingworth's point is also supported by the case of Swindon: all the sample worked locally but virtually all were at least 70 miles from their extended families. Thirty-two per cent of those separated from some or all relatives said they disliked the separation; 19.5 per cent further said that it caused hardship (either because the wife's parents were now living alone, or because two rents were being paid instead of the one paid in London). Yet when the sample went back to visit their families they reported that their dominant feelings were incredulity at their ever having lived in such bad housing and relief at getting back to Swindon. Their happiness about their new housing standards outweighed all other feelings they had about Swindon. This makes clear that Young and Willmott failed to control another factor present in Bethnal Green: that married couples were probably living with parents only because of the lack of alternative accommodation. Working-class people are often forced rather than choose to live with their extended families. In Swindon only 14.3 per cent of families wished to leave, and few of their reasons

[27] Worsley: J. B. Cullingworth, *Housing Needs and Planning Policy* (Routledge and Kegan Paul, 1960) pp. 163–8; Swindon: Cullingworth, 'The Swindon Social Survey', pp. 151–66.
[28] Similar results are revealed on a Macclesfield overspill estate, where the dissatisfied residents gave job and commuting factors and not extended family separation, as their grumbles. J. N. Jackson, 'Dispersal – success or failure', *Journal of the Town Planning Institute*, 45 (1959).

were directly attributable to family separation. He concludes: 'The intimate social life of a working-class area has given way to the more reserved home-centred life of the typical middle-class suburb. For the majority of families this change has been welcomed.'

Similar findings emerge from other studies of overspill schemes in which the jobs and services, so stressed by Cullingworth, were also provided. The 1967 survey of Cumbernauld residents found that 75 per cent thought they had bettered themselves by coming to Cumbernauld, 87 per cent had generally favourable reactions to the town, and over 90 per cent regarded the other residents as being as friendly as the people where they last lived.[29] And even where overspill groups are dissatisfied in their new environment this does not necessarily mean that it is the move itself they dislike. Thus Rankin found that in Kirkby, an overspill are area for Liverpool, 58 per cent of his sample wished to leave their present accommodation, while 34 per cent wanted to leave Kirkby altogether. But as with Cullingworth's samples, it was specific factors like the cost of commuting, and the actual layout of the new house that they objected to, for most did not want to go back to their old area.[30] And finally, whatever the nature of the grumbles, and despite the publicity given to 'new town blues', medical surveys show no discernible increase in neuroses among overspill groups.[31]

But does all this evidence prove that the people involved actually welcome overspill, as Cullingworth claims it does? In fact, he has demonstrated something less clear-cut; that on balance the housing benefits outweigh the social costs of overspill. Most overspilled working-class groups do experience a 'retreat into the home'. Cullingworth has not shown that the home-centred life itself is welcomed as an improvement on a life dominated by the extended family. It is now well established, both in British and American studies, that the stereotype of the suburbanite as a 'frantic socialiser' is only accurate for middle-class residents. By contrast, working-class families moving to suburbs have generally experienced a social isolation at least in the initial years.[32] The greatest

---

[29] A. J. M. Sykes *et al.*, *Cumbernauld 67: A Household Survey and Report* (University of Strathclyde, Dept. of Sociology, n.d.) pp. 16, 30–1.

[30] N. H. Rankin, 'Social Adjustments in a North-West New Town', *Sociological Review*, 11 (1963) pp. 289–302.

[31] See Lord Taylor and N. S. Chave, *Mental Health and Environment* (Longmans, Green and Co., 1964) Chap. 20; and P. Hall, 'Moving house in the aetiology of psychiatric symptoms', *Proceedings of the Royal Society of Medicine* (February 1964).

[32] The main North American studies are B. M. Berger, *Working-Class Suburb* (University of California Press, 1960); W. M. Dobriner, *Class in Suburbia* (Prentice-Hall, 1964); H. J. Gans, *The Levittowners* (Allen Lane, 1967); and S. D. Clark, *The Suburban Society* (University of Toronto Press, 1966) p. 140.

losses in social life are obviously felt by suburban housewives, left on their own amid strangers during the day.[33] And, again reinforcing Willmott and Young's arguments, working-class wives feel more cut off than middle-class wives from the families and friends near their previous homes. Yet this discontent must be kept in perspective: in Levittown, for example, general loneliness affected working-class women no more than middle-class ones and, like boredom, it afflicted only a minority.[34]

If we wish to attempt to reconcile the findings of Willmott and Young with those of Cullingworth and the North American sociologists, we must look back to the experiences of their samples before they moved, as their social malaise after a move is based largely on unfavourable comparisons with their previous situation. The loneliness of the Greenleigh respondents can only be understood by remembering that they come from Bethnal Green, where their extended families had in the past provided them with close and continual social support. It is difficult to compare them in this respect with the Worsley and Swindon samples, but Cullingworth implies that the latter were less willingly embedded in extended family networks than were the Bethnal Greeners. Taylor's study of migrating coal miners tests this kind of hypothesis. He finds evidence of a retreat into 'home-centredness' among the migrants, but whether this is experienced as a deprivation depends primarily upon the nature of the migrants' ties with their previous communities in Durham. Those less tied to extended family and community in Durham were more likely to adjust satisfactorily to their new environment.[35] Gans comes to a similar conclusion among the Levittowners: those who admitted to being lonely in their previous surroundings were the least likely group to be lonely after they moved.[36]

The crucial question, then, in an assessment of people's attitudes toward residential moves seems to be 'to what extent are they already involved in extended families of the Bethnal Green type?' And here again it has been suggested that the Bethnal Greeners may not be typical of present-day working-class people. Sociologists both in Britain and the United States have suggested that this type of extended family is on the decline, being replaced by what is termed the 'modified extended

---

[33] Clark, *The Suburban Society*, p. 141.
[34] Gans, *The Levittowners*, pp. 226–30.
[35] R. C. Taylor, *The Implications of Migration from the Durham Coalfield: an Anthropological Study* (University of Durham, Ph.D. thesis, 1966) Chap. 6.
[36] This study, like all those previously mentioned except Taylor's, base comparisons between before- and after-move experiences on the respondents' recollection of the former *after* they have moved. They are therefore likely to suffer from the customary defect of recall bias. The present study, like Taylor's, is a true 'before and after' study and is freed from this defect.

family.' This includes the same personnel as the 'traditional' extended family but its functions have been somewhat reduced. The functions are now: aid in times of crisis; and the provision of a certain sense of social solidarity between family members.[37] Aid in times of crisis can be supplied from a distance by a relation staying with the nuclear family for short periods. In Hubert's sample of middle-class Londoners for example, there was no relationship between geographical distance and the amount of help given by mothers to daughters during their confinement for child-birth; most mothers came to stay for at least one confinement.[38] The sense of social solidarity can also survive over long distances necessitating infrequent contact. Rosser and Harris conclude from their Swansea investigation:

> The [modified] extended family thrives on face-to-face contact, but it does not depend on it. It can exist as a recognised social entity for its participants even when contact drops to a barely-perceived minimum – the occasional letter or Christmas card, the unexpected visit after a long interval – and when relationships appear dormant or in a state of suspended animation.[39]

The continuance of the 'modified extended family' over long distance is made possible by the wide spread of car ownership and the speed and cheapness of modern transport systems.[40]

We can see now that the 'modified extended family' is very different indeed from the classical conception of the extended family. Indeed it may actually be rather closer to the other classical ideal-type, the nuclear family.[41] If there is a convergence of life-styles toward this type of family structure, as Rosser and Harris suggest, then the barriers to mobility set up by the classical extended family are removed. Indeed, they noted that younger respondents in Swansea were more favourably disposed toward moving away from long-settled working-class communites dominated by their extended kinship networks. They state

> The evidence from our survey and from our analysis of housing applications confirms . . . a marked willingness on their part to move out of these areas, and a strong desire to give their children an opportunity to grow up in the modern social and cultural

---

[37] Rosser and Harris, *Family and Social Change*, chap. VI.
[38] J. Hubert, 'Kinship and geographical mobility in a sample from a London middle-class area', *International Journal of Comparative Sociology*, 6 (1965).
[39] Rosser and Harris, *Family and Social Change*, p. 288.
[40] See also E. Litwak, 'Geographic mobility and extended family cohesion', *American Sociological Review*, 25 (1960).
[41] The study by R. Firth, J. Hubert and A. Forge, *Families and their Relatives* (Routledge and Kegan Paul, 1969) concludes that the extended kinship system of the middle-class sample was so structurally weak that no precise meaning could be given to the term 'extended family' (p. 456).

conditions of the affluent west of Swansea rather than in the grim and drab industrial east (for all its old-fashioned cultural strengths and virtues). Time and again we noticed in our analysis of housing applicants – and in our detailed interviewing – how young married couples preferred relatively distant housing estates, public or private, on the west to nearby estates close to their work and their elderly relatives . . . preferring obviously to get right away to a new social environment and a new way of life altogether.[42]

This is an important statement, though it is one which tends to outrun the authors' own evidence. It suggests that movement away from traditional working-class areas is not merely a product of housing need but also of decline in the attractiveness of the areas as communities. Hints of this were also seen in Cullingworth's articles, where a minority of overspill families had been actually glad to be away from the old community, dominated by extended families. Moreover, large-scale coloured immigration into many of these traditional working-class areas in the conurbations can only have furthered a decline in white working-class attachments to those areas. But to what extent this has occurred, and whether it is confined to younger people (as Rosser and Harris suggest) are unknown at present. We are left with contradictory interpretations of working-class attitudes to overspill. The most likely assumption is that working-class people are more divided over the issue than either group has suggested. This is certainly the conclusion to be drawn from Dennis' study of rehousing in Sunderland in which a majority of the inhabitants of some slum areas opposed rehousing but the majority of others approved it.[43] More research is obviously needed.

So far I have raised rather than settled problems regarding the preferences of working-class people. One point is clear – that their housing preferences are not dissimilar to those of middle-class people. In this respect they do not wish for absolute immobility, for they are also willing to change their housing in response to changes in their life-cycle. The remaining problem is how far will they move for this? Their community attachment is stronger than that of the middle class, and this may well constitute a far stronger obstacle to long-distance mobility. Such an obstacle among the middle class is normally removed by the emphasis non-manual workers place on their work-careers. Does this also neutralise the stronger community attachments of the working class? Let us turn now to a detailed consideration of overspill in which work and non-work

---

[42] Rosser and Harris, *Family and Social Change*, p. 60.
[43] N. Dennis, *People and Planning*, (Faber and Faber, 1970) Section IV. Note that the rehousing proposed was not of the overspill type, however.

factors are equally involved for manual workers, the experience of the New and Expanded Towns.

We have seen evidence that if housing overspill is unpopular, this may be because of its dependence upon rehousing alone. So let us now analyse the more inclusive type of overspill upon which the New and Expanded Towns have been based. In these towns (at least in the ones we will now consider) jobs and the normal services of a self-contained town have been provided as well as housing, and some of the overspill families will have actually moved as 'key workers', i.e. primarily for a job rather than a house.

We might also expect that these different factors may lead to differences between the types of people who will accept overspill. Consider for a moment the question of their age-structure. In this Chapter we have seen that among middle class and working class alike younger adults are more likely than older ones to move for housing (and possibly for environmental) reasons. But we might expect the reverse to occur in an industrial relocation where the alternative to transferring with one's job is to lose that job. For we have good reason to suppose that the older worker is more dependent upon his present employer than the younger one. It is obvious that the older employee, particularly the man approaching or over 50, is less able to sell himself to a new employer than his younger rival. His remaining working life offers less time to repay to the employer any cost incurred in training him, he is in any case less adaptable to new work routines, he probably possesses fewer paper qualifications (because of the recent expansion of eduction), he is suspect because he has spent longer reaching the same level as his younger rivals. Studies confirm the rather obvious point that late-middle aged and above men have greater difficulty finding employment if made redundant than younger ones.[44] Usually, older employees are well aware of this, and they try to make sure that they do not often appear on the labour market. Thus Margot Jefferys found that in the period 1945–51 the percentage of manual workers and lower clerical and supervisory staff who had not changed their job ranged consistently between 44 per cent in the 20–4 age-group to 78 per cent in the 45 and over

---

[44] For examples, see the two studies by Dorothy Wedderburn, *Redundancy and the Railwaymen* (Cambridge University Press, 1965) p. 80 and *White-Collar Redundancy: A Case Study* (Cambridge University Press, 1964) pp. 21–2.

26

group.[45] It should therefore be safe to predict that older men are more dependent on their employer and more likely to relocate with him.

Thus we would expect that in any particular case of total industrial relocation, these two age-related mechanisms would operate in contradictory directions, with younger workers more likely to accept job transfer for housing but less likely to for work reasons. This has been confirmed in a detailed American study of the relocation of a large group of automobile workers from San Francisco to Los Angeles. The authors of this study found that both factors operated in the predicted direction, with unemployment fears outweighing dislike of community disruption so that older workers were more likely to accept job transfer.[46]

Many of the New and Expanded Towns, particularly those in the South and Midlands, have attempted to base their growth as much on industrial as on housing relocation. Thus we might expect that they would contain more older workers and their families transferred with their employment than are found in most migrant groups. At first sight, however, the New and Expanded Towns appear to merely confirm our major conclusion so far: that geographic mobility is a function of the life-cycle of the nuclear family. For the population of the New and Expanded Towns is unbalanced in exactly the same way as are most migrant groups: young adults with young children are grossly over-represented. This can be seen from Table 2. We can see that the age group 20–9 (and therefore also the age group 0–9) is between two and three times over-represented when compared to the average age-distribution for the whole of England and Wales. As we shall see later, this unbalanced age-distribution is a considerable nuisance to the New and Expanded Towns. What explains this strange phenomenon? Have we not seen evidence which suggests that, though young adults will move for housing, older adults might move to preserve their jobs? So, either this prediction is incorrect, or the New and Expanded Towns have not really been based on industrial but on housing overspill. Let us consider, then, the relative contributions made by industrial and housing overspill to the populations of New and Expanded Towns.

Conventional wisdom about the early days of the London New Towns asserts that about two-thirds of their immigrants were transferred workers accompanying their firms, while the other third came through the Industrial Selection Scheme from the housing lists of the London boroughs. This figure seems to derive either from the statements of the Development

[45] M. Jefferys, *Mobility in the Labour Market* (Routledge and Kegan Paul, 1954) p. 102.
[46] M. S. Gordon and A. H. McCorry, 'Plant relocation and job security: a case study', *Industrial and Labor Relations Review*, 11 (1957).

27

Table 2:   *Age-structure of overspilled populations (percentages)*

Age group on intake	Swindon 1963–5	Haverhill 1963–4	Banbury 1962–6	Hemel Hempstead 1958	England and Wales 1961
0–4	23.0	24.5	23.6	13.0	7.8
5–9	9.8	8.7	11.2	10.0	7.1
10–14	4.6	4.6	5.9	8.3	8.1
15–19	5.4	4.6	4.8	4.5	6.9
20–4	21.7	16.9	12.0	10.0	6.2
25–9	16.4	13.2	15.6	15.5	6.2
30–4	7.1	9.1	8.8	6.4	6.5
35–9	4.2	6.9	6.9	8.4	7.0
40–4	3.3	4.4	4.0	6.6	6.6
45–9	1.8	3.0	2.1	6.6	7.0
50–4	0.9	1.9	1.9	2.5	7.0
55–9	0.6	0.6	1.2	2.1	6.3
60–4	0.5	0.2	0.9	2.8	5.3
65+	0.8	1.4	1.1	3.3	11.9
	100.0	100.0	100.0	100.0	100.0

Sources:

Swindon, Haverhill and Banbury figures all made available by Oxfordshire County Council. Hemel Hempstead figures in G. B. Taylor, 'Social Problems of New Towns' in P. Kuenstler (ed.) *Community Organisation in Great Britain* (Faber and Faber, 1961) p. 70. Swindon, Haverhill, and Banbury are expanded towns receiving overspill from London under the 1952 Town Development Act. Hemel Hempstead is a New Town receiving overspill from London.

Corporations or interested local authorities or from the firms involved. For example, J. H. Dunning has produced the figure of two-thirds transferred workers in one study, and 75–80 per cent in another, but in neither case does he show how he arrived at this figure.[47] Scargill estimates that firms moving into Aylesbury transferred 'up to 75 per cent' of their labour force, and here he is quoting the managements of the firms concerned.[48] If we assume for the moment that these are correct general estimates, can we reconcile them with the overall age-structure of the towns without abandoning any of our predictions about the effect of age? One possible

[47] J. H. Dunning, *Economic Planning and Town Expansion: A Case Study of Basingstoke* (Workers Education Association, 1963); and 'Manufacturing industries in the new towns', *The Manchester School of Economic and Social Studies*, 28 (1960), p. 155.
[48] D. I. Scargill, 'Town Expansion at Aylesbury', *Town and Country Planning*, 33 (1965) pp. 59–62. Note however that other writers estimates have varied between 50 per cent and 80–5 per cent. See respectively C. M. Brown, 'The Industry of the New Towns of the London Region' in J. B. Martin (ed.) *Greater London: an Industrial Geography* (G. Bell, 1966) p. 241; and M. Wragg, 'Starting Life in a New Town', *Town and Country Planning*, 19 (1951) pp. 250–1.

way of doing this would be to claim that firms setting up in these towns have simultaneously expanded their labour force, and, though transferring most of their original staff, have recruited extensively through the Industrial Selection Scheme to fill their new needs. Though this has happened in some cases, it will not do as a general explanation. First, many of the relocating firms have used the relocation as an opportunity to automate and to reduce their labour force.[49] Secondly, we must remember that the age-structure of these towns is almost identical with that of purely housing overspill groups. The firms' labour force would have to be expanding at an enormous rate for the new recruits to so counteract the age-structure of the original employees. So this is not a plausible total explanation.

It is more probable that the estimates of transferring employees are overstatements, originating from the desire of both the interested public authorities and the industrialists to emphasise their own successes. Taylor is one writer who is a little suspicious of their estimates:

> The percentage of employees making the move with their firm appears to have varied from 50 to 70 per cent, although Development Corporations have probably tended to exaggerate the proportions. In some quite important cases where firms have established new branches in the New Towns it will have been small (5 per cent) because only a few key workers will have been needed to provide continuity and the managerial function.[50]

One question to ask, then, is how 'new' the industry is in New Towns. Is it new to the town or new altogether? The importance of this question becomes clear if we try to interpret the reason given by another author for the New Towns' unbalanced age-structure:

> The new industries which provide the bulk of the employment recruit, in the main, young workers, most of them recently married and starting families. The middle-aged group is small.[51]

If by 'new' he means simply 'new to the town' this does not seem very plausible. We want an explanation of why these firms have been extensively recruiting at all, for obviously if they do recruit they will recruit younger people.[52] One explanation would be that many of the relocating organisations were in effect new branches or departments. Fortunately, Dunning has provided us with accurate information on this point with regard to manufacturing firms in the London New Towns in 1958. In his survey 188

---

[49] *Swindon: a Study for Further Expansion*, A study undertaken by joint teams of officers of Swindon Borough Council, Wiltshire County Council, and Greater London Council, October 1968, p. 101.

[50] Taylor, 'Social Problems of New Towns', p. 64.

[51] J. H. Nicholson, *New Communities in Britain* (National Council of Social Service, 1961) pp. 62–3.

[52] As older people are more reluctant to leave one job to seek another.

firms out of 271 were 'plant removals' (i.e. probably total relocations), with only 69 being new branches of existing companies.[53] The fact that one-quarter are branch factories helps to account for the extensive new recruiting, but cannot account for all of it. We must add in the factor of *selective recruitment* occurring even in total relocations.

Selective recruitment occurs in the period between the company's first announcement of its intention to move and the actual moving date. Many of those employees who have no intention of moving will leave immediately and be replaced by men eager to make the move, probably as a result of their bad housing. Most of the turnover experienced by industry is the continual vacating and filling of a few jobs. The result may be that practically 100 per cent of short-service employees may move in the end due to these special reasons. There is indirect evidence for such selective recruitment in a statement made by Brown concerning his briefly reported survey of 130 firms who had moved to London new towns. Commenting on the high turnover rates experienced by the firms after they had moved, he says

> a number of firms felt embittered against workers who joined
> the firm and acquired a house through the Development Corpo-
> ration, but after a short period transferred to another position.[54]

Dunning makes the same point, noting that it is mainly lower grade workers who do this.[55] Of course, it is only those who leave the company shortly after its relocation who have come in for our attention – they may represent the 'tip of an iceberg' of employees at all levels who only joined the relocating company after they knew of its relocation. Such people would be likely to be in the 'family life-cycle squeeze', when either sub-sidised council housing or easy-terms private mortgages would have maximum appeal. In short, they may be a 'normal' overspill group, moving for housing primarily, and with job alternatives being only a subsidiary part of their relocation decisions. Thus a director of one of the first firms to move to Crawley New Town has described most of his labour force as

> living in conditions ranging from barely tolerable to utterly
> impossible; living with the whole of their furniture in one room;
> in attics with leaking roofs; a few in furnished rooms at outra-
> geous rents; with mothers-in-law, or even living apart from their
> wives and children.[56]

---

[53] Dunning, 'Manufacturing industries in new towns'.
[54] Brown, 'The Industry of the New Towns of the London Region, p. 241.
[55] Dunning, 'Manufacturing industries in new towns', pp. 155–6.
[56] C. H. Cuttriss, *The Relocation of Industry with Reference to both the Human and the Economic Factors* (Town Planning Institute, 1955).

This is almost certainly an exaggeration by a man anxious to prove how socially beneficial his own relocation was, but the general point I am making is confirmed by surveys of New and Expanded Towns inhabitants themselves. The 1967 survey of Cumbernauld asked residents why they had moved there: 55 per cent mentioned housing reasons (i.e. reasons classified by the authors either as 'attraction of house' or 'desire to leave former residence'), only 18.5 per cent mentioned 'availability of job', and a tiny 3 per cent mentioned a job transfer.[57] Cumbernauld is less self-contained than most New Towns, of course, and it is not surprising that few will have moved there for the job and that even fewer will have transferred with their job. But in Stevenage, which is relatively self-contained, the same result (though less exaggerated) emerges: in a sample of residents 57 per cent mentioned housing as a reason for having moved there, compared with 42 per cent who mentioned job reasons.[58] In the Expanded Town of Swindon, the proportions among Cullingworth's sample of overspilled council tenants were 73 per cent mentioning housing and 19 per cent mentioning employment,[59] while the Swindon planning authorities estimate that in the future only 20 per cent of the council houses needed for migrants to the Expanded Town will be for key workers.[60] The consultants' proposals for the expanded town of Ipswich enabled us to bring this argument to its culmination. They include the results of two small studies of overspill families. The first sample is of potential candidates for overspill, families registered on the Industrial Selection Scheme register for Greater London; the second is of the employees of W. H. Smith's who accepted transfer with their company from London to Swindon. The samples differ very greatly in their reasons for moving: among the former 'housing is paramount', while among the W. H. Smith employees 'The principal motive was to continue working for the company.' Moreover, the age-stucture of the former closely resembled that of the normal migrants to New and Expanded Towns, greatly over-representing young married couples with small children. By contrast, the W. H. Smith employees were drawn from all employed age-groups.[61] The deduction from all this evidence is obvious: most migrants to New and Expanded Towns were not transferred workers.

We thus have grounds for doubting that the New and Expanded Towns

[57] Sykes, *et al.*, *Cumbernauld '67*, p. 15.
[58] Willmott, 'East Kilbride and Stevenage: some social characteristics of a Scottish and an English New Town', *Town Planning Review*, 34 (1964). The proportions among East Kilbride respondents were similar.
[59] Cullingworth, 'The Swindon Social Survey . . .', p. 153.
[60] *Swindon: A Study for Further Expansion*, Swindon Borough Council, p. 107.
[61] Shankland, Cox and Associates, *Ipswich Draft Basic Plan: consultants' proposals for the expanded town* (H.M.S.O., 1968) pp. 120–3. The plans to expand Ipswich have now been abandoned.

have provided a test of people's attitudes to what I have termed industrial overspill. We cannot use their experience to assess the impact of men's dependence upon employment on relocation decisions. The establishment of branch factories, the use of the Industrial Selection Scheme, and the occurrence of other kinds of selective recruitment have all combined to confuse the impact of age upon moving propensity. Unfortunately, they do so with other factors as well.

The occupational structure of migrant groups to the London New Towns has occasioned less comment than their age structure because it is close to the national pattern, except for a 50 per cent under-representing of unskilled manual workers and a 10 per cent over-representing of skilled manual and routine non-manual workers.[62] However, the relative absence of unskilled workers and their families from the New Towns does have a rather serious implication for the conurbations. For it is the unskilled who are worst housed there. The G.L.C., while reporting on the successes of its Industrial Selection Scheme, makes this point:

> most of the heads of households so moved are skilled or semi-skilled workers. The worst stresses in London are amongst unskilled workers living in poor conditions in some inner Boroughs.[63]

Nor can we assume that those left behind in the inner areas will then move into the dwellings vacated by the skilled emigrants for among overspill groups 'household splitting' has been a frequent occurrence. This means that the emigrants did not exist as a separate household before they moved, and thus 'split away' from the rest of the household on moving, leaving the conurbation dwelling still occupied. This occurs particularly with the young married couples who form such a large part of overspill groups: prior to the move they were forced to live with parents. Thus in one analysis of households in East Ham from which families had moved to overspill areas Cullingworth found that 46 per cent of the dwellings had not been completely vacated.[64] It is obviously essential to discover whether the occupational structure of the New and Expanded Town migrants can be considered a guide to future policy. From Thomas' analysis of the London New Towns we might doubt this. For Thomas has argued very persuasively that people have only migrated to the existing

[62] See B. J. Heraud, 'Social Class and the New Towns', *Urban Studies* (1968) p. 39, see also R. Thomas, *London's New Towns: a study of self-contained and balanced communities* (Political and Economic Planning, 1969) pp. 415–27, where there is evidence to suggest that as many higher occupational groups tend to live outside the New Town, their *real* proportion within the whole migrant group is higher.
[63] G.L.C. *Report of Studies*, p. 33.
[64] J. B. Cullingworth, 'Memorandum to the Milner Holland Committee', *Housing Review*, 14 (1965) p. 12.

New Towns because of relocation policies specific to those towns. The most important point here is that the London New Towns were able to choose the industry they wanted from among many applicants. As the Development Corporations were very conscious of the need for 'social balance' in the towns, they naturally looked for an employment structure which would avoid the anathema of traditional British town planning, 'the one-class community'. Yet, equally naturally, they tended to bias this just a little. Thus

> They didn't accept firms paying exceptionally low wages or those offering a high proportion of dead-end jobs, and certainly not firms whose industrial processes might have adversely affected the physical environment of the town.[65]

Hence the remarkable over-weighting of manufacturing industry in general, and the mechanical and electrical engineering groups in particular, in these towns.[66] Clean, technically advanced, export orientated firms naturally employ a larger proportion of professional, technical and skilled workers, and a smaller proportion of unskilled workers than industry in general. Moreover, as Thomas points out, the housing allocation procedures undoubtedly furthered this bias by leaving the nomination of key workers to the firms themselves. The firms almost certainly favoured their skilled workers in this way more than the unskilled, assuming that whereas unskilled workers could be recruited anywhere, skilled men in short supply must be transferred.[67]

Not all these conditions are to be found in the other New Towns, nor will they necessarily be a part of the future schemes. Choice between firms may have been possible for the London New Towns (and indeed for some of the South Eastern Expanded Towns) but it has not been significant elsewhere, while the present shortage of industry to relocate makes it unlikely in the near future. The New and Expanded Towns must now take what employment they can get, and their occupational structure is to some extent out of their own planned control. As Thomas shows in his other pamphlet, this can introduce strong distortions: the lack of office relocation outside of the South East under-represents office workers in the other New Towns.[68]

The other factor, that of discrimination against unskilled workers, is

[65] Thomas, *London's New Towns*, p. 386.
[66] Dunning, 'Manufacturing industries in the new towns'.
[67] Thomas, *London's New Towns*, pp. 419, 425. There is also the point that unskilled workers are discouraged by the high rents of new council houses (*ibid.*); see also V. Hole, 'The social effects of planned rehousing', *Town Planning Review*, 30 (1959).
[68] R. Thomas, *Aycliffe to Cumbernauld* (Political and Economic Planning, 1969) especially chap. 9.

even more imponderable. It is, of course, part of the selective recruitment process of migrants that we have already noticed. This selective recruitment by intending relocating firms naturally presupposes a prior selective turnover (probably of older employees). And the answer to 'why do some employees leave the company when they hear of the relocation?' may be 'because they were not asked, or not asked with enough sincerity, to relocate'. Clearly we must now go to intensive case-studies of company relocations if we are to solve such problems.

CASE STUDIES OF INDUSTRIAL RELOCATION

Previous case studies in Britain are not particularly helpful. In Luttrell's classic study of industrial relocation most of the case-studies reported on were branch factories intending to transfer only a few key workers.[69] There are brief reports on a number of successful relocations, i.e. where a majority of employees transferred.[70] But none of these makes clear whether this 'majority' is of original employees, or is swelled and biassed by selective turnover and recruitment. Nor are details given of the kinds of employee who accepted and rejected transfer (other than the obvious one that women employees do not relocate unless their household head is also employed there). All of them derive their material from the managements concerned and tend to paint a generally rosy picture of the relocation process. If we can believe their own stories, however, it appears that all the firms went to some trouble to help their employees financially with the move, to give them housing and educational advice in conjunction with the receiving authorities, and to 'consult' with employees (though this term is one that managements tend to use when they mean 'inform'). Their relocation policies may have resembled those of the present case-study firm which are reported in Chapter 5 – as I will argue, these policies had much to do with the 'success' of the present relocation.

Reinforcement for this point comes from the only thorough account of a relocation 'failure', Fox's study of the British Aluminium Company's offer to transfer men made redundant by the closure of its Milton Works (near Stoke) to a South Wales plant.[71] Despite financial incentives, advice and sponsored visits to South Wales only 31 of the 840 displaced men accepted transfer. Fox attributes this relative failure to explicit and im-

---

[69] W. F. Luttrell, *Factory Location and Industrial Movement* (National Institute of Economic and Social Research, 1962, 2 vols).
[70] Several of these are reported in 'Moving out of London' a series of articles published in *The Guardian* between 20 December 1963 and 3 February 1964, and reprinted as a pamphlet by The Guardian, Manchester, 1964.
[71] Alan Fox, *The Milton Plan* (Institute of Personnel Management, 1965).

plicit management attitudes: management did not positively want them to transfer and it failed to mount a 'selling operation' on the transfer. Indeed management in South Wales actually opposed the transfer and refused to allow the crucial encouragement to transfer of a guarantee of seniority rights. Workers will be reluctant to place part of their future in the hands of a management with such attitudes. Clearly, then, employers must make a whole-hearted attempt to persuade workers to move, if the worker is to regard the relocation seriously. From a Location of Offices Bureau study it seems evident that this does not happen in most office decentralisations: the proportion of staff moved by the London firms surveyed mostly fell below 10 per cent but where it was higher it was normally over 90 per cent. It would be useful to know the distances involved here (perhaps those transferring over 90 per cent moved only a very few miles), but in the absence of this information it seems reasonable to assume that in most relocations little attempt is made to persuade employees to relocate.[72]

A recent study which does break down the proportion of employees transferred by both distance moved and the level of the employee is that produced for the South East Joint Planning Team by Economic Consultants Ltd. This found that 'high level' employees were more likely to be transferred than 'low level' ones ('high level' includes skilled manual workers as well as higher grade office workers) and this disproportion increased with the distance moved: in those firms moving 61 or more miles, while 64 per cent of the higher employees transferred, only 8 per cent of the lower ones did.[73] When the difference is of this magnitude my suspicions are aroused on two counts. First comes the point I have already made – who was actually invited to move? Secondly, I suspect that the difference may be inflated by a failure to separate male from female employees. All we are told of the 'low level' staff is that they include 'clerical, office, semi-skilled and unskilled production workers'. Women would form the bulk of this group in most industries. The percentage of all employees accepting transfer of 61 miles or more is (at 14 per cent) very close to that of the 'low level' employees noted above, and hence the number of the low levels must greatly exceed that of the high levels. It is thus unlikely that the large female part of this group has been excluded from the analysis. It is not without interest that women employees are

---

[72] Economist Intelligence Unit, *A Survey of Factors Governing the Location of Offices*, p. 63. Where the relocation is short-distance, staff may not have to move house at all. Another study of short-distance relocations gives an exact proportion of relocaters among office staff (70 per cent, lower among routine clerical workers) but does not tell us how many actually moved house: Town and Country Planning Association, *The Paper Metropolis* (London, 1962).

[73] South-East Joint Planning Team, *Strategic Plan for the South East* (H.M.S.O., 1970) pp. 16–17.

only rarely transferred over a distance that would involve a change of residence, but it is hardly a surprising result, given the subordinate position of working women both in industry and in their own households.

The British studies, therefore, only give slight assistance. None report relocations in sufficient detail to enable us to separate the many influential factors involved in relocation decisions. Nor are we helped by a rather unsophisticated treatment of the data available. However, American studies generally show rather greater sociological expertise.

We must be wary of generalising from these to the British situation because of the many specifically American factors involved, like the much greater distances covered, the greater importance of formal seniority agreements, and the proportion of Negro and other ethnic minority groups. But from these studies we can certainly derive an interesting sociological fact, namely the importance of the worker's job comparison rather than the community comparison as the crucial determinant of his relocation decision. Thus in the study of Californian automobile workers already referred to, worries about finding an alternative job in the two locations dominated decision-making.[74] Weber's review of American interplant transfers (where the employee is offered transfer to another existing company plant) stresses the importance of a guarantee of seniority rights. Where transfer is offered to another plant some distance away, about half the workers will relocate if they are there guaranteed present seniority rights. However, where the worker is offered a choice between local and long-distance transfer, he will pick the former even if seniority is only guaranteed at the distant location.[75] This might seem to indicate that many workers will accept demotion in order to retain their local community ties, especially as another study by Smith and Fowler comes to the same conclusion.[76] But we must reckon with the pervasiveness of the idea of 'security'. Thus Smith and Fowler, while stressing community ties, also mention the importance of their sample's fear of job insecurity in the new location, but fail to see that the two are closely linked.[77] For all studies of job-seeking by unemployed workers stress the extent to which they rely on their local contacts with friends and relatives rather than on employment exchanges, newspaper advertisements and other formal means. Moving to a new locality weakens considerably the worker's

[74] M. S. Gordon and A. H. McCorry, 'Plant relocation and job security: a Case Study'.
[75] A. R. Weber, 'The Interplant Transfer of Displaced Personnel' in G. Somers *et al.* (eds.) *Adjusting to Technological Change* (Harper and Row, 1963).
[76] L. M. Smith and I. A. Fowler, 'Plant Relocation and Worker Migration' in A. B. Shostak and W. Gomberg (eds.) *Blue Collar World* (Prentice-Hall, 1964).
[77] *Ibid.* p. 502. This study is generally disappointing in its failure to intercorrelate the various determinants of relocation decisions.

36

ability to hear of and secure a new job. Thus the worker with strong social ties to his local community will derive from them economic as well as social support in the event of redundancy and relocation, and the worker with normal ties to family and friends will tend to refuse transfer if there is the slightest hint of insecurity in the new location.[78] The complexity of the relationship between work and community thus needs further investigation.

However, one deduction that can be made is the necessity for the existence of good industrial relations and reasonable confidence in management intentions on the part of workers. This may well be the correct interpretation of one of the few studies of British relocations which identifies a factor accounting for the difference between successful and unsuccessful transfer, Brown's study of 130 firms who have relocated from London to the London New Towns. Overall, these firms transferred half their labour force but the small firms performed significantly better: the average transfer rate among firms employing fewer than 20 workers was 86.9 per cent compared to only 40.4 per cent among the largest, those employing over 200 workers.[79] It is tempting to attribute the difference to differences in communication between top management and ordinary employees. In the very small firm personal contact will establish the employer's intentions in the new location; in the large firm a formal programme of persuasion and consultation must be instituted. If the formal programme of the British Aluminium Company described by Fox is at all typical of the large relocating company, large firms may fail in this respect.

Other studies give us few clues to the size and composition of the relocating workforce. Alongside the company-inspired optimistic views already mentioned are a number of generally pessimistic views of relocation.[80] But none of these cases gives further relevant details, and in view of the 'successful' relocations already mentioned we cannot conclude that in general workers will not move. This is the rather rash claim of Dorothy Wedderburn, on the basis of Fox's study alone:

> Geographical transfer is the most difficult to achieve, particu-

---

[78] See the discussion of this point in relation to British transfer schemes by W. W. Daniel, *Strategies for Displaced Employees* (Political and Economic Planning, 1970). Daniel concludes: it becomes surprising that (any manual worker) ... ever moves geographically rather than the other way round', p. 37. And indeed unemployed workers rarely consider moving house to find a job: see, for example, Wedderburn, *Redundancy and the Railwaymen*, p. 142.

[79] Brown, 'Industry of the New Towns', p. 241.

[80] Loasby 'The Experience of West Midlands Industrial Dispersal Projects' O.E.C.D., *International Joint Seminar on Geographical and Occupational Mobility of Manpower* (O.E.C.D., 1964, 2 vols). Guy Routh, 'Report on the Discussions at the Seminar', 1, pp. 140–2.

larly among manual workers. Even where housing is made available and some financial assistance is offered only a minority of workers are likely to move. (Fox, 1965).[81]

This is a somewhat over-general statement. In fact, we know very little about the mechanisms and motivations involved in industrial relocation. This is a large deficiency in the knowledge on which present regional planning is based: such is the justification for the present case-study.

SUMMARY AND CONCLUSION

In this chapter I have emphasised the importance in mobility studies of the family-life-cycle or family career. Young adults of all classes are favourably disposed to any kind of move which improves their housing position, but the incentive to move declines with middle age. This predisposition probably remains until a slightly higher age among those families whose household head enjoys a progressive work-career, and these are mostly middle class. Among this group we can distinguish locals and spiralists, according to the nature of their work-careers, and the latter are positively willing to move long distances to further their careers. Among the middle class we observed little serious opposition to migration, provided this did not represent a worsening of the family's housing and residential career. Among the working class, however, we could reach no firm conclusion on this point. Traditionally the working class has been thought to be deeply embedded in local community relations, intertwined with their extended family networks. Where this was so, hostility to migration was encountered, and often migration only occurred because of the forced alternative presented to the family: only by migration could housing improvement be secured. Yet other studies cast doubt on the strength of these local ties, and we saw some evidence that changes in family structure, toward the 'modified extended family', may have weakened the local ties of working-class people, particularly younger people.

We then turned to an analysis of overspill which included the movement of jobs as well as houses. Here we expected different factors to influence individual relocation decisions on the grounds that dependence upon a particular job would cut across the ties of dependence to local community, particularly its effect upon age. Though the young adult might be predisposed toward housing movement, we would expect the

[81] Dorothy Wedderburn, 'Redundancy' in *Industrial Society: Social Sciences in Management*, ed. D. Pym (Penguin Books, 1968) p. 78.

older man to be predisposed toward keeping his job. Yet we were not able to test such propositions thoroughly, because relocation to the New and Expanded Towns did not clearly present these alternatives to the individuals concerned, nor can we extract sufficient relevant evidence from the rather sketchy existing case-studies of industrial relocation.

Indeed, it was interesting to contrast the depth and the sophistication of the treatment of housing and community preferences in the work of writers concerned with regional planning with the short shrift given to work preferences. Yet the work preferences must be taken into account in any analysis of public attitudes to conurbation policy alternatives, for these policies can disrupt jobs almost as much as they disrupt dwellings and communities. Moreover, the New and Expanded Town policy is nominally based on job overspill, though we have seen that it does not work out like this. The government's present overspill schemes cannot depend much on new jobs and new branch factories; if they are to succeed they must attract total relocations. If this policy is to be subject to cost–benefit analysis we must be able to analyse its 'purest' form, the situation where an organisation's relocation is total in the sense that employees are offered a genuine choice between transferring and losing their jobs. The present case-study relocation is an example of this 'pure' situation.

Before turning to the case-study, we can try to build up our knowledge of relocating propensity from the literature on industrial sociology. Much of the discussion of the present chapter has skirted around problems connected with the 'meaning' of work to modern men, particularly the nature of their dependence upon work in general and their present employer in particular, and the relative importance of satisfaction derived from work and non-work areas of life. Where non-manual workers were discussed those issues could be presented in a reasonably simple and direct form, for, as already mentioned, the centrality of work in their total life experiences has clearly emerged. As regards manual workers, however, the situation is far from clear. Thus the following chapter will discuss the facts and theories emerging from industrial sociology which will enable us to assess the nature of the work dependence of manual workers.

39

3
The worker's dependence upon employment

At the end of the last chapter, I observed that to establish how dependent the worker is upon his employment, and therefore how likely he is to accept job transfer, we must establish the meaning and importance to him of his work. There are two principal dimensions of this problem. First we must establish how important is his work life in general when compared to his life outside his work. Secondly, we want to know whether the important aspects of work and non-work tie him down to a particular employer or locality. A skilled worker who can find equally satisfying work with many other employers is not very dependent on his present employer. A man who derives his non-work satisfaction from his nuclear family alone can transport it to another locality – he is independent of his present locality. So in this chapter, I will use the findings of industrial sociology to analyse (*a*) the relationship between work and non-work in general and (*b*) the extent of dependence upon present employment.[1] I will keep separate the two terms *work*, referring to work in general, and *employment*, referring to particular, present employment.

There is now a consensus in industrial sociology concerning the broad outlines of the situation of most manual workers. In general they are 'satisfied' without being 'happy' in their work, 'calculatively involved', and have their 'central life interests' outside of work. Satisfaction surveys generally show between 70 per cent and 90 per cent of workers saying that they are satisfied with their work, though this reply generally means that work has come up to some minimum level of expectation which may fall far short of genuine enjoyment and self-fulfilment.[2] A sense of self-fulfilment is much more likely to be found outside of work, where the man's 'central life interests' lie.

The term 'central life interest' was coined by Dubin to explain the attitude of a sample of American manual workers who preferred non-work activities and relationships to those experienced at work. Interestingly, his study was replicated by Orzack on a sample of male professional nurses also in the United States. The two sets of results are almost totally opposed: only 24 per cent of the workers had central life interests at work,

---

[1] Local community attachments were discussed in the preceding chapter.
[2] I have analysed this in my *Consciousness and Action in the Western Working Class* (Macmillan, 1972).

compared to 79 of the male nurses.[3] It is tempting to generalise from these results, as Etzioni does, to argue that lower occupational groups find their central life interests outside work while higher groups find them at work.[4] This was certainly the gist of the argument contained in the previous chapters.

The link between central life interest and 'calculative involvement' has been most effectively made by the 'Affluent Worker' research team. In their study of Luton manual workers they introduce the following ideal-type:

> workers' involvement in the organisation which employs them is primarily a *calculative* one . . . Thus involvement is of low intensity, and in terms of affect is neutral or 'mild' rather than being either highly positive or negative . . . Their jobs do not form part of their central life interests; work is not for them a source of emotionally significant experiences or social relationships; it is not a source of self-realisation.[5]

Most of the authors' sample of Luton workers conform quite closely to this ideal-type, and all the evidence reviewed so far would lead us to assume that manual workers as a whole were 'calculatively involved', with their calculations dominated by economic considerations.[6]

It is now tempting to jump straight to a conclusion on this issue. For has it not been demonstrated that the manual worker's commitment is negligible, that the salience of work compared to non-work experience is low? And does it not follow that the worker is relatively independent of any particular employment for his sources of satisfaction, and therefore unlikely to relocate? Indeed, there is one writer on migration who has argued thus. This writer is Jansen, who states of a non-migrant group:

> the group had few of the characteristics associated with migration . . . those working were concentrated in manual jobs and sought mainly instrumental benefits from the job, which would indicate that they were not very 'involved'.[7]

---

[3] R. Dubin, 'Industrial workers' worlds: a study of the "central life interests" of industrial workers', *Social Problems*, 3 (1956); L. H. Orzack, 'Work as a "central life interest" of professionals', *Social Problems*, 7 (1959).

[4] A. Etzioni, *A Comparative Analysis of Complex Organisations* (The Free Press, 1961), p. 53.

[5] J. H. Goldthorpe *et al., The Affluent Worker: Industrial Attitudes and Behaviour* (Cambridge University Press, 1968) p. 39.

[6] Of course, the 'Affluent Worker' research team were arguing that their sample was unusually 'calculatively involved' even when compared to other manual workers. When discussing 'instrumental' and 'calculative' workers I will try to specify clearly whether the comparison is with other manual workers or with non-manual workers.

[7] C. Jansen, *Social Aspects of Internal Migration* (Bath University Press, 1968) p. 161.

41

But this is an invalid argument. A worker may be calculatively involved in his employment at a very *high* level of intensity, if the extrinsic economic rewards are of sufficient importance for him, and he may be heavily dependent on his present employment if that offers the best possible extrinsic rewards. Alternatively, strong attachments to intrinsic aspects of work would not necessarily indicate high dependence on employment. If the attachment is to the interest of the job itself, the level of dependence depends on whether there are similar jobs elsewhere; if the attachment is to social relations with co-workers we must also ask whether workers imagine they can establish similar relations elsewhere. One point must be conceded: high normative commitment to the organisation probably does indicate high overall dependence on that organisation. This means if we are to link together 'involvement' and overall commitment and dependence, we must consider what the object of the emotional attachment is and how bound up it is with the present employment situation. Thus we must analyse the place of the employing organization in the labour market.

But even if there is no simple conclusion, we have already made two deductions. The first is that the meaning of work for most manual workers is decidedly negative. It is probably not variations in work or employment enjoyment or satisfaction that should concern us, but rather the more forcibly-experienced sense of work or employment dependence. The findings of this case-study support this approach. Secondly, calculative involvement means that whatever the level of employment dependence found, its character is largely economic. Questions of economic dependence must therefore central in any analysis of working-class reactions to factory relocation.

EMPLOYMENT DEPENDENCE AND THE LABOUR MARKET –
THE COMPENSATORY MODEL

The state of the local labour market is obviously a crucial determinant both of work involvement and of dependence upon a particular employer. If, for example, the worker perceives no alternative jobs open to him, he will feel heavily dependent upon his present employer (unless his overall involvement in work is so low that he does not mind unemployment). And indeed, American studies of factory relocation show that, as the local unemployment rate rises, so does the relative willingness of workers to consider transferring with their companies.[8] This is an obvious enough

---

[8] See Chapter 2, where the American studies are discussed.

finding, and in the rest of this chapter I will concentrate on the rather more complex situations in which the worker is able to find some kind of alternative employment locally. The relative attraction of these job alternatives to the worker is the most important fact to discover.

Let us first look at the objective alternatives available in what might be termed a 'typical' urban labour market. Clearly, the jobs available at any one hierarchical level vary considerably in their character. Thus for example jobs on building sites, in small workshops, large factories and in service trades will usually differ in their wages, fringe benefits, work activities and indeed their entire working environment. Whether the individual worker believes that this vast variety of jobs is available to him is more doubtful. The building worker might never consider the possibility of working in a factory, the factory worker never consider working on a building site. Hollowell, for example, has shown that many long-distance lorry drivers are not interested in factory jobs.[9] It is more probable that within the overall labour market, sub-markets exist for workers with differing specialisations and orientations (apart from the question of their formal skills, of course). Though our knowledge of either the overall labour market or the sub-markets is still slight,[10] we do have some evidence to suggest that even within sub-markets, considerable variety between jobs exists and is perceived to exist by the workers. This evidence comes from two inter-related sources: studies which emphasise that high wages are often used (and explicitly so) to compensate for unusually unpleasant aspects of particular jobs, and studies noting the importance of technology in determining job variety. Nearly all the studies are confined to the manufacturing sector. I shall return to the question of technology. Let us now consider the evidence for the bargain over wages and unpleasant conditions.

What one worker considers pleasant may be considered unpleasant by another, but there do seem to be some job features that are almost universally disliked by workers. Unusually hot (or cold), dusty, steamy or noisy working environments are obvious examples of this, and indeed managements operating foundries, test shops, paint shops and the like generally feel that they must offer higher wages than the local norm to outweigh these disadvantages and attract sufficient labour. Shiftwork constitutes another example: most workers consider shiftworking to be injurious to their health and to their family and social life, and must be compensated for these disadvantages by shift premiums, generally rang-

[9] P. Hollowell, *The Lorry Driver* (Routledge and Kegan Paul, 1968) p. 105.
[10] I am at present engaged with Dr. R. M. Blackburn at the Department of Applied Economics, Cambridge University in an intensive study of one local labour market (Peterborough).

ing from one-sixth to one-third of basic wages.[11] Again, jobs assembling mass consumer durables, especially cars, are normally considered intrinsically unpleasant, for the manual operations are simple, repetitive and have to be performed fast and continuously. These workers are also normally compensated with high wages.[12] In contrast, the low wages of the small workshop are compensated for by the high work autonomy and the close personal relationships with the 'boss'.[13]

These studies emphasise the worker's consciousness of his uneven work rewards, claiming that he originally chose his employment because of this. And indeed their workers do tend to say this. But none of them dispose fully of two other possibilities. First, there is the possibility that workers might have arrived 'blindly and ignorantly' at their place of employment, but then selective turnover might have quickly weeded out those who did not like the work situation. This hypothesis is very similar to the first, and stresses the necessary congruence between 'rationalistic' orientations and reality. But secondly, both original recruitment and subsequent turnover might have been random, but the workers who 'happened to' stay became socialised into accepting their situation and then began to rationalise their previous behaviour. Present evidence gives no firm guide to the relative importance of job choice, selective turnover, and employment socialisation.[14] However, it is worth noting that, whichever occurs, the end-result might be the same as far as employment dependence is concerned. For if the worker is concerned to emphasise that the very conciously wanted the high wages and was prepared to endure the other work aspects, then probably he is now deeply attached to this particular set of work rewards. If the latter are unusual within the labour market, then he is very much dependent upon his present employer. This seems true at least for car-workers, as Hilda Kahn's study of the men laid off by B.M.C.

---

[11] For the most comprehensive account of shiftworking, see P.E. Mott *et al., Shift Work* (University of Michigan Press, 1965).

[12] There are many studies of car-workers providing evidence on this point. For an American example, see C. R. Walker and R. H. Guest, *The Man on the Assembly Line* (Harvard University Press, 1952) for a British study, see Goldthorpe *et al., Affluent Worker*.

[13] A recent study has shown that workers in small firms are conscious of this exchange of rewards: G. K. Ingham, *Size of Industrial Organisation and Worker Behaviour* (Cambridge University Press, 1970).

[14] For example, as against the group of studies just cited, several American studies of labour markets exist which emphasise workers' ignorance of alternative jobs available and the 'irrationality' of their job-choice. See, for example, L. G. Reynolds, *The Structure of Labour Markets* (Harper, 1951). For further references, and for a criticism that these studies were conducted in periods of less than full employment (when workers would be less inclined to shop around), see L. C. Hunter and G. L. Reid, *Urban Worker Mobility* (O.E.C.D., 1968) pp. 115–16. For a study emphasising the randomness of labour turnover, see Food Manufacturing Economic Development Council, *A Study of Labour Turnover* National Economic Development Office, 1968).

in Birmingham in 1957 showed. After having been made redundant in mid-1956 no less than 51 per cent (disproportionately composed of the higher-paid workers) had voluntarily returned to B.M.C. in late 1958, despite fears of further redundancies.[15] Furthermore, Turner has demonstrated that the British car industry has a low turnover rate.[16] Pay is the factor in job-choice that is most immediately apparent to the outsider, but this reasoning could be applied to any of the other factors as well, and thus we might hypothesise that any worker receiving an unbalanced set of work rewards, in which high rewards on one dimension are compensated by low rewards on another, will be heavily dependent upon his present employment.

Unfortunately, the study of worker orientations is now at the point where the interest and the plausibility of the argument exceeds the known facts. It is highly probable that prior orientations to work determine to some extent job choice, selective turnover and work involvement (including both work satisfaction and work dependence), and some evidence has been adduced for this. But at the moment some of this evidence is contradictory, while the actual extent of the determination (which must somehow be reconciled with the evidence of worker's ignorance of job alternatives etc.) is uncertain. Let me briefly illustrate these points by describing the background factors which have been suggested as influences on differential orientations. These are type of residential community, geographical mobility, downward social mobility, life-cycle position, and social, religious and political activities.

(*a*) French and American studies have demonstrated that attitudes to work are affected by the size and type of community in which the worker lives or was brought up (using principally urban–rural distrinctions).[17] Unfortunately their results are sometimes contradictory,[18] and in any case Britain may be too highly urbanised as a whole for similar differences to emerge. There is no comparable British evidence.

(*b*) and (*c*) The 'Affluent Worker' team show that their sample, which they consider to be more instrumentally orientated than most workers, have experienced much more geographical mobility and slightly more downward social mobility than the norm.[19] Both these arguments are highly plausible, but more evidence is needed. Though a desire for higher

[15] H. R. Kahn, *Repercussions of Redundancy* (Allen and Unwin, 1964) p. 141.
[16] H. A. L. Turner *et al.*, *Labour Relations in the Motor Industry* (Allen and Unwin, 1967) pp. 189–90.
[17] A. Touraine and O. Ragazzi, *Ouvriers d'Origine Agricole* (Editions du Seuil, 1961); L. Karpik, 'Urbanisation et Satisfaction au Travail', *Sociologie du Travail*, No. 2 (1966), A. N. Turner and P. R. Lawrence, *Industrial Jobs and the Worker* (Harvard University Press, 1965).
[18] For example, Karpik finds that small-town workers are less interested in job content than workers in larger towns. Turner and Lawrence find the reverse.
[19] Goldthorpe *et al.*, *Industrial Attitudes and Behaviour*, chap. 7.

wages is very often a component of worker geographic mobility it is often difficult to separate from the wider notion of the relative attractiveness of residential regions. The attractiveness of Luton (the residence of the 'affluent workers') may be similar to that of the towns of Northern Italy for the Italian agricultural worker in presenting to him an entire and desirable 'modern' way of life.[20] Indeed, O.E.C.D. surveys have been unable to relate in any simple way the level of wages to the incidence of worker migration.[21] The downward social mobility argument is even more interesting sociologically: the suggestion is that manual workers with white-collar backgrounds must seek high wages in order to maintain a life-style similar to that of their white-collar reference group. But here the 'Affluent Worker' team's actual correlation is weak, and is any case partly accounted for by structural changes in labour force composition.[22] Nevertheless, there is some supporting evidence for the connection in Wilensky's study of 'moonlighters' – people who hold more than one job at the same time. This group is extremely calculatively involved, for deliberate sacrifices of leisure time, health or intrinsic work interest are normally made in return for the high wages which two jobs can bring. Wilensky shows that 'moonlighters' have often been blocked in their striving for upward mobility, feel worse off economically than their parents, and tend to marry upwards ethnically.[23] These are all indications of their setting themselves higher reference groups for life-style strivings, and possibly of downward mobility. These are certainly arguments worth exploring further.[24]

(*d*) The 'Affluent Worker' team deliberately selected their sample from male workers between the ages of 21 and 46, and, as they suggest,[25] this probably increased the overall instrumentality of the sample's orientations. There is now considerable evidence to suggest that the 'life cycle squeeze', the period during which adult nuclear families have their maximum number of children at the lowest point of their occupational careers, makes them need higher wages than other people. Thus, male

[20] G. Baglioni, 'Trade Union assistance to workers migrating from the south to the north of Italy' in O.E.C.D. (eds.) *Geographical and Occupational Mobility* especially p. 36. Thus Northern agricultural workers still migrate in large numbers to the towns despite the lower wages available there for unskilled labour.
[21] This is the main conclusion of: O.E.C.D., *Wages and Labour Mobility* (O.E.C.D., 1965).
[22] As has been pointed out by D. E. Mercer and D. T. H. Weir, 'Orientations to Work among White-Collar Workers' in Social Science Research Council (eds.) *Social Stratification and Industrial Relations* (S.S.R.C., 1969) p. 136.
[23] H. L. Wilensky, 'The moonlighter: a product of relative deprivation', *Industrial Relations*, 3 (1963).
[24] Unfortunately, the present case-study does not do this very thoroughly. The evidence collected here suffers from exactly the same disadvantages as Goldthorpe *et al.*'s and Ingham's.
[25] Goldthorpe *et al., Industrial Attitudes and Behaviour*, p. 159.

workers between the ages of about 20 and 35 are disproportionately represented among both shiftworkers[26] and 'moonlighters',[27] both more likely to be calculatively involved in their work than the norm. This argument does seem well-grounded.

(*e*) Finally, Dalton's classic American study found that a whole complex of factors was associated with workers' responses to an individual pay incentive scheme. 'Rate-busters', i.e. those workers who produced more (and were therefore paid more) than the work-group's production norms, were more likely to be Protestant than Catholic, Republican than Democrat, were more highly educated, were larger property owners, less likely to be involved in local organisations, less likely to be immigrants, and more likely to indulge in conspicuous consumption.[28] It is unfortunate that these rich ideas were not followed up by subsequent research, for Dalton's own sample was not large enough to separate all these individual factors. But it is clear that orientations to work may be associated with diffuse attitudes toward life in general.

We can thus note the congruence between several of these sets of results, and especially the suggestions that instrumental attitudes to work may be part of the life-view of the worker who is cut off from local class or ethnic communities, and more receptive to middle-class or Protestant values of material achievement. Differential orientations of a very general kind do seem to affect worker behaviour – the problem is to establish the relative importance of these compared with other factors. The 'orientations' approach stresses the *compensatory* nature of labour market mechanisms, whereby individual workers 'trade-off' advantages and disadvantages of different employment opportunities. It must therefore be reconciled with those theories which emphasise the *hierarchical* nature of the actual labour market. We shall now consider these theories.

THE HIERARCHICAL MODEL OF THE LABOUR MARKET

The two main hierarchical elements in the labour market operate through employer selection and the internal labour market. The labour market is

---

[26] Mott *et al., Shift Work*, p. 317, Table 1.
[27] Wilensky, 'Moonlighter', p. 110. And, reinforcing the argument about religion as a determinant. Wilensky finds Catholics notably underrepresented among the 'moonlighters'. Note that the 'moonlighters' in the sample came from all major occupational levels, not just from manual workers.
[28] M. Dalton, 'Worker response and social background', *Journal of Political Economy*, 25 (1947). Dalton's findings are discussed at length in W. F. Whyte *et al., Money and Motivation* (Harper and Raw, 1955) chap. 6.

obviously hierarchical in the sense that social strata inhabit different sub-markets: manual workers simply do not compete with managers for jobs, and the two are non-competing groups. At the manual level itself, the distinction between skilled tradesmen and other manual workers is also usually obvious. The point at issue is not whether the manual labour market is to be termed 'compensatory' or 'hierarchical', for it clearly includes elements of both. Further, the compensatory model presupposes an existing hierarchy: as the 'Affluent Worker' writers have observed, the car assembler compensates wages for intrinsic job satisfaction only because he is blocked from achieving higher rewards by the class hierarchy. The point is rather to establish the exact importance of the hierarchy within the manual stratum: to what extent do sections of the manual labour force constitute non-competing groups? How precise are the differentiations made between the abilities and skills of workers within one apparent social stratum? These are the questions which the great growth of 'semi-skilled' manual occupations have thrust before us. We can start answering these questions by looking at management interests in the matter.

Managements in manufacturing industry, when trying to fill a routine machining job will be looking for someone from the unskilled and semi-skilled labour pool with either previous experience in similar work or with some apparent mental and manual skills. At the very least, they will probably require the man to be able to read and write, which they will not necessarily expect from a factory labourer. And as the job of the machinist probably has higher rewards on all dimensions (wages, status, job interest, promotion prospects, security etc.) than the factory labourer, he is being selected by management for a higher position, not just a different one. This process is boosted by the operation of the internal labour market.

So far we have implicitly assumed that, if comparable jobs exist elsewhere in the labour market, then the worker is able to move into them (assuming that they fall vacant). But in fact, the worker's freedom of movement across the labour market is severely limited by the intervening job-structures internal to other employing organisations. Jobs within organisations in the broad band of unskilled and semi-skilled occupations (and sometimes within skilled occupations as well) are normally organised into an organisation hierarchy in which the higher positions are filled by workers who have previously worked in lower positions. In some organisations, moreover, this procedure is formalised so that length of service determines who shall be promoted. This formalised and hierarchical internal labour market seems to be the product of three factors: the specialised nature of many semi-skilled jobs, particularly machine-minding; the fact that high status jobs like leading hand, reliefman etc. involve knowledge of all the jobs in the section; and the strength of workshop trade unionism in protecting its own members. What this means for the new employee who was previously employed in a semi-skilled position elsewhere is that frequently he must undergo some kind of trial period on low level jobs before he can move up, and sometimes he must simply wait his turn for promotion by seniority.

Empirical support for this hierarchical model is found in Doeringer's study of 24 U.S. manufacturing plants in which the typical company had only two normal 'entry posts' for manual workers, one at low-level un-skilled work, the other at tradesman level. Seniority was relied on almost exclusively for determining redundancies, lay-offs and downgrading, but promotion practices were rather more diverse. Only three relied exclusively on seniority and two on 'merit' for determining promotion while most companies relied on a mixture of the two. But upon entry at least, the internal labour market was exerting a strong influence, on skilled workers as well as unskilled.[29] This has been confirmed by a larger and more recent study of the Chicago area in which it was found that seniority was the greatest single determinant of variations between the earnings of individuals with the same occupations.[30]

Surveys of American worker attitudes have show that the importance of the internal labour market is usually well recognised. Reynolds sums up these studies:

> workers have a strong preference for staying on with the same
> company. When they think of advancement, therefore, they
> tend to think of opportunities within the establishment where
> they are presently employed ... The worker typically 'climbs
> the ladder' within an enterprise, then slips back to a greater
> or lesser extent if he changes employers.[31]

Because of the existence of the internal labour market, virtually every worker except the very newest recruit has something to lose by changing employers. Those higher up the ladder will slip back by the change, while those lower down will forfeit all their length of service entitlement to future promotion. But clearly it is the former who lose more, not only through slipping back down the hierarchy, but also through losing their stake in the company deriving from length of service – pension, sick pay, holiday pay and the more intangible social status. Thus the workers' ignorance of the exact state of the external labour market may fit into a 'rationalistic' model of worker attitudes. For evidence on these points, let us turn to the excellent study of 'the reluctant job changer'.

---

[29] P. B. Doeringer, 'Determinants of the structure of industrial type internal labor markets', *Industrial and Labor Relations Review*, 20 (1967) pp. 209, 211–12.
[30] A Rees and G. P. Shultz, *Workers and Wages in an Urban Labor Market* (Chicago University Press, 1970).
[31] Reynolds, *Structure of Labour Markets*, pp. 139–40.

The authors of this study go to great lengths to distinguish between the concepts of job satisfaction and job stability. They consider this necessary because of the fact that, as we have already noted, 'satisfaction' with work does not necessarily denote any positive feeling of commitment to work and thus, in their results, a worker's reluctance to leave his employment is not significantly correlated with his work satisfaction.[32] Quite separate from satisfaction, and with much more impact upon attitudes to employment-changing, is a constellation of factors all contributing to work 'stability'.[33] Seniority, length of service, vested interest in pension, holiday, and sick pay benefits and 'fear of the unknown' all interlock to constitute a reluctance to change employment. Thus a preference for stability contains both easily-quantifiable aspects and attitudes to employment that are more difficult to pin down. The latter, however, seem to crystallise around the notion that, in the absence of any meaningful committed satisfaction, work provides self-identity for the worker through stability and predictability. As Caplow has remarked about semi-skilled workers (and he is being quoted by Palmer) 'for the machine tender stability (as an index of reliability) is often the only kind of personal achievement which can be made a part of his reputation'.[34] *The Reluctant Job Changer* provides a great deal of evidence to support this. Here, for example, is one of the associate authors, Herbert Parnes, describing workers' immobility in the three firms studied:

> In all three firms, reluctance to sacrifice seniority is the principal explanation of the workers' immobility. The other important consideration is psychological and sociological – the fear of a leap into the unknown. As many as a fourth of the workers in each firm point out that quitting their current job for a higher paying one would entail the risk of encountering less favorable conditions on the new job than those they now enjoy. The fears are rarely specific. The point is that the worker knows what is expected of him where he is, he is familiar with the routine, he knows his supervisor and the 'gang of fellows' with whom he works, and the prospect of plunging into a strange environment is disquieting. In contrast, fringe benefits are much less frequently alluded to.[35]

The effect of all these inter-related economic and sociological factors is to build up the ties which bind the worker to his present employer. The

[32] Gladys L. Palmer *et al.*, *The Reluctant Job Changer* (University of Pennsylvania Press, 1962) p. 34.
[33] *Ibid*, pp. 59, 157, and *passim*.
[34] *Ibid*. p. 4.
[35] *Ibid*. p. 78.

skilled worker to some extent receives self-identity in his work through his occupation in the country at large; the unskilled and semi-skilled receives his from his present employment.[36] Perhaps then the unskilled and semi-skilled worker (and in some cases even the skilled worker) is heavily dependent upon his employer if his length of service has exceeded some minimal level.

How far has the argument taken us? Has it not led us to contradict the earlier argument that most workers did not find their 'central life interest' (self-identity?) at work? Are we perhaps led to the conclusion that the work dependence of manual workers is markedly similar to that of the non-spiralist office workers analysed in the previous chapter? After all, we have noted the importance for manual workers of length of service and internal promotion channels as determinants of their dependence. These are also important for the office workers. However, while there are similarities we cannot argue for the identity of the two groups until we have compared the relative attachment of the two groups to work as a whole against non-work as a whole [This will be done at the end of the chapter]. What now of the implied contradiction between the argument of this section and the previous one?

The contradiction is not a real one. Indeed, it seems to be of the essence of calculative involvement and of non-work central life interests that workers should be able to derive from work the kind of self-identity I have just described. For if workers are to cope successfully with the absence of work activities that might provide meaningful creative self-fulfilment, they must learn to set less store by all intrinsic work activities. The best way of lowering one's 'emotional investment' in work is to increase its stability and predictability. Hence, it is found that workers are reluctant to move to other jobs within the same organisation as well as to jobs in other organisations.[37] Job-change can often be construed by the worker as (in Parnes' words) 'a leap into the unknown', inevitably involving an increase in his emotional investment in work as well as possible demotion. Of all the feelings involved in this kind of 'self-identity' only the enjoyment of a social status conferred by management and workers can be regarded as a positive rather than a substitute commitment (using Baldamus' terms).

Yet a paradox, though not a contradiction, remains. *Manual workers, in their attempt to reduce their dependence upon the intrinsic meanings of work as opposed to non-work actually increase their dependence upon a particular employer as opposed to other employers.* This makes it especially

[36] *Ibid.* p. 159. Note however, that here the authors point out that the skilled worker has a dual attachment to company and occupation, and that long-service men, whatever their skill, are unlikely to voluntarily leave their employment.
[37] Reynolds, *Structure of Labour Markets*, p. 145.

difficult to weigh up the relative overall dependencies of the worker on present employment and present non-work ties. I shall return to this difficulty at the end of the chapter.

The existence of the internal labour market is obvious; the problem is how important it is in Britain. Palmer's study is American and may reflect peculiar American realities. In particular, we might suspect that seniority would play a less important role in Britain, for seniority rights do not dominate industrial relations here in the way that they do in the U.S.A.[38] Nevertheless 'promotion from within' is an important phenomenon in modern Britain even for manual workers: as in the U.S.A., most firms probably limit the number of 'posts of entry' jobs and appoint the re-mainder from within.

This happens even at the skilled level where a recent study of 14 British engineering firms found that only 58 per cent of skilled tradesmen had served apprenticeships, the rest having being upgraded from the ranks of the unskilled and semi-skilled. This same study also finds ample evidence for the importance of the internal labour market as a determinant of wage-rates: the wage-rates within firms bore a closer relationship to the internal bargaining structure of the firm than to 'going rates' in the local labour market.[39] We are not dealing with a purely American phenomenon.

Of course, the dominant characteristics of British industrial relations are their informality and flexibility, and it is probable that for promotion as well as for bargaining there are no single set of rules governing most of industry. The situation is probably at its most flexible at the semi-skilled level where there seem to be few recognisable inter-industry criteria for selecting for jobs such as machining, storekeeping, crane driving and slinging, fettling, process operating or semi-supervisory positions. But while this undoubtedly weakens the structure of internal labour markets, it may not lower the level of the worker's dependence upon his present employer. If there is little recognisable structure in the labour market at this level, there is no pattern for the worker to predict and the 'risk' element in changing jobs becomes greater. As Palmer and many others have shown, workers generally seek to minimise risk rather than maxi-mise possibilities in the labour market, and thus their level of psycholo-gical dependence upon present employment may be almost as high where the internal labour market is ill-defined as where it is rigid.

The growing importance of fringe benefits, the worker's 'golden

---

[38] This is clearly seen in the case of factory relocation. In the American studies referred to in Chapter 2 above, and particularly that of Weber ('The interplant transfer of displaced personnel'), questions of seniority dominated all negotia-tions with trade unions.

[39] D. Robinson (ed) *Local Labour Markets and Wage Structures* (Gower Press, 1970) chaps 2, 3, 5 and 7. The apprenticeship figures are contained in Table 2.6, pp. 58–9.

chains', has been better-documented in Britain. Various studies have shown that pensions, sick pay, holiday pay, 'staff status' and many other benefits have been increasingly conferred upon manual workers. For example, in 1966 55 per cent of manual workers in the private sector and 65 per cent in the public sector were covered by occupational pension schemes.[40] Thus fringe benefits tied to length of service are certainly increasing in importance along with up-grading from within. There are two main determinants of this: shortage of labour and technological developments. The latter can be analysed in more detail for the study of technology is well-advanced in industrial sociology.

TECHNOLOGY AND EMPLOYMENT SATISFACTION

Any attempt to analyse variations in the nature of work involvement and dependence among manual workers must come to grips with the excellent and detailed treatment which has been given to technological determinants of job satisfaction in industrial sociology. For our purposes job satisfaction is a concept of rather limited use, as Gladys Palmer observed. But it is possible to re-interpret the the research results linking technology to satisfaction to make predictions about the nature of employment dependence. Before I attempt to do this, however, I will present in outline the principal findings of those writers who have analysed the technological determinants, as well as the principal criticisms they have aroused.

Joan Woodward in England, Alain Touraine in France and Robert Blauner in the United States have been the principal writers who have shown that worker and management relations and job satisfaction have varied with the technological structure of their place of employment.[41]

---

[40] For a review see Dorothy Wedderburn, 'The Conditions of Employment of Manual and Non-Manual Workers' in Social Science Research Council (eds.) *Social Stratification and Industrial Relations* pp. 4–30.
[41] J. Woodward, *Industrial Organization: Theory and Practice* (Oxford University Press, 1965).
  A. Touraine, *L'évolution du travail ouvrier aux usines Renault* (C.N.R.S., 1955).
  R. Blauner, *Alienation and Freedom: The Factory Worker and his Industry* (University of Chicago Press, 1964).
  More detailed and less theoretical descriptions of the changes brought about by automation in factories can be found in literature stemming from each of these countries. In Britain see the series of reports on automation of the D.S.I.R.:
  (*a*) D.S.I.R., Automation (H.M.S.O., 1956).
  (*b*) A. T. Welford, 'Ergonomics of Automation' D.S.I.R. *Problems of Research in Industry*, No. 8 (1960).
  (*c*) E.R.F.W. Crossman, 'Automation and Skill' D.S.I.R. *Problems of Research in Industry*, No. 9 (1960).
  In France see P. Naville, *L'Automation et le Travail Humain* (C.N.R.S., 1961).
  In the United States see J. Bright, *Automation and Management* (Harvard University Press, 1958). Subsequent writers have generally confirmed their findings.

All three work from a typology of technology which is basically three-fold (though Woodward's is slightly more complicated). Using Touraine's terminology, I set these out below:

Phase A: comprises traditional craft industries, where manufactured units are tailored to customers' individual requirements, or are prototypes, or consist of large pieces of equipment in several stages (Woodward, p. 39). The product is
integral, which means that its size and shape is continually
changing in the production process as new, physical parts
are added to it. As the product is unique or made in small
batches it cannot be standardised, and many minor decisions
are left to the skill and discrimination of the men who actually
build it. Thus the workgroup is composed of craftsmen, assisted by mates. The group's existence is recognised and
deferred to by both management and workers, as is its hierarchy determined by skill. Thus 'formal' and 'informal' organisation coincide (Touraine, pp. 62–3 and 179–80). High job
satisfaction results from workers' ability to use their manual
skills (Blauner, Chapter 3).

Phase B: introduces standardisation into the production of
the integral product. Large orders are received for the product
which is manufactured in large batches, or mass produced on
assembly-lines. Wherever possible, individual manual skills
are replaced by machine operations or are fragmented into
single-movement operations taking place sequentially along
assembly-lines. Thus the workforce is homogeneous: large
numbers of workers are now doing identical, low-skilled tasks,
either looking after individual machines as in the textile
industry (Blauner, Chapter 4) or performing simple operations
along with many other workers placed along assembly-lines
as in the motor-car industry, (Blauner, Chapter 5 and
Touraine, pp. 66–76). The jobs are intrinsically 'alienating'
(Blauner), while the formation of solidary work-groups is
prevented by the formal organisation of machinery. Thus there
is a separation between the formal and the informal work-
group (Touraine, pp. 62–3 and 179–80; Blauner).

Phase C: as technological progress proceeds, more and more
manual operations are taken over by machine, until in *Phase C*
the worker no longer touches the product. In the case of the
integral product, machinery such as the 'transfer machinery'
of the car industry (Touraine, pp. 33–5 and 47) takes over
a whole sequence of manual operations and the worker

becomes purely a 'machine minder'. But most factories at this stage of automation manufacture dimensional products 'measured by weight or volume (which become integral products after further processing; a quantity of acetylsalicylic acid, for example, became a number of aspirin tablets'. (Woodward, p. 38). This is the continuous-process plant, where chemical reactions inside the machinery form the product, and where again the worker becomes a machine-minder. But, in this phase, the worker has to develop new skills in order to look after such complex and expensive machinery successfully, and so job satisfaction rises again (Blauner, Chapter 6). Moreover freedom of movement is restored to the worker, while his task is again linked to that of other workers and supervisors. The formal and informal work organisation again coincides, and the 'social reinteg-ration' of the factory takes place (Blauner, Chapter 7; Touraine, p. 180).[42]

These points apply primarily to the production workers involved. Most skilled maintenance workers would seem to be in *Phase A*, with strong and officially approved work-groups, high traditional job skills and high job satisfaction.

It is impressive that, although the three authors were working almost completely independently of each other, their findings can be combined.[43] Our 'artificial theory of technological determinism' depends, first, on the functional model of 'effectiveness' relied on by Woodward. She states that companies making a certain type of product for a certain type of customer, will function more efficiently if they adopt particular layouts and types of machinery. Next she states that these combinations of machines (or technology) will be operated more efficiently if management adopts a particular structure of control and arrangement of worker tasks to go with them. At this point her analysis ceases to be very thorough, and I take over the next step in the argument from Blauner and Touraine. They demonstrate that workers desire certain types of rewards from their employment, namely, that they seek satisfactions deriving from the intrinsic skill content of the job and from the social relations with co-workers and with management. *Phase A* and *C* technologies are operated more efficiently by an allocation of work-tasks which permit the fulfilment

[42] See also on this point M. Fullan, 'Industrial technology and worker integration in the organization', *American Sociological Review*, 35(1970).

[43] The only cross-references in their work are several footnotes by Blauner to Touraine, which have the appearance of hurried additions at a late stage of writing.

of these desires, the use of worker skills and the formation of solidary work-groups (which, in the case of *Phase C*, often include technicians and managers too). Thus, with an efficiency model and a model of worker desires, statements can be made about the technological determinants of worker attitudes and industrial relations.

Perhaps I should say here that this is my own theory, for the theoretical perspectives of the three authors are very different from each other. Furthermore, none of these authors is a 'technological determinist' in the strict sense – they have merely chosen to vary technological factors while holding others constant. It is, of course, possible to reverse this procedure, holding technology constant and varying other factors. But this does not refute the theories of any of these authors.[44] Also as technology is not the sole determinant, it is quite possible that under certain circumstances it might not be the most important one. Thus we might find, as Goldthorpe and his collaborators did, that the influence which technology exerts is minor compared to the influence of other factors. The important finding of the 'Affluent Worker' team on this point is that their motor-car assembly-workers (*in Phase B*) are more satisfied with their employment than are process workers (*Phase C*) and even slightly more satisfied than are craftsmen (*Phase A*).[45] Their interpretation of this finding, and it seems a convincing one, is that the motor-car assemblers are not greatly worried by their lack of intrinsic job satisfaction or of solidary work-groups because they are interested primarily (and almost solely) in the financial rewards offered by their employment.[46] The authors urge us to look to variations in orientation to work as well as to technology in order to explain work attitudes. Whether we regard instrumentalism as being a reaction to non-work pressures (as do the 'Affluent Worker' team) or a reaction to work deprivation itself (as Touraine does), we cannot analyse it properly unless we look closely at the worker's own perception of his situation. I propose to do this now, and to bring together the material I have presented on orientations, technology and the internal and external labour market in order to make predictions about employment dependence.

I believe that the findings of the 'technological determinists' can be re-interpreted so that they reinforce the argument already developed on the hierarchical structure of the labour market. To do this, we must pay more attention than did the 'technological determinists' to the effects of technology upon the wage-structure and the internal labour market.

[44] As Turner and his collaborators suggest.
[45] Goldthorpe *et al., Affluent Workers* p. 72. Though there is a group of skilled workers, setters, who are slightly more satisfied than the assemblers.
[46] *Ibid.* p. 80.

PREDICTING EMPLOYMENT DEPENDENCE

I will organise my argument around the three phases of technology identified above. It is convenient to start the analysis of each phase by considering the occupational groups studied by Blauner: the printers in *Phase A*, the automobile assemblers and the textile machine operators in *Phase B*, and the chemical process workers in *Phase C*. Note that most of the statements made below are comparative ones: they seek to establish not the absolute level of employment dependence of each group, but rather its level relative to that of the other groups.

As Blauner and many other writers have noted, printers have exceptionally high job satisfaction which stems largely from their ability to control the work process in which they are involved. Indeed, they would seem to constitute an exception to the statements made earlier about the nature of the work involvement of most manual workers, for their enjoyment of the intrinsic activities and relationships of work makes it doubtful whether they are largely instrumentally involved.[47] But if we want to know whether their intrinsic and extrinsic work rewards tie them to any particular employer, we must find out whether in addition to controlling the work process itself they also control the supply of labour. If they can control both the supply of new recruits into the trade and the wage-rates paid to them, they can also make themselves economically relatively independent of any particular employer. The evidence is that, by and large, they can do this, and that these controls plus the control over the work process itself make them occupation rather than organisation involved.[48] If all skilled workers had similar powers, then all skilled men would depend very little upon their present employment.

But, of course, printers, in this as in so many other respects, are the 'ideal-typical' case of the tradesman to whom other tradesmen only approximate. In Britain, it is probable that a fairly large proportion of skilled tradesmen lack formal apprentice training, and also that wage-drift and plant bargaining have occurred on a considerable scale.[49] Both

---

[47] Of course, they are also among the highest paid manual workers in all countries, so we must be careful to separate their economic from non-economic rewards in any careful analysis of their involvement.

[48] Printers have been extensively studied by sociologists. The major study is that of S. M. Lipset *et al.*, *Union Democracy* (Free Press, 1956); a British study is that of I. C. Cannon. 'The Social Situation of the Skilled Worker' (unpublished Ph. D. thesis, University of London, 1961).

[49] On both points, see Robinson, *Local Labour Markets*. On apprenticeship see G. Williams, *Recruitment to Skilled Trades* (Routledge and Kegan Paul, 1957) chap. 4. It is unfortunate that, though Williams collected the necessary information, she does not give the exact proportion of apprentice-trained men in the industries studied. On wage-draft see, Royal Commission on Trade Unions and Employers' Associations 1965-8 ('The Donovan Commission') *Report* (H.M.S.O., 1968) especially chap. 3.

these would serve to weaken the control of any skilled trade as an organised group over the labour market. Accurate prediction is impossible here, but it seems probable that the actual level of dependence of any group of skilled tradesmen is not necessarily as low as that of the ideal-type of tradesman often presented in industrial sociology. In particular, we would anticipate that the dependence of the upgraded skilled man upon his present employer and of craftsmen with ill-organised union protection would be higher than that of the 'typical' printer. McCarthy's study of the closed shop in Britain indicates this. Though skilled workers in the printing and shipbuilding industries have usually been able to enforce strong entry controls upon employers, craft unions elsewhere, and certainly in engineering, have been forced over the years to accept a much weaker version of the closed shop, the 'post-entry control' where those already working in the industry are accepted as trade union members.[50] And as upgrading seems frequent, the internal labour market is also important for skilled workers. Of course, all craft unions have attempted to flatten out the job hierarchy within their craft, and internal differentiation seems minor compared to the large gap between craftsmen and their mates. Yet if wage-drift and plant bargaining have undermined the uniformity of intra-industrial wage rates, then the relative wage dependence will vary very greatly according to the state of the local labour market. There is thus more uncertainty regarding the labour market position of the skilled man than we perceived at first.

But in our analysis of the labour market position of the skilled man, we have moved away from an analysis of technological factors to occupational factors. Thus these remarks would apply as well to maintenance craftsmen in any technological phase as to production craftsmen in *Phase A*. Indeed, in all technological phases occupational factors must be considered if we wish to understand the worker's overall involvement in his employment, including his satisfaction as well as his dependence. For example, a man's satisfaction with his employment is not unrelated to his occupational status within the labour market. Thus, when dealing below with semi-skilled and unskilled workers I will tend, for reasons which will become apparent, to classify together with Blauner's *Phase B* workers all other unskilled workers. All factory labourers will be thus included in *Phase B* for example, even if they are servicing *Phase A* or *C* technologies. Similarly a great proportion of all semi-skilled workers will be considered together with *Phase C* workers. Turning to the heterogeneous *Phase B* group, let us first examine the automobile assembly workers studied by Blauner and others.

[50] W. E. J. McCarthy, *The Closed Shop in Britain* (Basil Blackwell, 1964) pp. 134–43.

58

Automobile assembly workers are men without recognisable and transferable skills, with unusually high wages and unusually poor scope for intrinsic work commitments. On-the-job learning is at a minimum – one American study found that 15,000 job classifications covering 80 per cent of workers in the automobile industry required less than one hour of training time[51] – and the labour force is homogeneous. There is very little internal promotion and consequently no internal labour market. Hence their dependence upon their employer is only great if they wish to maintain their unusually high earnings. In this respect they are similar to all those who are unusually instrumentally involved in their employment. The intensity of this involvement, the reluctance to abandon this particular set of rewards, is thus the determining factor, and we have to establish a great deal more about the importance of worker orientation and involvement before we can predict this. However, we can plausibily predict that among those most willing to abandon this employment will be the workers in the 40–50 age-group just emerging from the life-cycle squeeze.

The textile workers analysed by Blauner are probably far more typical in their work situation of the entire spectrum of jobs in *Phase B* technologies than are automobile assembly workers. Their intrinsic work roles are less alienating than the extreme case of the motor-car 'track' but are still simple, repetitive and undemanding. But as their extra-work situation was so unusual – living in company towns in the rural South of the United States – we had better hypothesise instead the extra-work situation of the 'typical' machine-minder in an urban factory. Here we would not generally find relations with workmates being coterminous with relations with friends and relations outside work, nor, more importantly, would we necessarily find such a depressed wage situation as Blauner. In a competitive labour market, the low skills and (probably) slightly lower than average working conditions of these jobs probably determine that their wages will be relatively low. And the enormous size of this group of workers in the labour market means that there will be a large number of employers in the labour market offering roughly the same economic conditions of employment. These, then, are the men whom we would expect to find least dependent upon a particular employer (except, of course, in a high-unemployment market when they would bear the brunt of that unemployment). Add to these the large unskilled number of non-production workers like material handlers, labourers, cleaners etc., and we have the least dependent type of unskilled or semi-skilled worker.

[51] R. L. Raimon, 'The indeterminateness of wages of semi-skilled workers', *Industrial and Labor Relations Review*, 6 (1953) p. 182.

Finally, we must consider the process workers, notably those in the chemical and steel industries often claimed to be 'the workers of the future'. Here I feel the 'technological determinists' go seriously astray for the first time. They assert that *Phase C* technologies create high employment satisfaction because they promote high intrinsic work satisfaction. We have already seen the necessary link between intrinsic job and work satisfaction denied in the case of car-workers – it is possible to argue similarly for the process workers. Though some studies have confirmed the high job satisfaction of process workers, not all sociologists agree.[52] The variety of intrinsic job contents contained within *Phase C* technologies is obviously rather large, and in many cases involves boring and machine-controlled routines. But more importantly, we should be sceptical about the *importance* of high intrinsic job satisfaction, where it is found. Most non-skilled manual workers do not expect to find interesting jobs. Resigning themselves to alienating work, they become instrumentally involved. If they do encounter interesting work, we might expect them to regard it as a welcome 'bonus', contributing little to their overall employment involvement. And this is what one recent study of process workers has found.[53] We might expect instrumental workers to be more concerned with economic considerations. The basic problem of Blauner's data on satisfaction levels is the generalising effect of satisfaction with employment: if a worker is satisfied on the whole, he will probably generalise this to specific aspects of work. But the high satisfaction of process workers may be due to factors other than those studied by Blauner. In view of this it seems to me surprising that so little attention has been paid to another factor in the situation which clearly helps produce high employment satisfaction (and also high employment dependence). This factor is the *secure wage* paid to process workers compared to what is available to them elsewhere.[54]

There are four main causes of the high steady wages in process production plants:

(*a*) The need to recruit men with high mental, non-traditional skills;

(*b*) the hierarchical ordering of jobs needing differing amounts of skills;

---

[52] Confirming studies are S. Cotgrove, 'Alienation and Automation', unpublished paper, University of Bath; and D. Wedderburn and R. Crompton *Workers Attitudes and Technology* (Cambridge University Press, 1972). For the contrary view see P. Naville, 'The Structure of Employment and Automation', *International Social Science Bulletin*, 10 (1958) pp. 16–28. Naville has elsewhere argued that the effect of automation on workers is profoundly ambivalent, and in increasing the distance between worker and machine, and between the worker's natural rhythm and that of the machine, it may increase alienation. *Vers l'automatisme social?* (Gallimard, 1963), chap. 11.

[53] Wedderburn and Crompton, *Workers Attitudes and Technology*.

[54] Wedderburn and Crompton note this factor, but neglect its significance.

(*c*) the need to avoid labour turnover and the cost of training replacements;

(*d*) shiftwork.

Managements view process production jobs as needing, above all else,
'responsibility' from the worker.[55] Tolerance varies considerably, of
course, but usually the worker is effectively in charge of expensive
machinery on which any error may have a disastrous impact. He is moni-
toring this equipment and, unusually for a manual worker, he is frequently
taking decisions about re-adjustments to controls. Thus, though without
traditional manual skills, he needs fairly developed mental skills. Moreover, this is probably highly specialised equipment, which means that
management cannot recruit men already trained in such jobs, nor can it
even rely on obtaining new recruits who have ever experienced similar
mental demands before. Thus management trains on-the-job and considers that experience on lower-skilled process jobs is the best qualification for entering higher-skilled jobs. Men, from the general unskilled
and semi-skilled market, recognised in some sense as 'responsible' and
'intelligent' but without any formal skills can thus be promoted through
a steep internal hierarchy.[56] Thus in Doeringer's American study the
process industries – steel and chemicals – recruited almost exclusively
at the low-skill end of the hierarchy, filling all other jobs by upgrading.[57]
Add the fact that process plants generally need to be kept running continuously, and that the men must accordingly be paid a shift bonus. The
result is that the higher-rated process operators (and the other types of
worker in *Phase C* technologies) will be earning a higher and steadier
wage than they could obtain elsewhere in the labour market. Nor need
we consider this in a purely economic light: the internal hierarchy is also
a status hierarchy, and if it is stabilised the worker may have a well-
developed notion of his professional status.[58] Again, I am emphasising
the hierarchical model.

If this very plausible argument is correct, the employment satisfaction
of most workers in *Phase C* technologies will be based on a comparison
with what is available to them elsewhere and will be a product of their
dependence. Such men will be extremely dependent on their employer

---

[55] J. S. Bright, *Automation and Management*.
[56] In a short article, W. W. Daniel has also observed that new technologies provide
considerable upward movement for men from the general unskilled and semi-
skilled labour pool. W. W. Daniel, 'Automation and the quality of work', *New
Society*, 29.5.1969, pp. 833–6.
[57] Doeringer, *Industrial and Labour Relations Review*, 20 (1967) p. 209.
[58] Touraine has noted that *Phase C* technologies enable semi-skilled workers to
pursue careers and to derive a sense of professional status rivalling that of the
skilled worker: *La Conscience Ouvrière*: (Éditions du Seuil, 1966) p. 111.

and will accept relocation. My case-study supports this argument. Nor need we confine it to chemical process operators.

First, a generalising effect occurs within companies which contain advanced technologies. This has been documented in the case of fringe benefits, which are most generous for all workers in the advanced sectors like the chemical industry.[59] Managements may wish to retain the services of their more responsible operators by providing generous pensions, sick pay and holiday pay related to length of service, but they usually accept the conventions of personnel policy and grant them to all em-ployees. There may be similar pressures on managerial promotion policy: where such desirable processing jobs exist at the top of the hierarchy, employees will probably press for the recognition of fixed rules for promo-tion at all levels, and particularly for the restriction of entry-points for outsiders. I know of no previous research documenting this, but will present supporting evidence from my own case-study later on. At present, we can give it the status of a plausible hypothesis.

Secondly, the 'golden chains' and the internal labour market may spread to other firms, through competition in the labour market. The response to hoarding of labour by other employers is to hoard oneself. However, arguments concerning 'the worker of the future' are rather dangerous. The 'typical' worker of tomorrow will no more be a process operator than the 'typical' worker of today is an assembly-line operator — the job market is far more diverse than this. These trends are probably developing but their overall importance is unclear.

In this section I have used technological and occupational factors to reveal variations in the ties of manual workers to their particular employ-ment relationship. I now want to attempt two further tasks using the material outlined in the previous sections. Firstly I must introduce the question of the importance of those ties relative to ties to non-work spheres of life. This is of particular importance for the prediction of reac-tions to industrial relocation, which is the main theme of this book. And secondly I must attempt to give some absolute values to employment dependence and to relocating propensity among manual workers.

PREDICTING RELOCATION PROPENSITY

Nowhere in this mass of evidence concerning manual workers have we seen any indications of the kind of spiralist career pattern, often found among managers and professionals, in which non-work spheres of life

---

[59] Wedderburn, 'Conditions of Employment of Manual and non-Manual Workers', pp. 14–15.

are subordinated to work in the sense that the latter determines both place of residence and types of community relations.[60] Furthermore, the only manual workers who might be considered to place intrinsic work activities and relationships among their 'central life interests', the well-organised skilled tradesmen, are as highly involved in their *occupation* as in their present employing organisation. However, the importance of the internal labour market and the contribution of steady employment to even the most alienated worker's concept of self-identity, do increase the importance of employment to the worker. Furthermore, even the most instrumentally involved workers may be highly dependent upon their present employment. We can see this by examining the Luton 'affluent workers'.

The 'affluent worker' is dependent upon his employment if, as I have argued, he wishes to maintain his level of economic rewards. But further than this, he may be relatively independent of the kinds of non-work ties which might prove an obstacle to further subordinating his life to work. An example of the latter is provided by job transfer, to which highly localised family and community relations might represent obstacles. If a worker is deeply embedded in an extended family or in other local social ties, he will be relatively unwilling to disrupt them by moving. But many of the 'affluent workers' will have already weakened those ties in choosing their employment (assuming for the moment that they did so). The Luton 'affluent workers' were relatively self-contained: that is, their social lives were largely confined to their own household and nuclear family, which are of course transportable.[61] Furthermore, certain types of instrumental involvement entail more weakening of localised ties, principally shift-working. Shiftworkers tend to be less active in voluntary associations and other non-family activities than dayworkers (though the differences are sometimes surprisingly small).[62] Highly self-contained workers may be especially dependent upon their present employment because their nuclear families cannot provide the economic support, and particularly the assistance in finding alternative employment that a close extended family might provide.[63] A previous history of geographical mobility, and also of downward social mobility (and possibly even Protestantism!),

[60] See Chapter 2 above for an analysis of 'spiralism'.
[61] Goldthorpe *et al.*, *The Affluent Worker in the Class Structure* (Cambridge University Press, 1969) chap. 4.
[62] Mott *et al.* found that shift work interfered with formal social activities (e.g. in voluntary associations) but not with informal ones (e.g. visiting friends) chap. V; F. C. Mann and L. R. Hoffman, *Automation and Worker* (Henry Holt, 1960) find the predicted differences between shift and non-shift in the case of visiting friends but not relations or co-workers (pp. 124–7); Goldthorpe *et al.* find that shiftworkers do less overall entertaining at home. *The Affluent Worker in the Class Structure*, pp. 97–8.
[63] W. W. Daniel, demonstrates the importance of this support. *Strategies for Displaced Employees*, pp. 36–7.

plausibly associated with instrumentalism, will increase this social and economic isolation. In all these special senses, then, the instrumental worker may be more dependent upon present employment *vis-a-vis* non-work spheres of life than other manual workers. Many *Phase C* workers will be in a similar position because of their shiftworking.

We can now make some tentative predictions about variations in relocating propensity among manual workers. One prediction seems reasonably secure:

(a) workers in *Phase C* technologies, that is process and transfer operators, and all others with positions near the top of internal promotion lines are the most heavily dependent of all upon their present employment, and will be the most likely to relocate.

At the other extreme, we may also expect:

(b) skilled workers whose trade exercises tight control upon the labour market are the least dependent upon any particular employer, and will be the least likely to relocate.

In between, however, are several worker groups whose relocating propensity is rather uncertain. We may say of these:

(c) skilled workers whose trade is not such a powerful protector of labour market interest are in an intermediate position; among this group those without formal qualifications, particularly those upgraded by their present employer, are probably most dependent of all upon him and therefore the most likely to relocate;

(d) workers in *Phase B* technologies who receive unusually unbalanced work rewards (for example, the motor car assembly workers) are dependent upon their present employer to the extent that they seek to maintain this set of rewards;

(e) machine-minders, labourers, and other workers *in Phase B* technologies not receiving particularly high rewards on any dimension are relatively independent of their present employers; among this group, the older, long-service workers will be more dependent than the younger, short-service workers.

Some, though not all, of these predictions can be tested in the present case-study, for the case-study firm contains several of these groups.

The absolute level of the relocating propensity is as important as worker variations in employment dependence and relocating propensity. This is much more difficult to establish with any degree of accuracy. Dependence might take two forms which we have already discussed, either economic (as in instrumentalism or as a consequence of the internal labour market) or social-psychological (as in the need for a stable self-identity obtained through work). The first would affect only those workers who cannot obtain the same (or a better) set of rewards in the external labour market, the latter would affect most long-service workers. How important for the overall gratification of the worker are these ties of dependence? There is no simple answer which can be given now. The extent to which the worker is 'consumption-minded', and the form his consumption takes, will obviously greatly determine his reaction to the economic ties of dependence. If, for example, the worker is committed to instalment purchasing of consumer durables, particularly a house mortgage, he may be more heavily dependent on maintaining his exact level of earnings than he who buys all his pleasures outright. These forms of consumption, particularly house purchase, are certainly increasing among the working class, but to go from this fact to a statement that dependence upon an exact level of earnings is also increasing would need detailed analysis of family budgets – which has not yet been attempted. Similar uncertainties beset analysis of the social-psychological aspects of employment dependence. The stress I have laid upon this factor derives mainly from the work of Gladys Palmer and associates, but in their work the social-psychological dependence of the ordinary worker is emphasised much more strongly than in most industrial sociology. What might be called the 'conventional wisdom' of industrial sociology, heavily influenced by Marxism minimises the significance of these ties between worker and employer. Thus it is still very much an open question how much status deriving from his present employment the worker enjoys both in his work and non-work life.

One point emerges clearly, however. Whatever the overall relationship between work and non-work in the life of the urbanised manual worker, any opposition to work ties would derive from one particular area of non-work life, namely the worker's kinship system. The worker's commitment to community relations outside of his kinship network is usually regarded as minimal by sociologists, and so does not constitute an obstacle to work-ties. Indeed there is one particularly neat piece of research which demonstrates that where the worker does have such strong community ties these actually depend heavily upon a satisfactory work career. This is Wilensky's study of 'middle-mass' Americans that is the upper manual and lower non-manual groups.[64] Wilensky analyses their job histories in terms of the orderliness of their careers, that is the extent to which their jobs have been

---

[64] H. L. 'Wilensky, 'Orderly careers and social participation: the impact of work history on social integration in the middle mass', *American Sociological Review*, 26 (1961) pp. 521–39. For a more speculative article using related data, see another Wilensky article 'Work, careers and social integration', *International Social Science Journal*, 12 (1960) pp. 543–74.

functionally or hierarchically related. While only a minority of the sample had job-histories that showed any significant measure of orderliness, those that had orderly careers participated more in the affairs of the local community than those with disorderly careers. Furthermore, by asking respondents to recall their social relations before they began working, Wilensky established that the causation ran

$$\text{orderly careers} \longrightarrow \text{social participation.}$$

Wilensky's measures of social participation mostly exclude family relationships, and we can thus say nothing about the vitality of extended family ties, but the vitality of this sample's other social relations depend upon favourable experiences in employment. Perhaps, then, there are some features of work centrality, which were assumed to be a middle-class phenomenon, among the working class as well. If this were so, non-kin social relations would probably present no great obstacle to relocation for the working class either, for where they were important to the worker they would also be dependent upon his work success.

However, the major obstacle to relocation among the working class, particularly in Britain, seems to lie in extended family relations, ignored by Wilensky. In adding the last two features of the theoretical model underlying this chapter – that is, the localisation of employment dependence and relocating propensity itself – we increase the uncertainties. For as we saw in the previous chapter, the move in working-class family structure toward the 'modified extended' type and the consequent weakening of the locality ties has been hypothesised rather than proved. Some such changes have almost certainly been occurring, but their exact extent is unknown. In view of the uncertainties surrounding recent trends in both work and non-work spheres of life, further research uniting the two is essential. I hope that this case-study will fill in some of the gaps in our present knowledge, for the case-study firm is peculiarly well suited to test many of the elements of the theoretical model I have set up. The relocation decisions of employees were peculiarly clear-cut: the employees could choose to retain their employment at the cost of breaking community ties in Birmingham or to retain their local ties at the cost of losing their employment. By establishing the nature of their jobs, their relations with the local community, and the reasons for their relocation decisions, we can come to conclusions regarding the relative importance of their ties to work and non-work aspects of life. Moreover, the technological structure of the firm was well-suited for casting light on the relationship between the internal and the external labour market which I have emphasised in this chapter. The firm contained a large section of continuous-process plant, as well as skilled maintenance workers, and unskilled workers on less advanced technologies. Thus *Phase A, B* and *C* workers were well represented, and the nature of their work involvement can be compared in a test of the 'hierarchical model' of the labour market outlined above.

However, I shall confess one limitation: the 'compensatory model' of the labour market has not found a good testing-ground in this case-study. The case-study firm did not offer an unbalanced set of work rewards to the manual worker, and thus the trade-offs of differentially-involved workers could not take place. I therefore had to be content to illuminate the rival, and neglected set of hypotheses, derived from a hierarchical model of orientations and the labour market.

As expected, the analysis of the work commitment of manual workers has turned out to be rather more complex than that of non-manual workers. After much effort I have produced predictions about the employment dependence and relocation decisions of manual workers, which will be tested in this case-study of relocation. Before discussing the actual relocation decisions, I shall analyse the structure of the firm's labour force according to the model set out in this chapter. The next chapter will describe the structure and recent history of the case-study company. The following one will describe the relocation process itself. These two chapters will 'set the scene' for the analysis in Chapters 6, 7 and 8 of the relocating decisions of the labour force and the after-effects of the relocation for both movers and non-movers.

4
The case-study company

The relocation of the case-study firm was actually only a part of the considerable processes of change which transformed the company during the 1960s, and only by understanding the changes can we analyse the nature of the work involvement of the diverse occupational groups within the company. So let us start at the beginning of the company's history and move quickly to the crucial 1960s.

THE COMPANY SETTING

Alfred Bird and Sons Ltd originated in a Victorian family incident. The wife of Alfred Bird, a Birmingham chemist, was allergic to eggs, and in 1837 he discovered a way of making custard without eggs. Within a few years he was selling locally both this Custard Powder and a Baking Powder which he had started manufacturing in 1843. The expansion of the company in the late nineteenth century lost its impetus after the First World War, and long-service senior management who can remember the family ownership period generally agree that the company was 'sleeping', though its profits were maintained.

Revitalisation came through take-over. In 1945 the General Foods Corporation of America set about finding an organisation willing to manufacture some of its products in Britain. A link was formed with the Bird company which culminated in 1947 in its complete take-over. At the same time, additional premises were acquired for the processing of coffee products. There were now two works, about one hundred yards apart and separated by a main road. Later, two more premises were acquired, one to serve as a finished goods warehouse, and one to house the research department. These also were in separate buildings, though close to the others. The straddling of a major road very close to the city centre brought major difficulties when traffic into towns began to increase rapidly in the 1950s. Apart from present inconvenience there was always the threat that Digbeth High Street, the main road, might eventually be widened at the expense of the dessert works. To see how inconveniences and vague fears were translated into actual relocation, we must trace the very rapid growth of the firm in recent years.

General Foods did not at first make a great impact on the company after the take-over. Several of the former directors remained and the new American products, ground coffee, cereals and other instant desserts, did not sell noticeably better than the Birds' desserts. Indeed, throughout the 1950s most were discarded one by one. But with the introduction of Maxwell House Instant Coffee in 1957 the firm experienced immense changes. The Instant Coffee sales and profits rose by about 20 per cent annually until 1964.[1] By 1962 the company was able to declare to the Ministry of Labour that coffee was its principal product. But Maxwell House was not unchallenged – indeed it was introduced some years after Nestlés had marketed Nescafé Instant Coffee, and has always had a smaller share of the market than the latter.[2] Competition with another major international corporation necessitated the learning of advanced techniques of manufacturing and marketing now practised by leading companies. The changes which this brought about for managers and workers were numerous. The most important was the relocation of the company itself. Its cause was quite simply that the factories in Birmingham could not accommodate the further expansion of the coffee plants which was confidently forecast by the marketing department. Yet it is impossible to understand the reaction to the move (which is the main subject of this study) unless the other changes produced by the coffee expansion are understood.

Table 3: *Alfred Bird and Sons Ltd: number of employees 1951–64*

Year (beginning of)	1951	1953	1957	1961	1963	1964
No. of employees	924	947	1,001	1,137	1,373	1,493

Table 3 shows the total number of employees with the company in various post-war years. The total fluctuated around the thousand mark throughout the 1950s, and then the total steadily increased year by year until it reached 1,500 in mid-1964. Accurate figures for each works are not available, but most of the increase took place in the coffee works (called Miller Works) and in the offices section of the desserts works (called Devonshire Works), where all the offices, except the research department, are housed. So the first change is one of size. This had effects on all parts of the company, though these effects were rather different for managers and shopfloor workers.

[1] In 1964 there was a short recession in the market for instant coffee which will be described below in Chapter 5, but thereafter sales continued to boom as before.
[2] That is to say about 30 per cent of the market, compared to Nestlé's 60 per cent.

69

MANAGEMENT

Among management the increase in total numbers reflected an increase in the number of specialists employed: accountants, chemical engineers, food chemists, and, lately, computer programmers and systems analysts. The marketing department also expanded greatly, and although some of its specialised functions such as consumer research are contracted out, it has attempted to attract university graduates to work out advertising strategies. In the last few years the company has developed an extensive programme of recruiting young managers direct from the universities. The lure is high salaries. Accurate figures are not available, but comparisons with other food companies through this period would probably become gradually more favourable to the company. Recent surveys in which Birds have participated indicate that the company is probably among the higher salary payers in the British food industry. A direct comparison is available between Birds' salaries and those prevalent nationally for 1964. Then, in a national survey conducted by the (then) Ministry of Labour, the average salary of administrative, technical and clerical employees was £1,008 in all manufacturing industry and £983.6 in the food, drink and tobacco industry.[3] The average Birds salary at the same time was £1,143.[4]

Good pay was accompanied by other favourable conditions of employment, notably the generous fringe benefits that will be discussed later on when we come to manual workers. Thus it is no surprise that in Survey 1 most of the salaried staff liked their employment at Birds as we can see by turning to Table 4. In the first column are the responses to an 'open-ended' question: 'What do you think of Birds as a company to work in?' As among the manual workers, nearly all respondents gave an answer favourable to the company. The remaining columns are based on fixed-choice questions and contain the percentages agreeing with the most favourable to the company of three alternatives. As most of the remaining responses fell in the middle category, i.e. 'neither satisfied nor dissatisfied' in the case of Question 88 and 'average' in the other four cases, there is little discontent revealed here. These, then, are in the main highly satisfied staff managers and supervisors. It is interesting to note, moreover, that

[3] Department of Employment and Productivity, *Labour Costs in Great Britain* (H.M.S.O., 1968) Table 12.
[4] These figures lump together men and women, and the latter earn considerably less. At Birds women constituted 38 per cent of this group, compared to 32 per cent in all manufacturing industry. In the food industry, women formed 39 per cent, so the differential of about 14 per cent between the salaries available at Birds and in the food industry generally probably reflects the real differences if we control for the effects of sex.

Table 4: *Male salaried staff viewing favourably various aspects of employment (percentages)*

Qu. 85	Qu. 88	Qu. 91	Qu. 92	Qu. 90	Qu. 93	
Birds a 'good' or an 'excellent' company	Satisfied with own job	Security good	Supervision good	Pay good	Promotion prospects good	N
84%	75%	58%	64%	61%	50%	62

they were also conscious of their financial dependence upon the company. Sixty-five per cent thought that it would be difficult finding similar wages elsewhere in Birmingham, a slightly higher figure than among manual workers.[5] So salaried staff seemed both satisfied with, and dependent upon, the company before the relocation. Though this is not altogether unexpected, given the sample bias discussed in the appendix leads us to expect a high relocation rate among the salaried staff.

However, it is worth noting one disquieting element in this general picture of staff contentment, which looms larger in later chapters dealing with the relocation and its aftermath. 'Office politics' appeared to be rising to an unusual level of intensity in the years immediately preceding the relocation. The evidence for this comes mainly from the informal interviews with 'key' managerial informants. It is difficult for the outside observer to assess the exact degree of conflict within a management group, but what is significant is that the managers themselves believed there was a very great deal of conflict among them.

The 'office politics' which were retailed to me were probably fairly normal for modern industry in most respects (though this is a subject on which little reliable and general information exists). Yet the general assumption that the 'solution' to problems of inter-group rivalry was dismissal of the losing group seems extreme. This assumption emerged most clearly in the language used to describe rivalries and 'purges' by the managers themselves in phrases like 'He's for the chop', 'we slashed that department', 'he was axed', and 'that was a real blood-bath' which were heard frequently during my field work. Moreover, there did occur authenticated cases of 'purges'. For example, around 1961 the English marketing director was involved in a dispute about the functions of his department with the American management of General Foods. He lost, and 'resigned' together with most of his department. Or again, the following years saw a crisis in the research department, and the staff there was

[5] See Table 16 (in answer to Survey 1, question 23).

reduced at a time of expansion elsewhere in the company. This resulted in most of the research staff demanding future job assurances before they would commit themselves to moving to Banbury. Another case occurred shortly after the move itself when three of the junior staff in the production planning department were dismissed while their seniors were shuffled out of positions of responsibility.[6] These purges were part of the folk-lore of the company in management circles and were frequently alluded to in conversation.

Yet the actual content of the legendary incidents was rather less dramatic than the folk-lore. In several instances 'dismissed' men were offered alternative employment within the company at no less a salary. They generally and rightly viewed this alternative as status-demotion and refused the offer. Moreover – and this is surprising in view of the folk-lore – the number of purges was remarkably small. Of course, all purges are officially described as being something else – a series of voluntary leavings – so it is just possible that some escaped notice. But this is unlikely given the eagerness with which managers picked up and transmitted gossip about job changes. So we are left with a total of three authenticated 'purges' in the period documented in detail in this study, that is between 1960 and 1968: one in marketing, one in research, and one in production planning. It is difficult from this to assert that Birds as a company was dominated by purges, especially as the first two incidents contained as many 'protest resignations' as actual dismissals.

If we turn to the cases of individual 'resignations', it is more difficult to separate the forced from the unforced. It is usually considered in the interests of both the manager and the company to conceal actual dismissals. Moreover, there is no clear dividing line between the two – indeed the typical forced resignation probably takes the form of hints from his superiors which are sufficient to tell the manager that his future with the company is not good. Thus, managers were very keen to anticipate future dismissals by acting on the slightest of such hints by leaving. Over-dramatisation probably followed: in at least two cases, described by other managers as cases of 'axing', the 'dismissed' person obtained a post with another prominent, progressive food company which certainly amounted to promotion. Male salaried staff turnover, running between 10 per cent and 15 per cent per annum, was probably high at Birds[7] but this may

---

[6] This is reported in more detail in Chapter 7.
[7] Adequate surveys of salaried personnel are not available, but a 'normal' annual turnover rate among male office staff is probably just below 10 per cent. See Organisation for Economic Cooperation and Development, *Wages and Labour Mobility*, pp. 62–3.

tell us more about the relations managers had with each other than with the company's official policies.

The company had changed qualitatively as well as quantitatively in the 1960s and in the offices this brought in larger numbers of younger men with more 'paper qualifications' than their predecessors. Many of these men and many of the older less-qualified men saw office politics as being dominated by the rivalry between these two groups. It is particularly interesting that many of the managers held stereotypes of each other similar to those of the 'thrusters' and 'sleepers' described by a P.E.P. report.[8] Younger, better-educated men were often described, favourably, as 'dynamic' and unfavourably as 'self-seeking' and 'ruthless'. Older, long-service men were labelled as 'dependable' and 'steady' or as 'half-asleep' and 'unimaginative'. And though the numbers of staff in the sample were too small for a thorough statistical analysis, marked differences in response between the two groups seemed to emerge there too. Thus, whereas half of all the staff thought that security and promotion prospects were good, only a third of the over 40s and a quarter of those with less than G.C.E. 'A' level or equivalent thought this. As one of the 'dependables' said 'The company is now going for paper qualifications. They forget that experience is also necessary. People like me are being overlooked now for promotion, and sometimes we begin to wonder if we're wanted here at all.' Indeed it must be said that some of top management were attempting to rid the company of the men they described as the 'deadwood' – whom it would be appropriate to 'axe'. However, these advocates of a 'tough' policy were trying to apply it equally to the 'thrusters', and to institute a general 'hire and fire' policy. Like most American corporations, General Foods attempts 'systematic job evaluation' for managerial as well as factory jobs. By close work measurement, it hoped, sub-standard performance could be perceived fairly quickly and dealt with.

The threat of dismissal is often understood by the new type of manager as being a part of his informal 'contract of employment'. One man said of the marketing department: 'You get paid extremely well, and part of it is for the risk. You accept this as part of the contract. It's your job to increase sales. If you don't, you know that you'll be out.' But top management was also attempting intermittently to use dismissals to remove what it termed 'deadwood' remaining from the earlier 'pre-efficient' days.

Most of those who resented the pressures toward this new system made in effect a different 'contract of employment' by entering the very dif-

---

[8] Political and Economic Planning, *Thruster and Sleepers: A.P.E.P. Report* (Allen and Unwin, 1965).

ferent company of ten years previously. These men joined, and presumably chose to join, a company which was not 'thrusting' or modernising, neither paying highly nor sacking freely. If a 'hire and fire' policy became actuality (as well as myth or projected future policy), these men would naturally lose by it. For whereas the 'thrusters' were reasonably confident of finding alternative employment, the 'dependables' were not so confident. Moreover, their attitudes to the company were distinctly less 'calculative', in the sense that when they described the company as 'good' or 'bad' in certain respects, they were much less likely to use comparisons with other companies as their frame of reference. The 'dependables', then, were more reliant, financially and emotionally, upon the company. Without the uncertainty of office politics, they would be obviously more likely to relocate with the company to Banbury. Taking politics into account, the reactions of both groups to the relocation becomes more difficult to predict.

MANUAL WORKERS

The effect of the expansion on factory workers has been rather more complicated, and this is where the separation of the two works becomes important. Miller Works and Devonshire Works not only produced different foodstuffs – they contained two very different technical processes. Indeed the technology of the coffee plant in Miller Works helped produce a type of employment for coffee process workers which was radically different from that of all other unskilled and semi-skilled workers within the company.

Instant coffee manufacturing is technically very advanced, and at Birds it has almost reached the stage of a 'continuous process': that is, a raw material is converted into a finished product by a series of chemical reactions which take place inside the machinery without being touched by hand. This technology can be classified, in the scheme developed above in Chapter 3, as a *Phase C* type, and it has certain consequences for job structure. The function of production workers in such a process becomes that of controlling the chemical reactions by operating dials and switches. Although this does not demand traditional manipulative skills, it does require constant attention and the ability to take decisions. From management's point of view, the worker occupies a responsible position: the machinery is costly, and a mistake could result in great damage to it. Moreover, because the process is a continuous flow, a hold-up somewhere along the line, even if it does not damage machinery, will soon stop the whole process. The economics of continuous flow technology usually

74

mean that it is very expensive to stop the plant except for periodic maintenance and this is why such plants are generally kept operating day and night and all week. Shift systems of working are therefore required. The Birds coffee plant operates continually day and night for 20 days out of 21 if the demand for coffee warrants it.

By contrast the dessert processes are not so technically advanced: theirs is a *Phase B* 'machine technology', where individual machines do individual tasks and the link between them is provided by manual loading and unloading. The breakdown of one machine does not stop total production, and the alertness of the individual worker is less important. Production is not continuous: according to demand it operates on one, two, or three shifts, but on a regular five or six day week basis. The technological environment of other manual workers, excepting the maintenance department, is also not advanced. Low skilled packers and cleaners and warehousemen make up this group. It is the lack of skills which links together the desserts workers, packers, cleaners and warehousemen.

Craftsmen form a third group. Craftsmen are not employed on production work itself, only on maintenance work, which is mostly of a mechanical and electrical nature, though there are a few carpenters in the company.

The different technical content of these three groups of jobs helps produce rather different employment situations. Coffee process workers work on a continuous shift system whereby the worker will have six morning shifts of eight hours and then two days off, followed by six afternoon shifts and two off, then six night shifts and two off; then he returns to the morning shift, and so on. (The grouping of the coffee workers into four separate shifts means that with three shifts rotating at any one time and the fourth resting, the plant need not be stopped.) This necessitates an irregular working-life, where neither the operator's working days nor his working times of day are the same from week to week. These inconvenient shifts push up the wages of the coffee workers, which are further inflated because of the 'responsibility' involved in their jobs.[9] The costliness of the machinery and the need to keep it running constantly force management to hire a careful, responsible workforce. This could be seen in the first survey by considering the job histories of the coffee processers. Data on up to three previous jobs were collected from the personnel records of the sample. As usual in such analyses, it is difficult to classify the job titles given there, but one factor emerges clearly. None of the coffee

---

[9] 'Responsibility' or a 'control skill' has often been identified as the key new skill demanded of workers by highly-automated plants. See especially Crossman, *Automation and Skill* for an excellent analysis of the components of the new skill.

processers had spent either his last employment or his previous employment of longest duration on purely unskilled, i.e. labouring, jobs, though 30 of the 74 'other manual' workers had done so. The majority of the processers whose jobs were recorded (i.e. 13 out of 23) had worked on jobs which might be termed semiskilled,[10] while the remainder had been either drivers or non-industrial workers (mostly salesmen).

Thus the introduction of coffee processing within the company has distorted the traditional distinction made by many in industry between skilled and unskilled workers. This can clearly be seen by looking at the grades of various manual jobs within the company in Table 5. Job grades vary between 10 and 110 for manual workers. The number of the grade represents the (rounded-off) total of its points-rating according to job-evaluaton. It determines the wage paid to the job-holder and represents the company's opinion as to the skill of the job. Three main points of interest arise from this table. First, the coffee processers' grades rival the maintenance workers' and outstrip the other manual workers', and consequently so do their wages. Secondly, this prosperity is available to the worker without traditional skills. Thirdly, promotion to the highest grades takes place only on the coffee plant for the unskilled worker, and so any unskilled worker who seeks a high degree of promotion will at some point

Table 5: *Types of occupation in the company's grade structure. Male manual workers in the sample*

	Skilled	Unskilled and semi-skilled	
	Maintenance workers	Coffee processers	Other manual workers
Grades 10–20	—	—	Most jobs in Devonshire Works, and all cleaners, packers, labourers, and warehousemen 57%
30–40	Mates 29%	Blenders, column loaders, helpers 61%	Some Devonshire Works machine operators, storekeepers, commissionaires 35%
50–70	Carpenters, painters boilermen, technicians 16%	Roaster operators 13%	Drivers 8%
80–110	Fitters electricians, instrument mechanics 55%	Spray drier operators, extractor operators, relief operators 26%	—
	(*N* = 31) 100%	(*N* = 23) 100%	(*N* = 74) 100%

[10] For example steel erector, slinger, chargehand etc.

76

have to transfer there. All three factors were recent innovations within the company, and thus with the growth of the coffee plant there arose considerable scope for conflict, and for adjustment, between the manual worker groups. Indeed, it is the conflict which explains the subsequent composition of the relocating group; while it is the subsequent adjustment which explains its size. This process of conflict and adjustment centred on the arrival and the development of trade unionism within the company.

CONFLICT AND ACCOMMODATION IN INDUSTRIAL RELATIONS, 1959–62

Birds did not officially recognise any trade union for negotiating purposes until 1962. Before that date a few workers had usually kept union cards needed in other employment, but outside attempts by the Transport and General Workers Union and by the Union of Shop, Distributive and Allied Workers, to establish a company branch had failed. The company was convinced that unions were not, and never would be, needed. This was stated by the personnel manager in 1959: 'very few of our factory employees belong to unions because our rates of pay and conditions of service are substantially in advance of those which are the result of union negotiation'. Let us examine the truth of this claim.

The company has not kept systematic records of wage-rates and real earnings throughout this period, but enough remain to form a guide to the progress of wage rates. Two sorts of comparison can be made between Birds' rates and outside rates for manual workers: 1. comparisons of minimum rates with those negotiated by the appropriate trade group on the Joint Industrial Council for the Food Industry; 2. comparisons of actual average earnings with those issued by the Ministry of Labour for all manufacturing industry and for the Food, Drink and Tobacco industry. The comparisons available are given in Tables 6 and 7 respectively.

The figures reveal three distinct periods in wage trends. The first extends from the take-over in 1947 to about 1958; the second from that date to November 1961; and the third follows the events of November 1961 to the present day. The first period reveals a gradually improving wages position, in which average Birds' wages overtake the average for all manufacturing industries (though female wages were already ahead of this average in 1947). However, the personnel manager quoted above was speaking in 1959 and in that year the Birds' minimum was only just above that negotiated by trade unions at the Joint Industrial Council. The margin of superiority was 6d per week for the men, and 10d per week for the women. By March 1961 the differential had widened to 5s 3d for men and 1s 3d for

Tables of comparative earnings and wage rates

Table 6: *Minimum weekly wage rates for full-time manual workers set by the Joint Industrial Council for the Food Industry[a] compared to Birds minimum rates. Men and women (aged 21 and over, and 18 and over, respectively)*

Month end	Joint Industrial Council		Alfred Bird and Sons Ltd	
	Men s d	Women s d	Men s d	Women s d
April 1954	121 0	86 0	142 6	97 6
December 1959	164 6	116 6	165 0	117 4
March 1961	173 3	123 0	178 6	124 3
November 1961			260 9	196 0
May 1964	196 6	140 0	263 4	198 4

[a] The title of this group has changed several times. It is now known as Food Manufacturing (General) Group.

Table 7: *Average weekly earnings of manual workers: England and Wales and Birds (men and women)*

Year[a]	All manufacturing industry		Food, drink, and tobacco industries		Birds	
	Men s d	Women s d	Men s d	Women s d	Men s d	Women s d
1947 (March/April)	129 2	68 0	117 5	62 9	110 0	70 0
1953 (March/April)	191 11	101 0	167 1	94 2	170 0	130 0
1956 (October)	245 8	123 8			262 6	148 3
1962 (April/Aug.)	323 10	157 1	297 4	151 5	423 0	198 6

[a] Only the year 1956 offers a strict comparison, with surveys conducted in the same week. In the other years, the month at the end of which the Ministry of Labour survey was made is given in brackets, followed by that of the Birds survey.

women, but this was still well down on the 1954 differential. Unfortunately, the figures for average earnings obscure this lag in Birds rates, but other evidence points toward it. It seems particularly marked for craftsmen. The comparison with rates paid to craftsmen with a firm of contractors doing work in the Birds' factory in November 1960 is revealing: the differential between them and Birds' craftsmen was as much as

40 per cent in their favour. A manager comments on this situation: 'The trouble was that until November 1961 we paid them [craftsmen] very badly. I know what this meant because I had the job of employing them. I inherited ten vacancies and I simply could not fill them.'

Yet the craftsmen did not only complain about basic rates. Their position in the Birds' pay hierarchy was also being undermined. They were technically skilled men, accustomed to earning wages higher than un-skilled or semi-skilled men. But by 1960 this was no longer true in Birds. With coffee output increasing at the rate of 20 per cent per annum, the company was finding that it simply could not satisfy demand, and, for a period, was importing finished coffee from Canada. It could not afford coffee plant stoppages whether mechanical or human in origin, and was prepared to pay high wages to help ensure that these did not occur. In November 1960 an engineering manager warned against this tendency in a memorandum. As he said, his figures speak for themselves (Table 8). Higher management's response to this was to raise the shift allowances which, although increasing the rewards of shift fitting, maintained the equality between skilled and semi-skilled. Indeed resentment was in-creased. The new allowances were percentaged bonuses of the rate for the job, instead of the old fixed payment bonuses of between 4½d and 11d for each hour done on shifts. The new percentages meant that shiftworkers gained more as their job-rate increased. This naturally meant that both tradesmen and coffee processers gained more than other workers on non-continuous shifts. And above all, the new allowances were considerably higher than the old and all shiftworkers gained money while dayworkers did not. So now the grievances of the unskilled and the semi-skilled dessert workers were added to those of the craftsmen.

Previous research has shown that any upsetting of traditional job hierar-chies often produces discontent, even if all workers actually gain in wages as a result of the change. Investigators in a North Wales Steel mill found that where this occurred the workers who had been moved down a couple of places in the hierarchy, with increased wages as compensation, actually

Table 8: *Maintenance workers pay, October–November 1960 (Miller Works only)*

Worker	Average weekly gross earnings (£ s d)	Average weekly hours	Equivalent rate per hour (s d)
Shift fitter	21 17 0	49¼	8 11
Shift electrician	19 15 0	43¼	9 1½
Shift coffee production operator	20 11 0	43½	9 5

thought that their wages had 'got worse' as a result of the changes.[11] A recent survey of the position of shop stewards in British industry has noted their continual use of the concepts of equity and 'fair play'. For example, if new job rates are introduced they are usually disputed on the grounds that they must enable workers 'not to lose by the change and thus be able to maintain their comparative position.'[12]

These arguments are re-inforced by the events at Birds in 1961 and 1962. On 21 November 1961 a token strike against wage-rates was staged by 45 workers who said they were members of the Transport and General Workers Union and asked for negotiations to take place between the company and local union officials. Twenty-one of them were maintenance workers, the others were desserts workers. There were no coffee workers amongst them. The strikers constituted only 7.3 per cent of the manual labour force, and were answered by a counter-move from anti-unionists. A petition was signed by 381 workers, or 61 per cent, for the managing director asking him to resist the introduction of trade unions in the factory. Petitioners still with the company denied to me that any coercive pressure was put upon them but as many of the sponsors of this petition were foremen, presumably informal pressures did play a part. Nevertheless, as I shall show later, even in December 1964 there was a minority group of workers who could be described as 'anti-union'. The most striking fact about the petitioners was their composition: half were coffee workers, whereas all coffee workers formed only a quarter of the manual labour force. A director of the company comments frankly on the causes of the split:

> The division between the two Birmingham works was always
> very strong, and for a time management deliberately used and
> fostered it to counter the power of the unions. Management
> could always rely on support against the unions from the well-
> paid, pampered coffee workers.

But management was in a difficult position. It wanted to retain the new job hierarchy because this was felt to reflect the actual worth of the different jobs. Management considered the coffee process workers to be worth their wages, because of the high costs of the machinery they were operating. So how could management satisfy the grievances of the strikers, and prevent the further spread of union membership within the

[11] W. H. Scott *et al.*, *Technical Change and Industrial Relations* (Liverpool University Press, 1956) pp. 216 and 238–9.
[12] W. E. J. McCarthy, 'The role of shop stewards in British industrial relations', *Royal Commission on Trade Unions and Employers' Associations*, Research paper No. 1 (H.M.S.O., 1967) p. 17.

factory? There is no doubt that this is what it wished to do, as its subsequent actions showed.

The solution attempted was simple. It was to give everyone a large wage increase, without first negotiating with union officials, while preserving the new wage hierarchy. Reference to Table 6 reveals the extent of the wage increases: they are increases of around fifty per cent. The slightly greater increase of female basic rates compared to male reflects the importance of women in the strike and the fact that most women were on the basic rate. But increases were granted throughout the scale in about the same proportions. This increase took the union aback, as it was much more than the local officials had asked for. The company attempted to close the subject on the 24 November by sending a copy of the anti-union petition to the local union officials commenting: 'in view of the interests of our employees, and the overwhelming wishes of the great majority, Management does not consider that any useful purpose would be served now by any continuance of discussions between us'. Moreover, the company had stuck to its refusal to discuss these matters with employees who were trade union members.

The company now expected union influence in the factory to disappear, but this did not happen. By March the directors were privately admitting that union strength in Birds had been growing continuously since November, and estimating present membership to be around 300 or even 350, i.e. about fifty per cent of the labour force.[13] In fact it was only about 200, though there had still been a considerable increase.

One reason for the increase is easy to discover. Although the company had granted a large increase, more indeed than the union had asked for, its hand had obviously been forced by employee discontent. Although its wage increase was already finalised by the time the strike actually took place, management had received advance warning of the Transport Workers' interest in the company. It is thus quite possible that many employees gave the union the credit for the increase.

Moreover, the differentials remained and the coffee workers were still thought of as a privileged group. Significantly, there were no coffee process workers within the union until years later in 1964.

But the leaders of the Transport and General Workers Union at Birds advance another reason for their success in recruiting after the large wage increase of 1962. The chairman of the shop representatives committee puts it like this:

[13] Throughout, I will mean by 'the union', The Transport and General Workers Union. Actually the (then) E.T.U. and A.E.U. also later obtained recognition from the company, but their membership was small and their influence confined to small groups of tradesmen.

We came in because of wages, yes. But it was coupled with
another thing, with preferential treatment on the production
side. If you were well in with the foreman you got the good job.
If you were a yesman you were O.K. This is much better now. It
can't be done anymore because we're too strong. We've cured
the thing we came in for.

A manager in close contact with the problem agreed:

The union has brought security. We used to sack people without
due cause, there's no doubt about that. We can't do it now,
though. The union would soon step in. Not that it's all a good
thing, mind you. There's some that should go through incom-
petence.

Three types of grievance about preferential treatment were common at
this time. One concerned wrongful dismissal and occasioned a short strike
in February 1964. The other two were both intimately related to the
growth of the coffee plant itself. One was the wage differentials already
described, but the other, already implied by the T. and G.W.U. branch
chairman, was promotion, the problem of who got 'the good jobs'. For the
coffee plant was virtually the only possible channel of promotion for the
manual worker without traditional skills. Top-rated coffee processing
jobs were paid about £30 a week in 1964, a considerable wage for men
without formal skills. Shiftwork was the only major drawback to work
on the coffee plant and there is no doubt that coffee process jobs are
prized by most of the unskilled workers in the company; when one falls
vacant many of them apply for it.

But what are the criteria for this promotion? The 'skills' needed
(according to management) are steadiness, a 'responsible attitude', and an
ability to take decisions. These are rather difficult to measure: steadiness
and a 'responsible attitude' can often mean a co-operative attitude to
management. Ten of the first twenty coffee process operators had previously been chargehands within the company, and since then operators
had been recruited partly on the basis of their record of co-operation
with their supervisors. In such circumstances charges of favouritism can
easily arise; indeed it is difficult to see how they can be adequately
dispelled.[14] Moreover, the job-structure of the company brings additional
promotional difficulties. Night packers, for example, were doing extremely unskilled work, hoping (by and large) for promotion to more
skilled or responsible positions. Yet they could not obtain promotion
straight into 'responsible' jobs on the coffee plant. First, they would have

[14] Except by management accepting seniority as the basis of promotion – which it
was unwilling to do.

to work in intermediate positions elsewhere in the factory. But this would bring problems as one of their foremen points out:

> A lot of them apply for better jobs, but not many move. Any job they might get would probably be on an alternating shift basis [mornings and afternoons] on which their shift bonus is ⅛th instead of the ⅓rd you get on permanent nights. Their new job would only be a grade or two higher so they wouldn't earn any more, and they might get less. If they got a day job, they'd lose a lot. To make up their money they have to go for a grade 50 or 60 job, and there's not many of those around. 60 is a Quality Control Technician and they can't jump into that.

So 'favouritism' could easily become an explosive issue within the company.

This is why, when the union was formally recognised by management in June 1962, machinery was set up for the settling of individual grievances through union-management consultation. But no attempt was made by the union to secure negotiation on wage-rates and general conditions of employment. Management knew that sooner or later this would be requested, if the union could increase its strength. For the moment the union was pressing for redress of alleged preferential treatment which seemed more important to members. The grievance procedure was narrow in scope. If a member was not satisfied that his foreman had dealt with his grievance fairly, he took it to his union shop representative; it was then discussed at joint union-management meetings. If agreement could still not be reached, a Ministry of Labour arbitrator was brought in, as in the case mentioned above. The union agreed, for its part, to refrain from work stoppages and intimidation of non-union members. Neither side suffered any delusions: management knew from the first that the eventual aim of the union was to force a closed shop. Both knew that any negotiations would be moulded by their actual bargaining strength.

Management took the initiative. In 1963 the company acquired its first personnel director and he soon introduced a system of joint consultation within the company. Though its stated intention was to 'bring all em-employees closer together', it was rightly recognised by the union officials as a means of by-passing consultation with them. Some members of management are convinced that employee morale was rising after the beginning of 1962 and that the union was losing its impetus. One personnel manager commented:

> A.B. & S. have always been good employers except for the period from '59 to '61 or '62. Then there was bad handling of employee relations right at the top, and the necessity for unions grew. The things that were wrong then were put right in the first

> year or two of union activity, and then the need for unions diminished. About 18 months ago [i.e. in the early summer of 1964] the union was actually wavering in importance. It was very unpopular due to its mishandling of issues.

The evidence available is not conclusive though it is suggestive. First, although union membership was not falling, its rate of increase had slowed considerably throughout 1963.[15] Secondly, an analysis of the number of grievances raised under the 1962 agreement and of the level at which they were settled shows that in the first half of 1964 the number of grievances fell slightly, but the number of those carried past the foreman level and involving a union representative fell sharply. Thirdly, as already mentioned, in December 1964 the pre-move survey identified many anti-union employees. About one-third of male manual workers said that trade unions should not have a place at Birds. Their reasons were of three sorts: 40 per cent reasoned that they did not 'believe in' trade unions, 35 per cent that Birds in particular did not need them, and the remaining 25 per cent that unions had done 'no good' at Birds.[16]

This is the total evidence for a falling-away of union support in late 1963 and early 1964. It is suggestive but not conclusive. Yet the probable reason for it is the same as that behind the union's reluctance to concern itself more with the negotiation of general wages and conditions: practically everyone has been satisfied with them ever since 1962.

CONDITIONS OF EMPLOYMENT IN THE PRE-MOVE PERIOD

McCarthy's survey of shop stewards shows that their bargaining is usually based on comparisons with other workers in the same company, with workers outside the company in the same industry and with workers outside the company in the same region.[17] The first comparison has been the basis of trade union activity at Birds. But the second and third have not been made because, as the unionists agree, there are very few outside companies having better wages and conditions than Birds. This is of the utmost importance in interpreting employees' reactions to the relocation, and is worth analysing in detail.

We have already seen, in Tables 6 and 7, that Birds' wage-rates and actual earnings for manual workers were considerably higher than the

---

[15] Union membership records are not sufficiently consistent or precise to permit statistical analysis, and this statement is only a rough estimate.

[16] In response to Survey 1, question 95. This question was 'open-ended' and the responses were classified afterwards.

[17] McCarthy, *The Role of Shop Stewards in British Industrial Relations*, pp. 17–18.

national average for all industries, and for the food industry in particular, by about 1962. This has remained true subsequently. Yet the comparisons made by trade unions are generally local ones, except in the very largest companies with widely-dispersed plants,[18] and the real comparison made by employees themselves was with other wage-rates in the Birmingham area. Some detailed figures are available on the wage-rates of several Birmingham companies in October 1963 from a private survey in which Birds collaborated. The other companies are not named in Table 9 below but all are large and well-known.

It can be seen from this table that wage-rates for daywork at Birds are the highest for less-skilled men, and are either second or third highest in the top three skilled categories. A similar pattern between skill levels is observable among women. One additional point should be made: the comparative figures are for dayworkers only and thus cannot be compared with the average earnings of the large proportion of the Birds' manual male labour force working on shifts. The earnings of the Birds' workers on the continuous shift system are given in the last column of Table 9. It is the extra earnings due to shift work which is most difficult to parallel locally for there is not much shiftworking in Birmingham.[19]

But it cannot be denied that better immediate wages do exist in Birmingham. Table 9 also suggests that there may be a few companies in Birmingham which pay higher wages to semi-skilled and skilled workers. Nor is shift-working completely absent from the area. Moreover, the car firms at least (which were not included in the survey on which Table 9 is based) are known to pay higher wages for unskilled work than Birds, as one or two of the non-movers later discovered.[20] Thus, when we come to analyse the sample's attitude to their wage-rates we shall find that, although conscious that Birds was a high-wage firm, a large minority was also reasonably confident of finding similar wages elsewhere in Birmingham. Birds, although a high-wage firm, was also in a high-wage area where (at the cost of more unpleasant working conditions and greater initial insecurity) higher wages were probably possible for many manual workers. But the exceptional reward offered by Birds to manual workers was, and still is, a near-guarantee of high wages in the future. This was sometimes remarked on by the sample in answer to Question 23. Having

---

[18] S. W. Lerner and J. Marquand, 'Regional variations in earnings, demand for labour and shop stewards' combine committees in the British engineering industry', *Manchester School*, 31 (1963).

[19] In the Ministry of Labour's 1964 survey 17.9 per cent of workers sampled in the Midlands Region were working shifts. The national average was only 18 per cent but some regional figures were very much higher than this: *Ministry of Labour Gazette*, April 1965, pp. 148–55 and June 1965, pp. 258–63.

[20] See Chapter 8 below.

Table 9: *Wage survey, Birmingham area, October 1963 – manual workers (amended to include engineering award of November 1963)*
Comparison of weekly earnings for 42 hours on day work including average bonus where applicable

	Alfred Bird and Sons Ltd			Food Company A			Food Company B			Engineering Company A			Engineering Company B			Food Company C			Alfred Bird & Sons Ltd Average earnings on continuous shift work		
	£	s	d	£	s	d	£	s	d	£	s	d	£	s	d	£	s	d	£	s	d
Male																					
Minimum earnings (A.B. and S. Grade 10)	13	0	9	11	12	0	11	3	6	11	0	7	10	6	3	9	19	6	18	18	8
Mid-way semi-skilled (A.B. and S. Grade 30)	14	7	0	11	17	0	12	15	0	12	8	0	12	1	0	13	8	0	20	16	10
Top semi-skilled production (A.B. and S. Grade 60)	16	7	3	14	19	0	14	7	6	17	5	0	13	7	7	15	4	6	23	15	11
Skilled tradesmen (A.B. and S. Grade 100)	18	19	9	17	8	0	16	5	6	16	16	8	17	3	6	20	4	0	27	11	6
Top skilled rate (A.B. and S. Grade 110)	19	12	0	18	8	0	18	10	0	20	10	6	18	0	6	21	11	6	28	9	8
Female																					
Minimum (A.B. and S. Grade 10)	9	16	0	8	15	0	8	5	0	9	8	5	9	1	7	7	15	0			
Maximum (A.B. and S. Grade 30)	10	15	3	9	5	0	9	1	9	10	14	5	10	7	6	11	0	0			

N.B. By the time the interview survey took place in November 1964, the average earnings of all groups of Birds employees had increased by 15s–£1 per week, except for the very highest grade where the increase had been £2 – £3.

said 'No' (they would not have difficulty obtaining a similar job) they often added 'but the question is, how long would the wage last?' or a similar remark. The importance of job security for the manual sample and also for some of the managerial group was revealed in the answers they gave to open-ended questions. One unskilled worker said:

> One thing, though: you know where you are with this company. I dare say I could earn more at Longbridge [the B.M.C. main site] but once there you're in and out, in and out. I come in here and know what my job is here all day, every day.

Some workers actually denied that wages would be higher at the car firms. Their reasoning followed this man's:

> Oh yes, I know they pay well. But its by the hour like every-where. I bet with all those hours lost through strikes and sack-ings, you don't *bring home* more than you do here. (his emphasis)

It is not possible to test this belief but it was one circulating widely through the Birds labour force. Certainly the security of employment at Birds was above average: no permanent employee has been laid off there for ten years, and in the interviews the men themselves often compared this to the perpetual lay offs which seemed to them to occur at either of the major Birmingham car firms, B.M.C. or Rover. Moreover, temporary demoting of groups of workers because of market recessions did not even occur before the conditions of 1964 which are to be discussed in Chapter 5. So the only internal transfer of employees which could threaten earnings during this period was a transfer to a lower-paid job while the previous job continued. But the company's 'Detached Worker Policy' took care of this eventually, guaranteeing the worker his normal wage if this were higher than that of the new job.[21] Moreover, since the introduction of the trade union there have been very few dismissals of any sort.

Another advantage of employment at Birds was the company's gene-rous provision of 'fringe benefits' which were greatly expanded following on the events of 1962. Conveniently, we can make a direct comparison between fringe benefits in the company and those in manufacturing industry in Great Britain as a whole in 1964. The evidence for the com-parison derives from the Ministry of Labour survey already quoted. It is evident, first, that Birds offered a wider range of fringe benefits to all employees than did the average employer in manufacturing industry as a whole or in the food industry in particular. Thus all Birds employees were

---

[21] This 'Detached Worker Policy' was considerably amended in Banbury so as to give the worker a *guarantee* of his normal wages over a period if he was trans-ferred, whether or not his normal job continued. See Chapter 7 below for details of this granting of a central part of 'staff status'.

covered by a pension scheme and by a sickness pay scheme. Table 10 shows that this is not true in all places of employment, though most employers in the food industry do now offer such benefits. In particular, it is worth noting the great difference in manufacturing industry in general (though not in the food industry) between the treatment of manual and non-manual workers. For many years fringe benefits at Birds had been calculated on the same basis for all employees. In this respect Birds was certainly in the fore-front of a national trend toward the narrowing of works/staff differentials.[22] It is certainly significant that in the Ministry of Labour survey, the industry whose conditions most closely approximate to those of Birds is the chemical (i.e. continuous-process *Phase C*) industry.

But of rather more interest is the *actual amount* paid out by the employer in fringe benefits. The relevant comparisons are made in Table 11. Figures are given separately for the size-range which includes Birds, that is over 1,000 employees. This table is a useful guide to the various financial conditions of employment at Birds compared to elsewhere. The average wage/salary is far higher than national and industry averages. Birds also spends more per employee on both subsidised services and recruitment and training. The main subsidised services provided by Birds are canteen facilities, working overalls, and medical services, and we shall see below that these services were appreciated to a surprising extent by employees. The high cost of recruitment and training reflects the recent trends already

Table 10: *% of employers incurring expenditure on certain fringe benefits*[a]

	Sickness and injury pay		Pension funds	
	For operatives %	For administrative technical and clerical workers %	For operatives %	For administrative technical and clerical workers %
In all manufacturing industry	42.1	67.3	45.1	66.0
In food, drink and tobacco industry	79.2	72.9	62.5	75.7

[a] *Labour Costs in Great Britain in 1964* (D.E.P.) Table 6. The two benefits shown in the table are the only important benefits for the employee which are not provided by 100 per cent of employers. For example, holiday pay is now provided for by 100 per cent of employers.

[22] See Dorothy Wedderburn, 'The Conditions of Employment of Manual and Non-Manual Workers'.

Table 11: *Average annual amount of wages and fringe benefits per employee in pounds*[a]

	Total labour costs	Wages and salaries	Private social welfare payments	All subsidised services	All recruitment and training
All manufacturing					
1,000+ employees	953.1	868.9	34.2	15.6	16.6
Total	885.5	813.0	27.1	12.7	12.0
Food, drink and tobacco					
1,000+ employees	862.4	765.7	45.1	23.5	7.6
Total	803.9	721.1	36.3	18.9	5.2
Birds	1,156.8	1,035.0	36.3	32.8[b]	23.6

Source: Labour Costs in Britain in 1964 (D.E.P.) Table 7. Unfortunately, the Survey did not tabulate separately the costs of male and female employees. A more thorough analysis would separate employees into four groups: male and female operatives, male and female A.T. can workers. But the overall employee figures are probably a fair basis for a comparison between Birds and national averages, as Birds, is over-weighted both with female workers (for whom employers probably provide lower benefits) and administrative, technical and clerical workers (who receive higher benefits).

[b] Excludes costs due to the relocation.

89

described in this chapter: the growing need for scarce managerial skills and for 'responsible' operatives. Only with regard to the 'private social welfare payments', of which the most important is a pension, did Birds lag behind any other group shown for comparison in Table 11. This group is the comparable size-range in the food, drink and tobacco industry, and its high expenditure for private welfare probably reflected the well-known paternalism of some of the larger food companies; no other manufacturing group listed exceeded Birds in its expenditure per employee on this item. Birds was therefore unusually generous in its provision of material benefits.[23] Moreover, all these benefits are linked to length of service: for example, the two week holiday is raised to three weeks after five years service and to four weeks after twenty years; while the ratio of employer to employee-contribution to the pension fund increases with length of service. Birds well appreciates that fringe benefits tied to length of service can be 'golden chains'.

The trade union recognised the importance of the benefits; the chairman of the branch comments 'They got pretty fair pay in Birmingham, as good as anyone else, sick pay, holidays on the average of your yearly income. Nobody would deny that they were working for a good company.'

It was therefore predictable that Survey 1 would find a great deal of satisfaction among employees at Birds. Whereas many employees were enthusiastic about job and company, and most were well satisfied, very few were actually dissatisfied. This was most marked in the answers to the question 'What do you think of Birds as a company to work in?' As among the salaried staff and the women the answers clustered at the favourable end of the scale in response to this 'open-ended' question, as can be seen in Table 17 later. Many of these answers were extremely enthusiastic. Of course, most surveys of worker morale find high levels of satisfaction – it is a sociological truism to say that people generally approve of the social institutions in which they are involved – but satisfaction of this apparent intensity is unusual.[24] There was a more usual distribution of responses to the question 'How do you feel about the job you do at Bird's? Are you satisfied, dissatisfied, or don't you feel strongly either way about it?[25] Of the male manual workers 67 per cent said they were satisfied, while

[23] A regional breakdown of the results of the government survey would have been useful. We may suspect that higher fringe benefits are to be obtained in the prosperous Midlands and South, and that Birds was not quite so unusual an employer in its own region.

[24] For example, 81 per cent of the male manual responses here were categorised as 'Excellent' or 'Good', compared to 65 per cent in the all-male sample of the 'Affluent Worker' team replying, to a slightly different question, that their firm was 'better than most', Goldthorpe *et al.*, *The Affluent Worker: Industrial Attitudes*, p. 72.

[25] Survey 1, question 88.

only 23 per cent said they were dissatisfied. These results are rather similar to those of other surveys.[26]

Nor was much dissatisfaction revealed in the answers to the other job attitude questions, Questions 89, 90, 91, 92, 93 and 94 of Questionnaire I given in the Appendix. Respectively, 16 per cent were dissatisfied by the work their department was doing; 10 per cent thought their pay, and 8 per cent their job security, was bad; 11 per cent thought their supervisors performed badly; 17 per cent thought their own promotion chances were bad; 12 per cent thought there was too much pressure put upon them in their work.

Although the general level of satisfaction with the Birds employment relationship was very high, we might expect in the light of the company's history that it would not be evenly distributed among the working groups I have distinguished. Among manual workers might not the three groups distinguished – the craftsmen and their mates, the coffee processers, and the 'other manual' group – be differentially satisfied according to the differences in their work situation mentioned above? Or alternatively, had the more recent managerial policies described reduced the effects of these differences among manual workers? More important, perhaps, differences in the extent of job dependence (which I suggested in the previous chapter) might be a more significant part of work involvement than job satisfaction. So let us start the analysis of inter-group differences by considering the most important part of job dependence, wage levels.

INTER-GROUP DIFFERENCES IN EMPLOYMENT DEPENDENCE

Table 12 shows the take-home pay of the work groups in the sample in November 1964.

At the manual level the effect of the introduction of coffee processing is clearly visible. The top-rated coffee process operators earned as much as the fully-qualified craftsmen (the highest-paid manual workers of all are relief operators on the coffee plant, able to work any of the jobs on the coffee plant; one of them appears in the £125 column above). Their median wage is somewhat below that of the maintenance workers, but their general wage-structure is much nearer to theirs than to the 'other manual' workers. But Table 13 below shows that in terms of the previous

---

[26] For a review of survey findings see R. Blauner, 'Work satisfaction and industrial trends in modern society' in W. Galensan and S. M. Lipset (eds) *Labour and Trade Unionism* (John Wiley, 1960).

Table 12:   *Sample: job group by take-home pay in November
1964 (percentages)*

	– £75	£75 – 100	£100–25	£125+	Total respondents N
Male staff	3	15	28	53	60
Maintenance	16	36	48	0	31
Coffee process	0	74	22	4	23
Other male manual	44	53	3	0	74
Women	95	5	0	0	105
All	48	27	14	11	293

experience and skills necessary for their jobs, they rank with the 'other manual' workers.

Table 13 attempts to measure the transferability of skill of manual workers. If a worker receives several bonus points for the previous experience he brings into the company, he is a 'skilled man' in the normal sense of the word. Those receiving 6 or more points are fitters, millwrights, electricians and quality control technicians – all recognised as tradesmen in the outside world. It should be noted that 18 of the 21 maintenance workers appearing in the second column actually receive more than 20 bonus points for previous experience, whereas in neither of the other categories is there a worker receiving more than 10 points.

Now we can attempt to reconstruct the exact relationship between the external and the internal labour market for the sample of manual workers. It already appears evident that some workers, notably the higher-rated coffee processers, have benefited greatly from the internal labour market of the company, while it still seems reasonable to stick to the hypotheses put forward in the previous chapter that the *Phase A* and *B* workers, the skilled and the unskilled, receive their qualifications (or lack of them) from the external labour market. Thus the former should be much more dependent upon Birds for the presentation of their job status than the

Table 13:   *Sample: job group by job rating of previous experience necessary – male manual workers (percentages)*

	–6 points	6 or more	N
Maintenance	32	68	31
Coffee processing	100	0	23
Other manual	92	8	74
All	77	23	128

latter. These expectations can now be presented systematically, and in Table 14 below I set out the principal occupational groups which are distinguishable in terms of the amount of upward mobility they have experienced at Birds, which represents the extent of their dependence upon the internal labour market. Before interpreting these crucial results I must explain the method of grading the occupational groups used here. The first two groups, the grade 50+ coffee processers and the craftsmen whose previous jobs had been only semi-skilled, have experienced a great deal of promotion within the company. More significantly, if they were to leave the company they would certainly risk returning to the unskilled or semi-skilled level from which they originally came. The next three groups

Table 14: *Sample: degree of upward job mobility experienced at Birds – male manual workers*

Degree of upward mobility experienced at Birds		No. in sample
High	1 Grade 50 + coffee processers	9
	2 Upgraded craftsmen	2
Medium	3 Maintenance mates and technicians (grades 30–50)	14
	4 Grade 30+ coffee processers	14
	5 Grade 30–50 other manual workers (except drivers contained in 7)	27
Low	6 Craftsmen with craftsman backgrounds	15
	7 Outside drivers	5
	8 'Other manual workers' below Grade 30	42
	Total	128

have also experienced some promotion within the company, for all had started at Birds on lower grades than they occupied at the time of the survey. But their promotions have not been as spectacular as those of the first two groups, while all would have more chance of finding similar employment elsewhere. Mates, unqualified technicians, security men, storekeepers and experienced machine operators (who form most of these groups) are sought by most manufacturing firms, though as I observed in Chapter 3, there are no general rules governing the employment of such men and the element of a demotion risk exists for most of them who change employment. For the final three groups, however, there should be less risk in changing employment for the qualifications of these men – the remaining craftsmen, the drivers and the unskilled workers – have been gained in the external labour market. Hence this grading system is intended to indicate the degree of worker dependence upon the company. If I am right to emphasise the relationship between the internal and the external labour market, it is to be expected that this ranking will be directly correlated with propensity to relocate for job-related reasons. The higher groups in this table should be more likely to relocate to Banbury for job reasons.

However, I ought to add a hasty *caveat* which particularly concerns the position of the skilled tradesmen in the company. For it is unclear whether many really were 'tradesmen' in the full and conventional sense of the word. The company had no records of the exact training they had received and, unfortunately, this information was not collected in the interview survey, but it was generally believed that many ('about half' was the consensus figure) had not served apprenticeships. One of their managers expressed the implications of this rather cruelly by saying 'they are not high-grade tradesmen'. Certainly, they were not employed on very complex tasks: their jobs were routine maintenance, and difficult jobs were contracted out. Furthermore their tradesman's experience was not considered sufficient to enable them to do their jobs without special training. This can be seen by looking at the learning period bonuses they received.

In the company's job evaluation scheme, points were awarded to jobs on the basis of the training period needed, their 'learning period'. Wages received for these points are not obtainable elsewhere, because the skill involved is specific to Birds. Table 15 dichotomises learning period points; those in the second column are receiving at least £1 a week in wages for on-the-job learning. The most surprising feature of this table is that all the maintenance workers except for one painter receive about £1 a week for learning a skill which is purely specific to Birds, so even the skills of the tradesmen are not fully transferable. For example, a packing-line

Table 15:   *Sample: job group by learning period bonus points –*
male manual workers (percentages)

	−4 points	4 or more	N
Maintenance	3	97	31
Coffee processing	42	57	23
Other manual	80	20	74
All male manual workers	55	45	128

fitter, although he receives 24 of his 97 points for previous experience in his trade, also receives 10 points for on-the-job training: 10 per cent of his wage is therefore specific to the company. Additional points to be noted are that over half the coffee processers receive as much as £1 per week for learning company-specific skills (and all the five men receiving 20 or more points for the learning period were coffee processers), and in comparison with maintenance and coffee workers, the vast majority of the 'other manual' group needs little on-the-job training.

It should be remembered that most of those receiving four or more points on this criterion were also working continuous shifts, receiving a shift bonus of one-sixth of the basic rate.[27] This too is not readily obtainable elsewhere in Birmingham, where shift-working is not widespread. The workers in the maintenance and coffee processing departments, mostly receiving bonuses for on-the-job training and for shift working, were in fact earning between £2 and £6 per week not easily obtainable elsewhere. Hence there are grounds for believing that the skilled maintenance workers were rather more dependent upon the company than their title of 'tradesmen' might suggest. I noted in Chapter 3 that the real world of the tradesman was probably rather more varied than that suggested by the image they have often succeeded in foisting upon us. The Birds' tradesmen might be far from untypical if they were as company-oriented as they were trade-oriented.

If the maintenance workers were close to the coffee processers in being heavily dependent upon the company for the presentation of their financial rewards, we might expect the two groups to be similarly conscious of this. Table 16 shows this. Over half the sample, and about two-thirds of the higher-paid groups, thought that they would have difficulty in finding similar wages elsewhere in Birmingham. Only among the 'other hourly-rated' group, the unskilled men not working on the coffee plant, is there a majority believing that it would not be difficult to find similar wages elsewhere.[28] This is further evidence to suggest that the maintenance workers and the coffee processers were considerably more dependent upon the company than were the unskilled workers. This difference should be reflected later on in the relative proportions of each group relocating to Banbury for job-related reasons.

---

[27] A few workers in all departments were receiving a larger shift bonus of ⅓rd of basic rate for working permanent night shift. Only 13 out of the 74 'other manual' group were on continuous shifts (being mostly security guards) compared to three-quarters of the coffee processers and just over half of the maintenance workers.
[28] Of the 'other manual' group, only 6 per cent were not sure whether they could find similar wages, leaving 54 per cent definite that they would have no difficulty.

Table 16: *Sample: job group by difficulty of finding similar
wages in Birmingham – men only (percentages)*
Survey 1, question 23

	Yes, would be difficult	not sure or no, not difficult	N
Male staff	65	35	55
Maintenance	67	33	30
Coffee process	73	27	22
Other manual	40	60	67
All men	56	44	174

VARIATIONS IN JOB SATISFACTION

I argued in the previous chapter that the concept of job satisfaction had
only limited utility in industrial sociology mainly because, though most
people say they are 'satisfied' with their jobs, this actually tells us little
about the nature of their work experience or their employment relationship. In this chapter, we have seen that the vast majority of the manual
labour force at Birds was satisfied with its employment, but in my view
this does not indicate the extent of their real work involvement. This
comes out most clearly in an analyses of inter-group differences in job
satisfaction. The main results are shown in Table 17.

The slight differences in levels of overall satisfaction with the company
revealed in column 1 are not significant. Indeed, they are slightly mis-
leading because most remaining responses were not statements like 'Birds
is a bad employer', but were mild praise of the company, such as 'Its pretty
fair, all round' or 'They're not so bad'. Only ten responses altogether
from men could be interpreted as condemnation of the company, and
these were fairly equally spread throughout the groups. Thus in general
Birds seemed to have been successful in stemming discontent between
1962 and 1964.

All the other trends in Table 17 are somewhat unexpected. One is anom-
alous – that the coffee processers were least inclined to see the security
of their jobs as 'good'. This is due to the fact that the interview survey was
conducted at the time of a slight recession in the coffee market (described
in Chapter 5). This also affected the answers of the coffee processers to
the question about their pay. Neither result should be taken as indicating
long-term attitudes as the speed with which everyone seemed to recover
from the coffee recession shows.

Table 17:   *Sample: job groups viewing favourably various aspects of work – male manual workers. Based on Survey 1*

Questions: Job groups	85 Birds a 'good' or 'excellent' company	88 Satisfied with own job	91 Security good	92 Super- vision good	90 Pay good	93 Promotion[a] prospects good
Maintenance workers (*N*=30)	93	73	77	40	81	15
Coffee processers (*N*=22)	86	50	43	52	47	7
Other manual workers (*N*=67)	75	69	69	45	48	21

[a] Throughout I will be using the term 'promotion' in the sense used by the workers themselves to refer to upgrading within the manual stratum as well as promotion to the rank of supervisor.

The uniformly low opinion of the manual workers about promotion possibilities reflects the fact that by 1964 the coffee plant was well-established within the company but was no longer expanding. As there were very few coffee processers near retirement age, there was little promotion within, or on to, the coffee plant between 1962 and 1964. On the other hand, outside the coffee plant the problem of running old and new factory areas at the same time during the actual transfer of operations to Banbury was now looming up and promotion to the rank of temporary supervisor was being offered to workers. Without this temporary boost to prospects all working groups would probably have viewed their promotion prospects with the same degree of pessimism as the coffee processers in Table 17. The introduction of the coffee plant had at first greatly raised promotion possibilities for manual workers, but then depressed them again. Not surprisingly, worker expectations of promotion took somewhat longer to subside. Shiftwork was not considered an obstacle in desires for promotion: only five per cent of those who said that promotion prospects mattered to them said that they would not be prepared to work any of the shifts.[29] Thus by 1964, the coffee plant was firmly established within a generally-recognised hierarchical ordering of manual jobs. A coffee process operator sums up the consequences of this:

[29] In response to Survey 1, question 82.

When I first started on the coffee ten years ago you had to start
at the bottom, and we thought that we wouldn't get the top
jobs until those at the top got pensioned off. But of course
coffee has expanded and we've been able to move with it,
being fortunate to be there at the right time. But now we've
come to more or less a dead stop. So now the people who
come in start at the bottom, and there don't seem to be any
prospects of getting any higher for some time to come, and its
bound to create bad feeling both among those at the lower end
of the coffee plant and those outside it who want to come in.

The greater opportunities for promotion within the manual stratum on
process production have been noted by other authors.[30] Certainly, compared to the homogeneous labour force of, for example, motor-car assembly work, greater promotion opportunities are available. But the
structure can ossify, and in order to judge the exact extent of promotion
opportunities, the sociologist has to take into account not just the technology but its rate of expansion and the age-structure of the labour force
too.

These three results, attitudes to pay, promotion and security, all serve
to underline the unreliability of satisfaction scores as measures of real
commitment to a place of employment. All have been susceptible to
short-term shifts in conditions which left unchanged the basic nature of
the employment relationship. This is principally because the 'frame of
reference' used by employees for evaluating their satisfaction appears to
be a historical rather than a comparative one. By this I mean that they
answer 'satisfied' or 'dissatisfied' by comparing their present situation to
their past situation and not to that obtainable elsewhere in other firms.
A dissatisfied employee is more likely to think he did better in the past
than to think that he can do better elsewhere. And while knowledge of a
dissatisfaction based on this frame of reference may enable us to predict
such outcomes as industrial relations activity, it does not seem to lead to
predictions of work attachment, that is, propensity to stay or leave the
firm. At any rate we can test this proposition and in later chapters I discuss
correlations between work satisfaction and relocating for work reasons.

The levels of intrinsic job satisfaction and attitudes to supervision
revealed in Table 17 are at odds with previous reserach. In Chapter 3 I
discussed the work of writers termed, rather erroneously, 'technological

[30] See particularly Blauner, *Alienation and Freedom*, pp. 148–51, and Chapter 3
above. But for a view stressing the variety of promotion structures in praess plants
see S. Cotgrove and C. Vaughan, 'Technology, class and politics: the case of
process workers', *Sociology*, 6, No 2 (1972).

determinists'.[31] They distinguished three phases of technological development within factories, which they claimed produced different levels and types of job satisfaction. In this sample the coffee processers, and the plant on which they work, fit into *Phase C*, whereas the 'other manual' group is in *Phase B* (machine-minding). So, according to the 'technological determinists', the coffee processers ought to be more satisfied with the jobs themselves than the 'other manual' workers. But in fact in Table 17 the reverse is true. The reason for this is not hard to find and is produced by the processers themselves: that working conditions are rather worse on the coffee plant than they are elsewhere. The coffee plant is dirtier and dustier. Within a few minutes of entering its vicinity the newcomer notices dust lining the back of his throat and a slightly unpleasant taste of coffee waste products. In Birmingham working conditions were actually more cramped than they were elsewhere at Birds. Blauner's process plant in the chemical industry is new, clean and shining, its machinery working in near-silence. There the men apparently work in an atmosphere of clinical calm. It is not to be regarded as typical.

Nor were the Birds' coffee workers apparently aware of the high skill level of process jobs as described by the 'technological determinists'. They were no more likely to mention the variety of the job or the skills they used as reasons for liking it than were other workers. One processer neatly summed up the skills he needed: 'The thing about these jobs is the responsibility. That means you mustn't fall asleep!' A coffee plant supervisor made the same kind of point, though with more moderation: 'Common sense is needed on the coffee plant, not much else. But it isn't all that common and you can't rely on all workers to take the right decisions at the right time.' In short, 'responsibility' meant more to management than it did to the workers.

The 'technological determinists' also claim that workers in *Phase C* technologies are much more 'socially integrated' into their firms than are those in *Phase B*. This means that they will enjoy more expressive relations on the job with work-groups which include supervisors as well as workmates and exhibit a higher commitment (or loyalty) to the norms of the organisation.[32] And indeed we can see in Table 17 that the coffee processers have a slightly higher opinion of their supervisors than do the other workers, though the difference is slight and not statistically significant. But when asked whether any of their three best friends were Birds'

---

[31] The three principal authors referred to here are Woodward, *Industrial Organisation*. Blaunter, *Alienation and Freedom* and Touraine, *L'evolution du Travail* .... See Chapter 3 above.
[32] See Chapter 3 above.

employees, only one-third of coffee processors – the same proportion as in the other work-groups – replied that one or more was a Birds' employee.[33] Moreover, as in other surveys of manual workers, the desired qualities of the 'good' supervisor or workmate seemed to be of a rather neutral sort. The foreman was expected to 'leave you alone to get on with the job' and the workmate was expected to 'pass the time of day, you know, it makes the day go along faster'.[34]

In a rather superficial sense, some 'social integration' did exist within Birds. The company was felt to be 'friendly', and the 'atmosphere is easy-going'. But this degree of 'friendliness' was not socially very significant. For example, 60 per cent of the sample (and, incidentally, 60 per cent of the coffee processors) thought it would be a positive disadvantage to have Birds employees as neighbours, compared to 20 per cent who thought it would be an advantage.[35] 'Friendliness' rested more on an economic than a social basis. Its principal components seemed to be that 'you knew where you were with them', 'they treated you fair and well' and 'they'd always listen to your grievances'. The future seemed relatively secure with Birds because 'they wouldn't suddenly turn round and do something nasty'. The present situation could be relied on to continue. Moreover, the present situation was economically satisfactory, since Birds offered three sorts of rewards for manual workers not available to the same extent elsewhere in Birmingham. They were: high wages, high security of employment, and high fringe benefits. Employees themselves were quite conscious of these. Whenever they mentioned specific examples of the 'friendliness' or the 'fairness' of the company they related to one of these factors. Of particular interest was the frequent mentioning of trivial items as evidence of the company's attitude. It was extraordinary how the company's provision of working overalls, of canteen facilities and of cups of coffee during breaks, were picked out by employees as being especially generous. Obviously, these small factors were considered as being symbolic of the company's interest in employees.

Now we have seen that these conditions were relatively new, stemming from management reactions to the crisis of 1962. Indeed in the early 1960s there was a marked shift in the entire managerial 'style' at Birds. This was complete by the time the fieldwork commenced in late 1964, and then I was repeatedly struck by managers' insistence on uniformity of treatment

---

[33] In response to question 39, Survey 1. A higher proportion (56%) of Goldthorpe *et al*'s 'Affluent workers' reported having at least one 'close friend' among fellow workers. This probably reflects the smallness of Luton and its domination by the firms studied when compared to Birmingham and the insignificance of Birds in it. But note the differences in the questions asked in the two studies: Goldthorpe *et al.*, *The Affluent Worker: Industrial Attitudes*, p. 62.

[34] *Ibid.* especially pp. 64–67 on supervisors, and pp. 49–63 on workmates.

[35] In reply to question 14, Survey 1.

as the basis of personnel policies. There is, of course, a rival managerial ideology, summed up in the phrase 'treating each case on its merits'. The latter had characterised Birds' policies before the 1962 crisis as both the special treatment of the coffee workers, and the general allegations of favouritism by the trade union, had indicated. But learning the apparent lesson of 1962, management moved over to uniformity. This comes out with regard to the relocation policy itself in the next chapter – and, indeed, this uniformity of policy comes under criticism from some managers in Chapter 7. The emphasis has continued to the present day (1972) and has led to the granting of staff status to manual workers, thereby putting General Foods in the vanguard of the progressive industrial relations movement. It must be admitted, of course, that the major cause of the 1962 crisis was technologically based on the emergence of the new coffee processing plant. But I wish to argue that once management decided on how to react to the crisis, its ideology was the major determinant of worker attitudes throughout the company. The decision to attempt to buy-out the trade unions was, of course, a very American one, and the Birds memoranda of this period are full of American-inspired advice emanating from General Foods (some of it irrelevant to the British context, such as the advice to hold a union ballot under the provisions of the U.S. Taft–Hartley Act!). Another management preoccupation often classified as American was the costs of indirect labour, particularly staff costs, and the energy which in British companies might be put into combating wage increases on the shopfloor was here put into assessing managerial productivity and throwing out office files. These components of the Birds management style can clearly be treated independently of technology (though they obviously have more to do with profitability) in their effects upon worker attitudes and behaviour. Yet managerial style is rarely given much attention by industrial sociologists. Historically, this can be attributed to the narrowing of focus which occurred among the 'Human Relations' school of sociologists. Whereas they began by looking at human relations in a very general sense, they ended by concentrating on leadership styles among first-level supervision. It is comparatively easy to demonstrate that supervisory styles have little impact upon worker attitudes and behaviour;[36] it would probably be impossible to show this with regard to management's overall style, treated as an independent variable.[37]

There are therefore two implications of the satisfaction findings and

[36] Etzioni, *A Comparative Analysis of Complex Organizations*, pp. 118–25; Goldthorpe *et al.*, *The Affluent Worker: Industrial Attitudes*, Chap. 3.

[37] And indeed in the *Affluent Worker: Industrial Attitudes* there is evidence pointing to the importance of this factor: for example, the workers are much more likely to give reasons relating to 'good management and union practice' than reasons relating to 'good economic rewards and conditions of employment' for their firm's good industrial relations record (p. 77).

101

neither is significantly related to technology. First, the overall satisfaction level of employees was undoubtedly high, and though the emergence of the coffee plant provided an early impetus, managerial ideology has contributed more to this subsequently. Second, the inter-group differences in satisfaction are rather more complex and transient than the 'technological determinists' had led us to expect. Earlier, however, I stressed the role of technology in determining group differences in employment dependence, and I would expect these differences to have the more important effect on relocation decisions. It may be that a high level of satisfaction in a workforce is a necessary condition of successful relocation, but this may be only where that satisfaction is closely intertwined with dependence. Where they can be separated, the latter is likely to be the better predictor.

CONCLUSION

We can now summarise the nature of the employment relationship of the Birds workforce. As expected, it proved very different for manual and non-manual employees. Indeed the keynote of the employment situations of the two groups would seem to be complete opposites: for manual workers it would be 'stability', for non-manual 'uncertainty'. Both groups enjoyed fairly high wages and exceptionally good fringe benefits, but whereas manual workers could be reasonably sure of continuing to enjoy these in the future, many managers, clerks and supervisors were by no means certain of this.

When dealing with non-manual employees I have so far used fairly crude distinctions between 'locals' and 'spiralists', and 'thrusters' and 'sleepers'. As terms which divide up a very complex reality these have fairly obvious limitations, and the last pair of labels have the additional problem of being value-laden (when P.E.P. describe managers as 'thrusters' and 'sleepers' there is little doubt that the former are meant to be the 'goodies'). But an interesting feature of the very fluid situation in Birds management in these years is that the managers themselves thought in similar terms. Fully conscious of the problems brought about by rapid technical and market change, they tended to polarise into those who believed that new problems must be solved by new men, better-qualified and younger, and those who thought that experience in the company, and 'steadiness' rather than 'push' (their terms) were the best qualifications. Hints of such group identifications have emerged in this Chapter; they emerge more clearly in Chapters 6 and 7. They are my main justification for continuing to use the terms here.

In Chapter 2 I made some simple predictions about the nature of the employment dependence of non-manual workers, which can be summed up by the statement 'locals are highly dependent, spiralists are not necessarily so'. This statement holds in the light of what we have learned about the salaried staff of Birds. The spiralists and locals identified themselves as such, the former were calculating in their comparison of the company with others, the latter knew of their dependence upon the company. However, a major complication arises from the fact that the acknowledged rivalry between them had not yet ended and nor had it produced stalemate. We cannot therefore make any predictions about their likely relocating behaviour until we analyse both the company's relocation policy toward the problem (was it to be used as a method of discouraging unwanted men from staying with the company?) and men's own assessment of the rivalry itself in Banbury.

On manual workers, however, a great deal of detailed information emerged, broadly confirming the theoretical model presented at the end of the preceding chapter, and from which we can make predictions concerning their relocation choices. First, we have not found that unusual occurrence, a dissatisfied workforce, and so one possible obstacle to relocation was not present in this company. Indeed, we have found a workforce which was unusually satisfied in two ways. First, the ratio of satisfied to dissatisfied is higher than usual. Second, in many workers we have discerned traces of a genuine commitment to aspects of their employment which goes beyond the usual kind of satisfaction found at this level. The source of this, however, seems to be the economic rewards offered to them by the company. Because of the long-term 'golden chains' of generous fringe benefits, because future security seemed assured, economic well-being became generalised to include feelings of stability: 'You know where you are with this company.' We must not forget the contribution of the trade unions in this respect, particularly the Transport and General Workers' Union whose entry into the company ensured redress against preferential treatment and also persuaded management to be a wage-leader in the future. The effect of this economically favourable stability was to create a background favourable to the relocation. Thus all workers may be slightly more likely to consider relocating with the company than the predictions outlined above suggest.

Nevertheless, most of the variations between work-groups predicted there seem to have been reinforced in this chapter. The coffee process workers conformed very closely to the ideal-type of technology *Phase C* worker discussed throughout Chapter 3. Their dependence upon the company was high and thus their relocating propensity must be regarded as high. By contrast, the 'other manual' group, comparable to *Phase B* machine-minders, have appeared much less dependent upon Birds and thus must seem much less likely to relocate. However, the skilled crafts-men do not resemble the ideal-type of tradesman typified by the printer, and this is worth elaborating.

In Chapter 3 I noted that it was only the skilled trade controlling its own labour market and working methods that was committed to the occupation and independent of the employer. Here we have an example of skilled tradesmen without such powers. Probably only about half have served apprenticeships so their right to a skilled job could not be recog-nised by all employers. Some have indeed learned their trade in an in-formal way within Birds and are even less likely to find recognition. A significant pointer is also provided by the trade union affiliations of the tradesmen: a majority have been in the T. and G.W.U. rather than in one of the traditional craft unions, and in this union they have rarely followed a line independent of the unskilled workers. Thus they have not obtained control of either the external labour market or internal working arrange-ments to the extent, say, of printers. The fact that they all receive bonouses for on-the-job learning is an indication of management's ability to impose on them its view that these are to some extent specialised jobs outside their occupations' normal range. It is also a measure of their dependence upon the company, a dependence recognised by the men themselves even for the preservation of their immediate wage (Table 16). These tradesmen seem rather more likely to consider relocation than the 'typi-cal' tradesman.

With these expectations in mind let us now turn to the relocation itself and the reactions of the workforce to it.

5
The relocation

In July 1962 the company announced to its employees that it was considering a relocation. It hoped that the new site would be within twenty-five miles of Birmingham but anyone with knowledge of planning practice could see that this was unlikely to be allowed. No single site was mentioned until 10 October when a bulletin announced: 'Though nothing definite has been finalised, we are now negotiating an option to purchase a new large industrial site in the Banbury area.' Nothing had yet been said about what would happen to the labour force in the event of a move. Yet the move had not become reality and at this stage many employees doubted if it would happen.

Doubt was dispelled on 9 January 1963 when the company announced that negotiations for a site at Banbury had been successfully concluded, and that production at Banbury might begin before the end of 1964. Banbury might seem a surprising destination, in the light of government policy of steering industry toward the development districts. But the company had very much wanted to stay in the Midlands or the South as it wished to be near the centre of the company's market as well as Avonmouth Docks and major distribution outlets in Birmingham and London. As these areas contain little unemployment, the company was committed to transferring its labour force. The Board of Trade would be unlikely to approve. But of the four shortlisted sites – Banbury, Swindon, Wellingborough and Weston-Super-Mare – only Banbury did not need Board of Trade approval. Some time before a company had purchased the site, received outline planning permission, and then decided not to use it. Once granted, such permission cannot be revoked and an Industrial Development Certificate was therefore not needed. As the Board of Trade remained convinced that Birds should be moved to a Development Area, this loophole at Banbury became all-important and Birds and Banbury Borough Council (the owners of the site) soon agreed to ignore the Ministry. The whole site extended to 40.85 acres but only 18 acres of this was free from Ministry control. It was hoped that the Ministry would recognise the *fait accompli* and grant an I.D.C. for the remainder of the site, but this was refused. Even now the firm can only put half of its site to industrial use. The rest is landscaped garden and car park. Such are the anomalies produced by a pluralistic distribution of political power over the planning process!

The company chairman promptly stated the fundamental personnel policy.

> It is hoped that as many employees as possible will move to Banbury. Let me emphasise that this move is the direct result of increased demand for our products and there will be work for all who wish to relocate.

In May this principle was re-enunciated in the first Relocation Policy for employees and throughout the move was continually re-iterated by management representatives.

But there was considerable disbelief about this. Employees could see quite clearly that the new factory would entail more efficiency and more economy of men and material. For example, two factories, a warehouse and research department, all in different buildings, were to be brought together in one building. The whole of the maintenance department would be united in one factory area for the first time. One manager describes the plan:

> One of the reasons for moving is the chance of greater efficiency with fewer workers. If everyone had moved, we would have been in a mess, particularly in the services[1] department, which now maintains several buildings. 120 men were to be saved, and some shifts were to be cut down.

This plan was not as unscrupulous as it might sound. It was never intended that any manual worker should be told that he was not needed in Banbury. Management always assumed that many workers would not want to move, no matter what practicable incentives were offered them. It was hoped that the number of dropouts would be about equal to the labour saving required in Banbury. If, as appeared likely, the dropouts outnumbered the latter, then the company could safeguard itself by agreeing to take London overspill tenants in Banbury under the Industrial Selection Scheme. This purchased goodwill from Banbury Borough Council and was instrumental in persuading the council to provide council houses for the workers moving from Birmingham. But from the company's point of view workers from Birmingham, already trained, were preferable to untrained labour from London. Management also seems to have had a curious fear of 'trouble' occurring among these Londoners. Its memoranda contain several references to the 'rampant trade unionism' likely to be found among them. So management did genuinely want to transfer as many manual workers as it anticipated would be willing to move.

[1] That is to say the maintenance department.

But among the male staff there was some justification for suspicion of the company's intentions, for individuals were told that their services were no longer required in Banbury. The number was small: three men in the sample were told this. As the sample is made up of about 1 in 4 of all employees, it is probable that no more than a dozen in all were stopped from moving. But, of course, others may have received more subtle hints or may have realised for themselves that their relations with the company were becoming strained. These would tend to leave the company before, perhaps well before, the move itself and their departure might appear completely voluntary. One very disgruntled leaver thinks this was frequent:

> It is normally difficult to get rid of people with conspicuously above-average performance, even though they may not fit in with 'the team' and appear dangerous rivals to those above them. The fact of the impending move to Banbury makes it easier to explain away curious departures as 'not wanting to go to Banbury' (as was done quite untruthfully with another former member of our department).

But this type of forced decision is difficult to distinguish from the type based on voluntary personal assessment of future chances with the company and it is impossible to judge its frequency. As we shall see in Chapter 6, male staff took a long, hard look at their prospects before arriving at their decision.

At the other extreme, few employees received individual encouragement to move. Managers were generally aware of their superiors' opinion of their work but when they went to their superiors to ask for a long-term assessment of their prospects with the company, they did not usually receive direct encouragement to move. On the whole, the company refused to abandon its official policy of encouraging everyone equally to move. One manager praises the company for this: 'Considering the pressures we were all generating for the giving of personal assurances, the company did very well to hold by its policy.' There were a few exceptions to this, but these were some of the company's hesitant steps toward a 'hiring and firing' policy described in the previous chapter. This was not stepped up by the move. Indeed, some management wish it had been. In any case, younger and better-qualified staff could protect themselves by leaving for another job and many did so in the years between the first announcement of the move and its completion. Salaried annual turnover was distinctly higher in both 1962 and 1964 (though not in 1963) than it had been in earlier years. Most of those who remained were either fairly confident of their standing in the company, or had known at the time of their recruitment that the company was going to move. Thus almost all employees were offered the chance of relocation. The obvious question now is 'under what terms'? This takes us into the company's actual 'Relocation policy'.

The relocation policy was comprehensive and generous from the first. Quite apart from the content of the policy, its presentation was obviously the work of a professional selling organisation. Once this brought forth the comment 'They sell Banbury like they sell coffee'! A great deal of information was passed on to employees in an attempt to keep the move, and its attractions, before their eyes for a two-year period. The expertise was not original. It had been developed in the 1950s by the parent company which had relocated its headquarters from New York City to White Plains, New York State, and the presentation of the Birds' bulletins is exactly the same as in American ones. The policies were also derivative. This enabled Birds to mount a sophisticated publicity campaign without needing to recruit much specialised expertise.[2]

Two basic principles underlay the policy. The first was that no-one who wanted to move should suffer financially in so doing. The second was that every employee should be treated according to the rules laid down in the policy. There should be no treating of individuals' needs as they arose (which, it was felt, would lead to preferential treatment).

The basic financial incentive to move was the 'relocation allowance', which was the equivalent of five weeks gross salary or wages, calculated on average weekly earnings over the previous year. This was designed to give employees the equivalent of a month's gross wages after tax. The allowance was generally understood by employees to be intended to cover the cost of 'curtain and carpet' fittings. The company would also pay the cost of removal and installation of certain public utility services such as telephone, cooker and television aerial. Removal of goods and furniture and the employee's family were also paid for. An allowance of £10 was paid for expenses incurred in visiting Banbury to look at houses etc.; this had to be claimed for and receipts presented.

Private housing assistance often provided more real financial benefit than the cash grants. Aid was given to anyone selling a Birmingham house and to anyone intending to buy in Banbury. This included the guaranteed sale of a Birmingham house at a price indepently assessed at market levels; payment of legal expenses, stamp duty, agents' commissions and survey fees, incurred in buying and selling; and loans for house

[2] Subsequent American relocations of General Foods taking place at the same time as the British relocation have been briefly studied by staff members of the Harbard Business School. See *Harvard Business School*, Case Studies, Labor, Nos. 519 and 520 (1966). A somewhat uncritical account of these relocations can be found in E. S. Whitman and W. J. Schmidt, *Plant Relocation: A Case History of the Move* (New York, 1966), from which the similarity of the publicity campaigns can be judged.

108

deposits and to bridge any time-lag between the buying of a Banbury house and the selling of a Birmingham one – the former at the low rate of interest of 4 per cent and the latter at no interest but repayable within 60 days. As regards rented housing the March 1963 policy was vague, confining itself to the promise to assist employees to find accommodation 'comparable to that which they currently occupy'. The vagueness reflected the company's uncertainty as to whether it could persuade Banbury Borough Council to provide houses to let. But no official mention was made of the negotiations until the Transport and General Workers Union threatened to join them, having received information from Trade Union members of the Banbury Council. Then, in September 1963, the company announced that agreement had been reached with the local authorities and that 345 council houses would be available in Banbury to married employees living within the City of Birmingham.[3]

The council house negotiations had been complex and concessions had been made by the two principal parties, Birds and Banbury Council. There were two reasons for the company's concessions. In the first place most of the factory site itself had been owned by the Council. As we have seen Birds had desperately wanted the site. The company was also anxious to secure the goodwill of the local authorities, not only to obtain the council houses but also to make sure that County planning permission would be forthcoming for the company's future expansion plans on the site.

For its part, the council welcomed the arrival of Birds. It had been committed since 1961 to receive London overspill tenants under the provisions of the 1952 Town Development Act, and the more jobs there would be for these people in the future the better. Altough a little wary of an American-owned company, it welcomed a clean food factory which would also provide many jobs for local women. Providing the provision of council housing did not involve it in much expense it would be favourably disposed toward Birds.

The third party, Birmingham City Corporation, also approved of the project. The city's housing problems have been dealt with in Chapter 1. They are immense enough for the Corporation to welcome the removal of any house occupiers from the conurbation, whether they are council tenants or not.

So the compromise emerged. The company and Birmingham Corporation were to pay jointly half the subsidy on each house, while the Ministry of Housing and Local Government were to pay the other half. This was in

---

[3] Nearly all the male employees were married, and as it was the men who were mainly interested in moving, the restriction of council housing to married tenants did not cause much resentment.

accordance with the Town Development Act whose provisions governed this scheme. The 'exporting authority' was defined as the company and Birmingham jointly. The company's contribution on each house was £25 per annum for ten years, while Birmingham paid £6 per annum for 15 years. The company paid throughout the ten years whether or not the occupant remained working for the company. In other words, the houses were not 'tied'. Banbury's contribution was to build the houses but even with the subsidies received the Housing Department doubted whether the scheme would pay for itself.

If this had been the whole agreement, Banbury would not have gained much. After all, if the council refused to provide the houses the company would still have moved (as the site purchase antedated the housing agreement). Probably fewer employees would have moved with the company and more jobs would have been available to local people. So Banbury Council also secured a promise from the company to recruit any additional labour needed, beyond that transferred from Birmingham, through the London Industrial Selection Bureau 'insofar as their requirements are capable of being met through this source'. It was tacitly admitted by both parties that only manual workers were likely to be forthcoming through this scheme, so that, in effect, only the company's manual labour requirements could not be met from other sources. This led to the introduction of a terminal date of eligibility of transfer for Birmingham manual workers. Only manual workers with the company on or before 1 April 1964 were entitled to move.[4]

The stewards of the Transport and General Workers Union have alleged to me that the company had not really been trying to sign a council house agreement and was preparing to take most of its labour from Banbury or London. But it has already been demonstrated that the company wished to retain its Birmingham labour force. Moreover, the Banbury Housing Department are convinced that the company were genuine in their desire for houses from the start, and were impressed by the vigour of the company's negotiating. We must therefore reject the union's claim. But it is true that the company decided to move to Banbury before the council houses were finally secured, so it might seem that it was prepared to see large numbers of manual workers, at least, remaining in Birmingham. The answer to this, according to individuals involved in the formation of company policy, was that the company really wanted its workers to move but did not at the outset pay enough attention to ways of getting them to move. As supporting evidence they point to the company's

---

[4] This was later moved back to 17 July, as Birds were unable to fill all the council houses allocated to the company.

statements that it expected at least 700 workers to move long before clear policies were formulated as to how this could be done. One man said 'We were all saying we would move 650 or 700 because someone higher up kept saying it. But at this time I don't think anyone here knew how it could be done.'

The confidence came from the States, as indeed did the impetus to move in the first place. Many of the British managers were sceptical, as a North American director reports:

> When we first started talking about it, they [the British] said that it couldn't be done. You might move the office staff, they said, but the British workingman is much too attached to his own backyard to follow his job like that. Well, we set out to prove them wrong. We said 'They'll move if you offer them enough, and if they've got a damn good job'.

The prediction was based on the experience of General Foods in the States.[5] It is possible that without this naivety, without this assumption that British workers were really just the same as American workers, the move would not have been made, or if it had been it would have been to a Development District where labour would be locally available. It was certainly a brave decision to go to a small town where job vacancies had long ago outstripped the number unemployed. Without such confidence at the top, the delays involved in formulating every detail of relocation policy might have been worrying for the company. Not until September 1963 was the council house agreement signed; while an inevitable delay occurred in deciding which jobs would be transferred unchanged to Banbury.

It has already been noted that management had plans for reducing staff in the maintenance department and, it was rumoured, in the new Research Department. For a long time it was also feared that the company would want to discontinue jelly manufacturing in Banbury, and this turned out to be true. Quite apart from wholesale departmental changes, it was likely that the individual content of many jobs would be changed, involving a change in the individual wage-rate. New machinery, new use of space, the consolidation of factories, would all create different manpower needs. This was a detailed engineering problem, which could not be solved until the actual layout of the factory and the plant was decided on. Even by August 1964, the future of about a quarter of manual jobs was still

---

[5] Where about 30 per cent of eligible employees relocated to the Corporation's newly-consolidated plant over a much greater distance. This proportion would have been higher if many relocating employees had not been threatened with a pay-cut at the consolidated plant, i.e. they had not been 'offered enough'. See Harvard Business School, Case Studies, *Labor*, No. 520, pp. 6–9.

uncertain, and their Birmingham occupants had not yet been guaranteed the same job in Banbury. But by the end of 1964 when Survey 1 took place, of 273 respondents, 237 knew that their jobs were being continued in Banbury, 22 (mostly jelly workers) knew that they were not and only fourteen were still uncertain.

This raised the biggest loophole in the relocation policy and one noted at once by trade unionists and by most employees. The policy was not as frank about this as it might have been. The two clauses in the May 1963 policy which deal with this state:

1. Employees who transfer to Banbury will have first claim on their present job. In a few instances, because of modernisation, and expansion, some employees may be trained and reassigned to another position. Employees will be selected for those opportunities on the basis of seniority, ability and merit, in accordance with Company policy.

2. As a matter of principle, it is Alfred Bird & Sons intention to continue existing salary and wage rates for equivalent jobs on the Company's move to Banbury.

This avoids a direct statement that the actual Birmingham rate of pay of each individual is not guaranteed in Banbury, if the individual is not doing the same job. In fact, very few employees suffered an earnings cut because of the move while the subsequent introduction of 'Personal Grades' brought the company closer to a guarantee of earnings.[6] But neither of these could be predicted before the move and there were serious drawbacks to making an early decision to move. The terms for the non-movers were, however, much clearer.

Apart from considerations of generosity towards non-moving employees, the company had economic reasons for its policy regarding termination. It wanted non-movers to continue working until the factory actually closed down in Birmingham but, left to themselves, these employees would probably leave a job without prospects as soon as they could. So the company ruled that employees who stayed till within a month of the close-down of their jobs would be eligible to receive a termination allowance. If they stayed till the actual day of close-down, they would receive a bonus of 50 per cent of their final four weeks pay. The actual allowances were the same as were already offered for redundancies by the company before the move. It was considered that employees who left before the last month were voluntarily resigning and had not been 'forced' to leave, i.e. not made redundant. This was confirmed by the Government's Redundancy Payments Scheme which came into force on 6

---

[6] See Chapter 7 below for details of 'Personal Grades'.

December 1965, before many employees had actually relocated. Payment in both the company and the governmental schemes was based on both age and length of service. The bonuses for age are somewhat larger in the governmental scheme and accordingly, after 6 December 1965, the company was forced to pay out more to older employees than it had intended to do in its own relocation policy. But the differential was not great and the company was of its own volition paying substantial termination allowances before this was legally required.[7]

Pension rights were also important to some non-movers. If the employee chose to cash his benefit he received only his own contributions back and the pension was not transferable to other companies. This meant that unless the employee was very near to retirement he was bound to lose financially on his pension compared with someone who stayed with the company. If he cashed it he lost the company's contributions; if he arranged to leave his money and take a reduced pension on his retirement, he would have to start again in another company on the low benefit rates of the short-service employee.

The third major assistance promised to non-moving employees was help in finding other employment. This occupied the major portion of the relocation services manager's time for nine months even though many employees found it relatively easy to obtain other employment at a time of full employment. The policy was never the subject of serious negotiation or grievance.

EMPLOYEE REACTIONS

This, then, was a comprehensive relocation policy, modelled on the Corporation's American experience. The first principle of the policy was that no-one should lose financially by moving. Whether this was carried out depends on one's interpretation of the word 'lose'. Certainly, many movers found themselves out of pocket afterwards, but this was usually because they chose to raise their standard of living by buying a more expensive house or by furnishing it better than in Birmingham. As far as the buying and selling of houses was concerned, this was done at market prices with legal and other costs paid for. Some gained by the transaction and some lost but there were no heavy losses. In renting, the exchange was usually a new house for an old one, so this was a gain. The costs of

---

[7] A Ministry of Labour survey of redundancies in the period October 1961–September 1962 found that in only 57.4 per cent of cases were severance payments made and notice of more than one week given. *Ministry of Labour Gazette*, February 1963, p. 55.

moving were paid so that the only enforced expenditure was on the fitting of carpets, curtains etc., arising from the likelihood that all sorts of furniture and fixtures would not fit in the new house. This was supposed to be covered by the relocation allowance. At the lower end of the income scale this might only be £60, which was certainly not sufficient to provide new fittings. At this level we might find some hardship and evidence for this is discussed in Chapter 7. But for the majority, receiving between £80 and £200, the cost of such fittings would not necessarily involve them in loss. The conclusion must be that the short-term costs of moving could be met by the policy. Indeed, the 1964 questionnaire survey found general contentment with these aspects of the policy, as can be seen from Tables 3, 4, 5 and 6 in the Appendix.

Very few basic criticisms were made of the policy by employees. Only about one-third of the sample could mention any weakness in it and the most frequently cited criticism, that not enough was being done to find alternative jobs for the non-movers, was mentioned by only 1 in 9 of the sample and by 1 in 7 of the non-movers. The most important grievance was over the scaling of benefits according to income level. Relocation allowance varied between £60 and £400, and the travelling allowance also varied. 50 of the 82 complaints of unfairness referred to the scaling of these two allowances, but there were only 11 spontaneous mentions of the unfairness of scaling as suggestions for further relocation assistance[8] Typical of these was this comment: 'The company says it wants to take everyone, but it's obvious it wants some more than others'. Not surprisingly, these critics were at the lower end of the manual earnings scale. The Transport and General Workers Union, torn between the interests of its higher and lower paid members, raised the scaling of the allowances as a grievance but later dropped it, realising that it could not afford to alienate its craftsmen members by pressing the point. By announcing the differentials at the start the company gave a large section of the workforce a vested interest in defending them.[9] This was also the obstacle to some of the other grievances raised, usually by the union: younger men raised a grievance that the termination allowance was unfair to them and older men resisted them; women complained and men resisted them; single men complained and married men resisted. Whether or not the company had been cunning enough to predict the effects of the differen-

---

[8] See Tables 5 and 3 respectively in the Appendix.
[9] The company's offer to narrow differentials was confined to manual workers only. It was rather surprising that the union did not seize on this as a bargaining strategy in pressing for a 'fairer' system. By including salaried staff in the calculation, the maximum allowance for manual workers would have been reduced by much less.

tials, the result was certainly to fragment opposition to the whole policy. The scheme as a whole was mostly considered satisfactory, while each part of it found many defenders. Only slight changes were made to it.

Thus the relocation policy was sufficiently generous to form, at the least, a favourable 'background' to the relocation itself – few employees were not able to move because of the inconveniences or the costs of the transfer itself. Yet, with the obvious exception of the housing provisions, the policy itself did not contain positive incentives to move. Indeed, to anticipate the thorough analysis of moving decisions contained in the next chapter, the policy did not figure at all in the reasons put forward by the sample for their moving decisions. The non-movers, in particular, did not seem interested in it. Not only were the movers more informed about the Relocation Allowance – which might be expected – they were also more likely to know correctly the details of the pension rights of non-movers, [10] as well as to name more alternative Banbury employers than the non-movers. [11] Thus the policy – with the exception of housing factors – provided strong motivation for neither accepting or refusing the transfer offer. Decisions were made on the basis of the long-term work and non-work situation of the employees.

THE PROGRESS OF THE MOVE – SUCCESSES

For a very long time all the preparations for the move proceeded smoothly. More details of jobs in Banbury came through and they were generally favourable to employees in that most jobs were to be transferred relatively unaltered. The Personnel Relocation Services Manager started full-time on his job in June 1963 and interviewed every employee by the end of the year. The results seemed to bear out the company's expectation that about 700 would move but there was a suspicion that many who had said they would move were in fact still undecided, frightened that frankness would lose them promotion chances. This was particularly marked among salaried staff where only about a dozen of the men had said that they would not move, despite the fact that many were looking round for other jobs. The problem was then to keep employees to their statement.

This was done by encouraging employees to display an interest in Banbury and in the relocation which gradually added up to a real commitment to move. Coach trips were laid on to Banbury between July and September

---

[10] In response to Survey 1, questions 77 and 76 respectively. χ^2 significant in both cases at the 0.05 level.
[11] Survey 1, question 25. χ^2 significant at the 0.001 level.

1963 and the festivity of a daytrip in summertime naturally added to the attractions of Banbury. In May 1963 a housing questionnaire was sent out to all employees asking them to state their requirements in Banbury. Those who stated that they wanted to purchase a house were pressed to see the company's Community Relations Manager who was in contact with local builders. And after the signing of the council house agreement, prospective council tenants were interviewed in mid-1964 by an official of the Banbury Borough Housing Department and shown the types of housing available.

The company kept up a continuous flow of background information. Employees were issued with a folder containing company bulletins and pamphlets giving information on Banbury. They were subsequently issued with copies of all bulletins. A news-sheet notable for its professional presentation was brought out at regular intervals. News about the factory, houses, schools, and even jokes helped to keep the word 'Banbury' always before employees' eyes.

Information was not confined to formal channels. It is doubtful if many lower-level employees in most firms look at notice-boards or read company letters (though a saturation campaign like that of Birds might overcome this), but nobody could ignore the various personal interviews. A lot of the credit for this must go to the relocation services manager. The personal interviews were largely his idea in the first place and he worked excessively long hours to complete them. Though his methods nominally represented an 'open-door' policy, as the interviews were held at the employee's request, the relocation services manager made sure that he saw, and kept seeing, all the known waverers. If the initiative for interviews had always in practice lain with employees, moving decisions might have been made by default, and the easiest course – not moving – might have been adopted by more employees.

This conclusion is reinforced by Alan Fox's report of the transfer arrangements made by the British Aluminium Company when it closed down production at its Milton plant and moved to South Wales. An attempt was made to transfer some workers also, but in a rather half-heated way, using 'soft-sell' techniques. It failed: only nine workers eventually transferred. Fox comments:

> What evidence we have on mobility suggests that if . . . (the) . . . factors making for inertia were to be overcome in even a small minority of individuals, a strong counter-motivation had to be built up within them. This the company made no attempt to do. The material inducements . . . were such as to offset the cost of moving, but provided no tempting positive attractions and indeed were designed to avoid doing so. And if the Com-

116

pany did not seek to induce by material attractions, neither
did it seek to persuade by emotive appeals. It presented its
employees with a coolly-prepared profit-and-loss account,
stepped back and told them to do their own sums. Long
periods of official silence were allowed to elapse between the
various stages of the transfer operation, during which time
the men were left open to all the influences militating against
transfer, of which there were many.[12]

Birds overcame both the obstacles mentioned by Fox: the company made
the relocation financially attractive and through a 'hard-sell' programme
it hammered this home to all employees.

RELOCATION DIFFICULTIES

So when plans began to go awry in 1964, the majority had made their moving decisions and to some extent were committed to them. Difficulties
first arose over the timing of the relocation. The first announcements had
contained the hope that parts of the new factory would be in operation by
autumn 1964. This proved to be unrealistically early. In October 1963 a
relocation schedule was announced which put the starting of the coffee
plant back four months to the very end of the year. This proved to be the
beginning of an avalanche: in February 1964, the start-up of all operations
was put back several months and the first manufacturing was not to start
until March 1965. Successive schedules all contained further delays. In
fact, the first department did not move until May 1965 and manufacturing
did not start until the autumn of 1965. Most jobs were moved in that
autumn and in the following winter.

These delays would not have produced labour problems if employees
could also have delayed their personal moves, but this was rarely possible.
The council house building programme was not delayed and Banbury
Council was able to fulfil its commitments within the agreed period. If
houses remained empty after completion the company might have to pay
the rents as well as the subsidy until they were occupied. The company was
therefore very eager to persuade employees to move into them at once,
before their actual jobs were transferred.

House buyers were also trapped. It was generally expected that house
values would rise as the actual transfer date grew near, because of increased demand from Birds employees and from others (for Banbury was

---

[12] Alan Fox, *The Milton Plan* (Institute of Personnel Management, 1965) p. 61.

growing in population steadily throughout this period). Mortgages were also easy to find in 1963 and 1964, so some employees entered into house buying arrangements even before the dates originally given for the transfer of their jobs. Many more purchased a house on the assumption that they would be moving into it as, or just after, their job was transferred. All these people were surprised by the postponements of the transfer dates, having moved to the Banbury area with their families well before their jobs were transferred.

By November 1964 more than 200 employees were commuting daily from the Banbury area to Birmingham, a distance of about 40 or 50 miles. In the summer of 1965 the number reached 700.[13] The company realised that these people would be blaming the company for the inconvenience. Accordingly, in March 1964 it announced plans for aid and compensation for commuters to start from June 1st of that year. June had been the first month named for the commencement of production in the original relocation schedule. Buses were to travel between Banbury and Birmingham, serving all shifts and days of the week, and used free by all employees travelling more than 25 miles to work. Employees were encouraged to use the buses but if they could not, expenses for the use of a private car were to be refunded to the extent of 4d per mile in excess of the distance they would previously have travelled to and from work in Birmingham. As extra time as well as cost was involved, the company allowed employees to enjoy a working day reduced by $1\frac{1}{2}$ hours at normal rate of pay. But most manual workers were tied by the machinery to precise starting and finishing times. These were maintained but compensation was paid in the form of an Inconvenience Allowance of 20 per cent of their basic pay, payable monthly, with a maximum of £20 per month.

These policies proved workable but they failed to stifle all discontent. In the first place, the journey was still inconvenient. Employees' houses were scattered all over North Oxfordshire and the adjacent parts of Warwickshire and Northamptonshire. They still had to get into Banbury to catch the bus which did not make detours from the direct route. This took up to an hour and immobilised the family car for the working week unless car-pools were used. The 25-mile limit, which was later applied to private car expenses, was also unpopular with those who had moved less than that distance from Birmingham. The company reasoned that these people, usually top and middle management, had not committed themselves to the company in Banbury and were still able to leave the company and take another Birmingham job without moving house again. But they replied (unsuccessfully) that they had after all moved, and solely as a re-

---

[13] This included a couple of hundred women recently recruited in Banbury.

118

sult of the relocation: they should be compensated for this inconvenience. Moreover, the bus journey was itself considered unpleasant in the winter: the coaches were ill-heated and the atmosphere was smoke-filled. These were minor, but unforeseen, drawbacks of the move.

The 'inconvenience allowance' caused other complaints. It was scaled to income, and this seemed more unfair than the similarly scaled relocation allowance. The company had defended the latter by saying that it was intended to keep up the employee's standard of living (in carpets, curtains etc.) and the higher-paid needed more to do this. But, argued critics of the inconvenience allowance, the inconvenience of travel was the same for everyone, or at least it did not vary with income. The company was at a loss to reply. It could not publicly admit the real reason for the differentials: that it was still more concerned with attracting skilled workers and office workers to Banbury than unskilled. It had attempted to narrow the range of the differentials by fixing a maximum for the allowance but no manual worker reached the maximum. Once again, however, the announcement of differentials gave groups vested interests in defending them and all attempts by individual employees and by unions to modify it failed.

Naturally those commuting did not enjoy it. By the time of the questionnaire survey, 55 of the respondents in the sample were already living in the Banbury area and affected by the new travelling arrangements. Most were dissatisfied with the travelling they were then doing.[14] The most common grievance (mentioned 23 times) was that the company had not warned them in advance about commuting, but also 20 people said that the company was not providing enough aid to commuting: the conditions and itinerary of the coaches were criticised 10 times, while the scaled inconvenience allowance was criticised 13 times. But no-one was sufficiently discontented to consider moving back to Birmingham.[15]

So far, then, the problems and dissatisfactions I have presented as arising from the relocation policy have been minor and localised: by and large the company's treatment of the relocation evoked praise rather than blame. Nevertheless, there is no denying that certain undercurrents of tension and unease were to be perceived in the company at this time and were to be attributed to the relocation. Among staff, these centred on the rivalry between the 'thrusting' and 'sleeping' managerial groups already mentioned in the previous chapter. I have chosen to delay analysing these in detail until after the relocation was completed, because the relocation policy, by encouraging everyone to relocate, left the rivalry in a state of suspended anima-

[14] In response to the question 'Are you satisfied, dissatisfied, or don't you feel strongly either way about the travelling you are now doing?'
[15] In response to the question 'Do you want to go back near Birmingham to live?'

tion until Banbury was reached. Its climax in Banbury is described later in Chapter 7. Among manual workers, the unease was evident through the development of trade unionism in the period of the relocation, and this is what I will now discuss.

The trade union activists in the company – which at this period meant the shop stewards of the T. and G.W.U. – were suspicious of the relocation right from the start. This stemmed from the simple fact that they were not consulted in advance about the relocation or about the first relocation policy. Subsequently, the company's bulletins about the move tended to fall between two stools: they gave details about everything that had been decided but nothing about what was still being discussed. The company thought its relocation policies were fair and comprehensive; it was not prepared therefore to see them as a basis for negotiation. But, as we shall see, various groups and individuals wanted to dispute parts of the policy. Most manual workers used the trade unions as their voice, though the company was reluctant to negotiate. When the Transport and General Workers Union presented a list of suggested amendments to the policy, a senior executive of the company commented in a memorandum:

> The relocation policy is not a subject for negotiation . . . Some of these suggestions are worthy of consideration. Others are quite extreme. The main thing is that any future changes in policy should not appear to spring from Union demands, but rather as a Management decision based on experience and knowledge of employees' problems.

At this stage, the company was still engaged in a tactical battle against the union, attempting to resist further union recruitment by devious methods of propaganda. The ideology behind this which was presented to the outside was that the union could not be given special privileges: the company had to consider all employees union and non-union members alike, and it could not give unfair advantages. This is a frequent management strategy for resisting trade unions. Its paternalist flavour can be gauged from a November 1962 management statement:

> it was company policy that employees had a right to be consulted or to express their views upon matters which affected them . . . having obtained their views Management had to decide on a course of action, and in very few cases could they meet the needs of, or satisfy, everyone. Consultation with employees covered everybody in the organisation, Union members and non-Union members, Operatives, Clerical Staff, and Managers, and it would quite clearly be wrong to set up a formal consultation procedure with one section only. Management were giving consideration to this problem in

order to improve the flow of information throughout the organisation.

Such tactics, quite apart from the content of managerial policies, are not likely to produce co-operative trade unionists. In this case they evoked exaggerated suspicions like this comment by a shop steward:

> When we heard it was going to be Banbury nobody thought the company intended to take anybody. From then onwards there was suspicion all the way. And they were right: the intention was to leave behind as many as possible and then to take London overspill ... Communications about the move were very good. They had to be because there was this terrible suspicion behind everything.

There were men who looked for secret motives behind every company policy, steadfastly believing that the council houses offered in Banbury were 'tied houses'; that Banbury was a town of 'forelock-tugging peasantry' who would let Birds reduce wage rates; that 'once the company gets us down there, they can do anything with us'. These myths were difficult, sometimes impossible, to erase. The Relocation Services Manager said in exasperation 'It doesn't matter how many times I get them in front of me and tell them the houses aren't tied to the job. They just sit there and think 'You bloody liar.' Yet many of these men, and particularly those who shared milder suspicions, also said that they thought Birds was an excellent company. How could they hold both opinions?

The answer is not really specific to Birds but lies in the general power-relationship of management and workers. For all their trade union and labour market power, workers almost invariably have to react to policies already formed by management. It is very rarely that workers are able to initiate; because the first proposals are never their proposals, they tend to be wary of them. If it is to be otherwise management must invariably be able to produce policies which workers recognise as in their interest. Very few managements can be inspired enough to predict what these will be even if they were disposed to satisfy workers. The situation is somewhat different for managers who generally realise what new policies are being prepared through the information they are asked to provide. They can accordingly make their views felt before the policies are formalised at all.

Birds' failure of 1959–61 had shown management's fallibility in these matters. There was every reason for workers to be wary of the move to Banbury, even though they were content with the company in normal circumstances, especially as they were not consulted in advance about the move.

The union failed to get any substantial amendments to the relocation policy, and yet its membership grew from about 200 at the time of the first move announcement to around 350 in early 1965. The vast majority of the newcomers were probably joining for future security. They did not expect any specific ills to befall them but there was a general feeling of 'just in case'. One comment, 'I'm going to be in a dicey position once they get me down there' might have been made by almost all of them. This can be seen from the responses to Question 95 in Survey 1: 'Should trade unions have a place at Birds?', 'Why do you think this?'. Among those who replied 'yes', the 'just in case . . .' attitude was predominant. Seventy-one per cent of the reasons could be coded as 'self-protection', often phrased along the lines of 'you never know when you'll need it', while 15 per cent specifically mentioned the relocation. A further 5 per cent composed of non-movers, said they would need a union card if they sought employment in a closed shop elsewhere in Birmingham. Thus only 24 per cent of reasons were unconnected with the relocation, and most of these were statements that 'all companies should have trade unions'.[16] Extensive recruitment had now occurred among the hitherto unorganized.

The move was the result of the expansion of coffee manufacturing; without the expansion the company would still be in Birmingham. Plans had been made to double the 1963 volume of production in Banbury within a few years but in the summer of 1964 the coffee market experienced a recession. The causes are not altogether clear and expansion was back to normal within two years. At the time, however, long-term trends seemed to be at work and many managers gloomily predicted that the British coffee market was near saturation-point. On 10 July the company announced that one of the three coffee plants would be shut down and coffee workers would be transferred to other jobs.[17] The policy of the company as regards wages was clear: the 'detached worker policy' laid down that the worker's former wage would not be guaranteed if his former job was completely stopped. But the bulletin went on:

> It is intended to treat this as an exceptional circumstance outside the normal provisions of the detached worker policy but *without prejudice as to any future action or policy*. It is intended to protect the earnings of employees in these categories [i.e. the various groups of coffee workers] during the period of 7 weeks from 11th July 1964 as follows
>
> (*a*) Their *gross* pay each week shall *not be less than* the amount they would have earned had they been on their normal job.

[16] $N = 104$ reasons mentioned by the 84 out of 119 respondents who answered 'yes' to question 95.

[17] It is indicative of the different 'contracts of employment' offered to managers and workers at Birds that, though dismissal was not contemplated for the coffee workers, it was promptly handed out to the marketing director.

(*b*) They must be prepared and willing to work on any job for the hours required (including overtime) for the gross pay defined in (*a*).

(*e*) ... if there is any indication that this period is to be extended it must not be taken that these arrangements for payout will also be extended. (My emphasis)

Such a policy is industrial dynamite. The company was breaking its own rules, ratified by the trade union but was not intending to negotiate new rules. It was guaranteeing the wages of high-rated employees working alongside workers receiving the normally lower wages for doing the same job. A score of workers were transferred during this first close-down. The imminence of the move to Banbury had obviously forced the company to take such steps. No worker had been laid off at Birds since 1957, nor had there been even partial shut-downs on the coffee plant. The coffee workers naturally looked on present earnings as permanent earnings, and this assumption was at the root of their wholesale move to Banbury. Many had entered into mortgage and other hire purchase contracts to the limits of these earnings. The company was afraid that their reaction would be violent.

The coffee workers were mollified by the guaranteed wage but the other workers were aroused by it. The Transport and General Workers Union, which had no members among coffee process workers anyway, made repeated attempts to stop this guarantee. It would not change the policy at the first shut-down, but threatened trouble if it happened again. A further shut-down did occur: on 9 September the company announced that the small coffee plant would remain closed for a further four weeks. After three it was opened again but on 11 November it was closed for a further 7 weeks. On neither occasion was compensatory pay received by the coffee workers. The union appeared to have won, though the bulletin quoted above refused to guarantee wages in further shut-downs.

This was an important victory for the union. It was the first demonstration of its strength since 1961. Indeed, in May 1964 it had been severely weakened by the defection of about 20 electricians to the Electrical Trades Union, which had been recognised by management as representing the electrical department after a token strike on 11 May. The uneasy alliance between the craftsmen and the unskilled workers was breaking down, and the Amalgamated Engineering Union was also attempting to obtain a foothold in the company. The contemptuous description of the Transport and General Workers Union as the 'dustmen's union' was often heard at this time among craftsmen. Now the Transport and General Workers Union had justified its continued existence, at least to unskilled workers.

The biggest effect of the victory was a surprising one: the coffee workers began to join the Transport and General Workers Union. One of them describes the background to this:

> We reckoned that we'd always been treated pretty fair by management. If one of us had a grievance, he'd take it to his supervisor, and it was pretty sure to be treated quickly. We had a very good atmosphere on the plant – I'm not saying we still don't. But when that coffee recession was on, management soon began to take more notice of the blokes in Devonshire Works than us. Why? Because they had the union behind them. Well, we put our heads together and decided that our tactic should be 'If you can't beat 'em join 'em'. So we joined.

The chairman of the shop representatives' committee agreed:

> I don't think that the coffee workers would have come in but we interfered with them. The coffee people will tell you now they're only in the union – they are quite open about it to me – they say 'we only joined the union to have some say in it, because in any case the union was interfering with us, and we couldn't get back.' We were reducing differentials and getting fringe benefits fairer. Like the detached worker policy ...
> When they moved the coffee workers *en bloc* [during the recession] they wanted to pay them the rate. And we said 'Oh no, they aren't getting it. This is against the policy of the company.' We wouldn't have it; we interfered with them so they joined. Since then they have used the union a lot on their behalf.

Union membership figures bear out these statements. There were no members among the coffee process workers until the 18 October 1964. On that day 38 of them joined. Most of the rest soon followed.

The increasing unionisation during the relocation period, culminating in the recruitment of the coffee processers, marked the start of a new type of industrial relations. Now management had to learn to live with unions rather than play off unionists against non-unionists. The months surrounding the coffee recession marked the period of my most intensive contacts with managers in their official capacities and it was easy to detect quickly changing attitudes to trades unions among them. In the personnel department and in line management in the factories individuals were learning to live with a situation in which consultation with trade unions was becoming the usual method of doing business. This was one of the consequences of the relocation which management had not expected with its fears of 'rampant trade unionism' among new recruits in Banbury. But I suppose it is a fairly predictable consequence of relocation, especially one to a small town like Banbury. Such a relocation increases the level

124

of dependence of the relocating worker upon his employment, by making alternative employment more difficult to find.[18] Where trade unions are already available they will therefore be steadily joined 'just in case'.

THE TEMPORARY WORKERS AND THE CLOSED SHOP

But in the Birds case unionism received a boost from a wholly unexpected direction, and one that carried the trade unions to a closed shop. Originally, only factory workers with the company in April 1964 were eligible to make the move. This means that all workers who joined the company after that date would be made redundant within a short period. Because the moving dates were continually postponed, this period was always assumed to be shorter than in fact it turned out to be. It was difficult to attract workers for so short a period and the company had to accept all applicants. Most of the newcomers were young men, many of them Irish, who had had a previous job-history of drifting from job to job. They were extremely independent and they would often leave a job rather than submit to discipline. The Birds labour force had always had a reputation for docility, and some of the supervisors proved incapable of adapting to the new men. One of the temporaries summed up the situation: 'Birds? It's the best company for fun I've ever worked in.'

The temporaries were mostly members of the Transport and General Workers Union. Their shop representatives soon became the most militant section on the union committee and it proved difficult for the established leadership to contain their challenge. Unofficial strikes resulted in the summer of 1965. There were three of these. Two were refusals to work with non-union members, while the third attempted to get the rate of sickness benefit increased.[19] All were unofficial and were disowned by the established union leadership in the factory. But the public attitude of the leadership was somewhat hypocritical as it took over from the strikers the attempt to force a closed shop. It was in a very strong position to do this. If a stoppage occurred, transport drivers of other companies declared Birds' products 'black' while the union decided whether the strike was official. This took longer than it took for the Birds finished

---

[18] Bearing particularly in mind W. W. Daniel's point that the extended family – from which the worker is separated by the relocation–provides the usual channels of obtaining alternative employment. See above, Chapter 2.

[19] Sickness benefit was of some importance to the non-movers. The number of days of paid absence was tied to length of service, and many employees were now eligible for a considerable period of paid absence. Thus the non-movers were eager to use up their rights.

goods warehouses to fill and production to stop. At this point the union asked for a closed shop. If the company refused this, the union declared itself unable to restrain its militants who came out on strike again. This happened twice and the company realised it could continue happening indefinitely. It therefore capitulated.[20] Employees joining the company after 15 August 1965 were advised to join the appropriate union. This is not quite a union shop: new employees could only be 'advised' and nothing was said of existing employees. But both sides came away from the agreement with the knowledge that there would be trouble if the company actually employed someone who refused to join a union. The other loophole, the position of existing employees, has not yet caused trouble partly because the informal pressures towards joining were very strong and only six have resisted. Management is divided on whether it would actually support an obstinate anti-unionist if this cover became an issue.

The trouble was led by temporaries and non-movers, but this did not mean that the union would decline in influence once the company was in Banbury. Once a negotiating procedure is established between union and management, and respected by both sides, it tends to be the normal method of doing business. The unionisation of the coffee workers illustrates this: they still say they are satisfied with the company but they are frequent users of union channels. In Banbury they use the Transport and General Workers Union to negotiate all their grievances.[21] Nor does militancy remain in Banbury – there has not yet been a serious dispute of any sort between unions and management.

Nevertheless, the non-movers did at first infect the last of the moving workers with some of their attitudes. There was a great decline in productivity in Birmingham towards the end. The decline occurred even in departments where most of the workers were to be transferred to Banbury. For several months the greater part of two factories, one in Birmingham and one in Banbury, were kept running simultaneously, and management had great difficulty in spreading its supervision over them both. The temporary promotion of manual workers to supervisory posts was the only solution and, quite naturally, a few of these temporary foremen were neither able nor willing to enforce discipline.

---

[20] It also overestimated the strength of union membership at around 600, or two-thirds of the manual labour force – in fact it was only about 350, or less than half.

[21] The phenomenon of 'dual allegiance' – where the workers most favourable to their employer are also the most active union members – is, in fact, normally found where unions are well-established and not where they are striving for recognition. See Theodore V. Purcell, *Blue-Collar Man: Patterns of Dual Allegiance in Industry* (Harvard University Press, 1960).

Another obstacle to the maintenance of discipline was the discontent of some of the regular foremen. By August 1965, sixteen first-line supervisors were members of the Transport and General Workers Union and had appointed a shop representative. They did so because of the unease which the move brought. Imminent re-organization of the manufacturing department was expected and they wished to guarantee themselves protection in case this worked against them. One of them said:

> We are joining because we think we're going to be messed
> about something awful. Trouble at Birds starts at the top and
> works down. The hourly paid man is the safest in the factory.
> Its getting down near our level now.

But why should salaried men 'on the staff' join what is predominantly a manual workers' union? One who didn't join explains it in terms of lack of ambition:

> I don't think that joining the union is any help in this [in
> securing your future]. If that's your feelings then I think you
> ought to be on the shop floor. But there is a group of foremen
> here promoted from the shop floor who are quite happy to
> remain where they are. These are the people joining the union.
> The better educated, the more ambitious, don't join ... The
> foremen who join are not the most resourceful of people and
> they won't be bothered to go to ASSET and start their own
> branch.

Some members of management suspect that some of these foremen turned a 'blind eye' to the activities of the unofficial strikers. Certainly the latter seemed to be able to make use of company telephones and other facilities for arranging their plans.

The factory system may be viewed as a system of controls over the effort of workers.[22] If the controls are taken away it is very doubtful if the worker will continue his effort. And once having been taken away it is difficult to re-impose them. Birds experienced this difficulty, particularly as regards the women recruited from the Banbury area and brought daily by coach to work in Birmingham. There they were introduced to the relaxed discipline and declining morale of the non-movers. One of the managers who continued in the Birmingham factory until the end commented.

> The first impressions the Banbury workers had of us was
> disastrous. We had girls working here, coming in from
> Banbury every day, who must have sent the news back to

---

[22] See W. Baldamus, *Efficiency and Effort* (Tavistock, 1961) for a persuasive analysis of this sort.

Banbury that Birds was the softest spot you could ever work in. They could vanish half an hour before the buses to take them back; they could be late at the Banbury site and know the bus would wait for them.

Of course, had this relocation been over a greater distance, the consequences of the building delays would have been much worse for the company. Daily commuting would not have been possible and presumably parts of either the new or the old plant would not have been in operation for long periods. It is probable that any relocating company will experience severe problems at the time of the move itself. But if parts of this Chapter have read like a chronicle of disaster, it must be borne in mind that the crucial benefits (and costs) of relocation are felt over a much longer time-span, after the relocation itself is over. Birds' most important personnel problem at the time of the relocation was not how to run two factories at once for a short period of time, but was rather how to transfer a work-force adequate for many years to come.

6
Movers and non-movers: relocation decisions

Previous chapters have explored the history of the company prior to the relocation. Knowledge of this history is essential for an explanation of employee reactions to the relocation offer. Two points stand out. First, by 1964 Birds was a company which was generally liked by its employees; secondly, employees' ties of dependence to the company varied in strength between the occupational groups distinguished in Chapter 4. The first point explains why, overall, so many employees made the move to Banbury; the second helps to explain why some moved more willingly than others, and why others did not move at all.

From the point of view of personnel management the move was a success, for the company was able to transfer almost as many male employees as it needed in Banbury. Far fewer women transferred, but then this had been anticipated, and extensive female recruitment from Banbury itself had been planned from the start. About 65 per cent of the male manual workers transferred to Banbury, and about 60 per cent or 85 per cent of male salaried staff, depending on the date chosen for the calculation.[1] The company would choose the higher figure as representing the true measure of its success so its final proportion of movers would be around 72 per cent, for men.[2]

Let us now clarify the actual relocation decision facing employees. Stated generally, it was either to keep a job and change house and locality or to retain house and locality and lose a job. The choice was virtually between working for Birds (and living) in Banbury and working for another employer in Birmingham. This was for three reasons:

(a) The company intended to close down completely its Birmingham establishment.[3] As it had difficulty in selling part of its Birmingham premises it did retain a caretaker staff after the move, and one of the present sample was still employed there over a year after the move, but

---

[1] See the discussion of sample bias in the Appendix.
[2] The percentage of women moving was just over 25 per cent in both the sample and the whole labour force eligible to move.
[3] Except for its Midland Region Sales Office, which has not been included in this study at all.

this was an unforeseen occurrence and employees certainly did not expect the company to continue to employ them in Birmingham.

(*b*) Commuting from the Birmingham area to Banbury was considered impracticable by nearly all employees. From Solihull (the closest Birmingham suburb) the trip would take between one and one and a half hours each way, and from central Birmingham two hours would be needed. None of the movers in the sample was commuting by the time of the second survey, though four employees not in the sample were still doing so.

(*c*) Banbury, a small market town of about 25,000 inhabitants, offered few alternative employment opportunities and so a move there was considered by the sample as tying them to Birds as an employer.

These factors crystallised relocation decision on four discrete choices between

1 working for Birds or working for another Birmingham employer;
2 Banbury or Birmingham as places to live;
3 maintaining or severing any close extended family and community ties in Birmingham;
4 the company's relocation terms for movers and non-movers.

The company's relocation policy has already been discussed and it will not figure prominently in this chapter, except in so far as it affected the comparison employees made (in choice 2) between the housing available to them in Birmingham and Banbury. In this chapter I shall analyse choices 1, 2, and 3.

THE ALTERNATIVE JOB SITUATION

To the question 'Why did so many employees move?' there is a simple general answer: 'To keep their jobs at Birds.' This was the overwhelming response to the first question of the 1964 survey. Table 18 shows the factors mentioned as reasons for moving by those who said in the survey that they intended to relocate. We must note in this table that respondents often gave more than one reason for their decision, and that the 27 employees who said at the time that they were still undecided about moving also answered this question.

However, if we look at reasons given against moving by the intending non-movers and by those who were still undecided, in Table 19 we find that factors connected with the respondent's own job decline in importance among the whole group to one-seventh of all reasons, though they amount to one-quarter of the men's reasons.

Table 18: *Sample: reasons for moving by sex (percentages)*

	Own job	Banbury or Birmingham as places	Hous-ing	Finan-cial	Child-ren	Other	N	No. of persons answering
Men	51	17	10	4	2	14	224	144
Women	55	8	9	2	5	29	55	41
All	52	15	10	4	3	17	279	185

We have already seen that Birds was in many senses a 'good' employer: it is thus no surprise that employment factors constituted stronger reasons for relocating with Birds than for leaving the company. Before we turn to investigating the precise nature of these factors, it is as well to dispose fairly quickly of the factors entering into the relocation decisions of the women employees. As can be seen in the two tables above, these differed markedly from the men's.

As most of the women were not the principal bread-winners in their families they simply never considered following their jobs to another town.[4] A minority of 27 per cent (30 out of 110 respondents) did relocate, however, and most of these did so for one of two reasons. Either they were married to, or were the unmarried daughters, of, Birds employees (13 of the 30); or they were young, single girls moving as a rather restrained 'adventure' in living away from their parents (8 cases). This leaves 4 older single women who were genuinely attached to their careers in the Birds offices in much the same way as many of the male managers, 3 married women who found jobs for their husbands at Birds, 1 woman supporting her husband, and 1 whose husband commuted to Birmingham after they moved (to Warwick). These motives for moving are very different from the men's.

EMPLOYMENT SATISFACTION

If we return now to the male employees, we must obviously explore the nature of the job-related factors which the large majority gave as their reasons for moving. What was the nature of this strong job attachment? The first commonsensical question we could ask might be 'were they then satisfied with their employment?'. And the answer to this is that

[4] Although they were as satisfied with Birds as an employer as were the men in the sample.

Table 19: *Sample: reasons against moving (percentages)*

	Other person's job	Own job	Housing	Banbury or Birmingham as places	Family or friends in Birmingham	Too old	Finance	Other	N	No. of persons answering
Men	6	24	16	6	9	6	10	22	67	48
Women	31	7	9	17	11	9	2	13	96	71
All	21	14	12	12	10	8	6	17	163	119

most of them were, as we have already seen. But if we seek to interpret their relocation decisions in the light of their job satisfaction, we came against the simple and consistent set of findings that *relocating propensity is not correlated with employment satisfaction*. Movers were not significantly more likely than non-movers to have favourable opinions of the company as a whole, of the work pressures upon them, of supervision, of intrinsic job content, of security, or of promotion chances.[5] Yet this lack of association is not surprising in view of the data and the arguments already contained in Chapters 3 and 4. For there I noted the general 'weakness' of measures of job satisfaction as predictors of the overall commitment to their jobs of workers. Indeed though in this company as in most others studies by sociologists there were very few 'dissatisfied' workers, this tells us more about the workers' psychological defence mechanisms than about their actual involvement in work. For among manual workers we saw in Chapter 3 that though 'dissatisfaction' might indicate negative attitudes 'satisfaction' did not necessarily indicate very positive ones. Furthermore, Table 17 indicated that the satisfaction of the present sample with various aspects of their employment seemed unusually susceptible to small and sometimes temporary changes in the company, which we suspected left their overall employment relationship largely unaffected. The latter, I maintained, was much more affected by the employment dependence of the worker. To test this hypothesis we must see whether employment dependence fares any better as a predictor of moving decisions than employment satisfaction.

First, it is worth pointing out one positive implication of 'satisfaction' findings. The fact that very few Birds employees were dissatisfied with their overall employment does at least inform us that their work attitudes did not in themselves constitute a serious obstacle to relocation, though we have yet to show that they might be an inducement to relocate. Though a satisfied workforce might not necessarily accept a job transfer offered by its employer, a workforce dissatisfied with its overall enduring conditions of employment would surely reject it. Dissatisfied labour forces are not often found but those which exist are unlikely to accept a relocation offer. Perhaps, therefore, job satisfaction constitutes a necessary, but by no means a sufficient cause of relocation.

[5] Being the responses to, respectively, questions 85, 94, 92, 88, 91 and 93 of the first survey. Indeed, among these, the only *perceptible* difference is that concerning attitudes to promotion, where those more concerned with promotion are more likely to move than those who are not, and the most likely to move are those who are concerned *and satisfied* with promotion. But even here χ^2 is significant only at the unacceptable level of 0.20.

THE EMPLOYMENT DEPENDENCE OF SALARIED STAFF

I shall again conduct my analysis of employment dependence separately on salaried staff and manual workers. First, I will deal with the salaried staff, that is the managers, supervisors and clerks in the company. The samples bias referred to in the Appendix makes any comparison between movers and non-movers among this group rather dubious. However, some points still stand out clearly from the data.

The first is that their relocation decisions were dominated by job factors. Unlike the manual workers, the overwhelming majority of the non-movers (8 out of 10) as well as the movers (43 out of 52) gave job-related reasons for their decisions. There seems no good reason for assuming that the group of non-movers missing from the sample – those who had already left the company before the sample was selected – would have had non-work reasons for leaving thus early, and so this evidence reinforces what was said in Chapter 2 about the centrality of work in the lives of the middle class. In this sample of non-manual workers it was almost always work factors which decided whether they would uproot themselves and their families.

The second point emerges the more clearly *because of* the sample bias. Among the moving salaried men were two fairly distinct groups of men, and one of these was greatly added to by the relative newcomers to the company, those who had joined the company after the relocation was arranged.

Seventeen of the sixty-two salaried men in the sample had joined the company in the full knowledge that it was shortly to relocate, and only two of this seventeen did not themselves relocate. These short-service men were naturally younger than the others and they were also slightly better qualified, though only three of them had received University education. Like the other younger salaried men, they were pursuing *careers*. 'Job prospects' constantly recurs among their reasons for moving to Banbury. The older men were in fact slightly more likely to mention job-factors as reasons for their move (indeed, all those over 40 mentioned them, compared to 80 per cent of those under 40), but their reasons were more negative in tone, and more often concerned with preserving present job status rather than seeking great future improvements. Such statements as 'Its 17 years since I worked for another firm, I can't leave now' and 'I don't want to lose what responsibilities I've got' contrast strongly with younger men's 'I can get good experience in marketing here. Then maybe I move on' and 'I've been as good as told that I do have prospects with the company'. Not surprisingly, the majority of the older men felt dependent on the company for the preservation of their job-status. However, this did not prevent the oldest workers, the over-60s, from staying behind in Birmingham – three of the six in the sample did so. All knew of their dependence, all accepted jobs which (in Survey 2) they said were worse than their Birds job. Yet they were sufficiently near retirement age to accept this. This problem of dependence loomed largest for the poorly-qualified in middle and late-middle age: only one man out of the 16 who had at most G.C.E. 'O' Level qualifications between the ages of 31 and 60 did not move, compared to 4 out of 18 in this age-group with higher qualifications.

Yet we cannot say that the younger men, though they did mostly relocate for job reasons, were heavily dependent upon the company. If the expected promotion prospects did not occur, they were quite willing to look for another job in another company.

This clearly separates them from the rest of the movers, for it involved contemplating another change of house and district as well as job. All the non-manual male sample stated that it would be difficult finding a job with similar pay in the Banbury area.[6] They accepted that moving to another area was a necessary (and not always undesirable) consequence of their desire for progressive careers. By contrast most of the older staff, and particularly a small group of long-service foremen, were less favourably disposed toward the move. These men generally recognised that they were 'tied' to the company by virtue of their age and lack of external qualifications. The relative distinctness of these two types of moving salaried men will emerge very clearly in Chapter 7 when we analyse their post-move experiences at work.

The analysis of the moving decisions of salaried men just presented has been short. This has been partly because of the constraints imposed by small numbers and a biassed sample. But it has also resulted from the simplicity and the predictability of the main findings: some men relocated because they were heavily dependent on the company for the preservation of their job-status, the remainder because they were embarking upon careers. Only the latter appeared to think they had much choice in the matter.

We must now turn to a rather more complex analysis of the manual workers. In this case, we will treat separately the two major determinants of employment dependence, age and the relationship between the internal and external job-hierarchy.

---

[6] In answer to question 24, Survey 1. Three-quarters of the manual workers also stated this.

THE EMPLOYMENT DEPENDENCE OF MANUAL WORKERS

My main hypothesis is that manual workers relocated to the extent that they were dependent upon the company for the preservation of their job-status level. To establish this we turn first to the degree of the worker's upward mobility within the internal labour market, for the more his promotions have occurred within his present firm, the more dependent he will be upon it.[7] In Table 20 I have attempted to establish the sample's degree of upward job mobility within the company by comparing its Birds' jobs at the time of the survey with the three previous jobs held outside the company.

Table 20: *Sample: moving decision by degree of upward job mobility experienced at Birds – Male manual workers (numbers)*

Degree of upward job mobility at Birds	Occupational groups	Movers	Non-movers	Total
High	1 Grade 50+ coffee processers	9	0	9
	2 Upgraded craftsmen	2	0	2
Medium	3 Maintenance mates and technicians (Grades 30–50)	12	2	14
	4 Grade 30+ coffee processers	9	5	14
	5 Grade 30–50 'other manual' workers (except drivers contained in 7)	18	9	27
Low	6 Craftsmen with craftsman backgrounds	14	1	15
	7 Long-distance drivers	2	3	5
	8 Below grade 30 workers (all from 'other manual' group)	24	18	42
		90	38	128

[7] Unless, of course, he obtains a universally recognised qualification such as a formal period of apprenticeship.

136

In fact, the overall association between upward job mobility at Birds and relocation decision is an extremely weak and insignificant one. It is the presence of two of the groups of maintenance workers – groups 3 and 6 – which weakens the association. Without them the x^2 association becomes significant at the 0.01 level. Thus, ignoring the maintenance workers for the moment, among the coffee processers and the 'other manual' workers dependence upon the company's internal labour market for the preservation of job status seems to be significantly related to moving decision. How then, do we explain the behavior of the maintenance workers nearly all of whom relocated, regardless of the degree of internal company mobility experienced? Let us use the other indicator of employment dependence outlined in Chapter 4, the learning-period bonus, in an attempt to answer this.

The job-learning bonus is a pay bonus given to Birds workers for learning and retaining job skills specific to their own job. Thus if a worker leaves the company he will probably forfeit at least this amount of wages in taking another job. This bonus is therefore a useful partial measure of wage dependence. Table 21 correlates this bonus with work-group and moving decision, dichotomising the bonus at 4 points (i.e. a weekly bonus of around £1). There is a strong correlation here between learning-period bonus and moving decision: almost all those receiving four or more points bonus relocated, while just over half the remainder did so.[8] The difference appears in all three major work-groups, though naturally we should not attribute much significance to the maintenance worker results, where the only man not receiving at least 4 bonus points (a painter) did not relocate. It seems, then, that there is a marked association between the workers' dependence upon the company and their relocating behaviour. Can we now convert this statement of association into one of causation, and

Table 21: *Sample: moving decision by job group and learning period bonus – male manual workers (numbers)*

Work group:	Maintenance workers			Coffee processers			Other manual workers			All manual workers		
Learning bonus:	−4 pts	4+ pts	All	−4 pts	4+ pts	All	−4 pts	4+ pts	All	−4 pts	4+ pts	All
Movers	0	28	28	5	13	18	33	11	44	38	52	90
Non-movers	1	2	3	5	0	5	26	4	30	32	6	38
All	1	30	31	10	13	23	59	15	74	70	58	128

[8] x^2 significant at the 0.001 level.

Table 22: *Sample: reasons for moving by occupational groupings. Male manual workers, movers only (percentages)*

	% Mentioning job reasons[a]	% Mentioning housing	% Mentioning other factors	N respondents
Coffee and 'other manual' workers				
Grade 50+ (all coffee processers)	100	0	37.5	8
Grades 30–50 except drivers[b]	74	22	43	23
Grades below 30	44	32	52	25
Maintenance workers				
Craftsman (Grades 70–110)	87	0	67	15
Mates and technicians (Grades 30–50)	92	17	42	12
All			Total responding	83

a As in Tables 18 and 19 the percentages add up to more than 100 per cent, as respondents could give more than one reason. Also the respondents are those who either said they were relocating or were still undecided in answer to Survey 1, question 1.

b The two relocating drivers who gave their reasons for their decision have been excluded from this table. Neither gave a job-related reason for moving, which reinforces the interpretation I give of the results in the table.

demonstrate that the highly dependent workers who relocated did so because of their dependence? To do this we must look at the movers' own reasons for their relocation decisions. These are presented in Table 22 by occupational groupings. The latter have been distinguished in accordance with the argument about employment dependence contained in this section. If it is indeed true that the maintenance workers and the higher-graded workers in other departments were more dependent upon Birds, then we might have expected the movers from these groups to be more likely to give job-related reasons for their decisions than the movers from the other groups. And this is precisely what Table 22 reveals. This table shows that those workers who were more economically dependent upon the company were more likely to relocate for job-related reasons. But, of course, I have not yet shown that those reasons actually entailed recognition of economic dependence for they may have been connected with other aspects of employment. The reasons given are not in themselves clearly worded enough for us to decide this. But I also asked workers whether they thought they could find similar wages to their Birds employment elsewhere in Birmingham, and the answers to this question should help us to decide whether the workers themselves were conscious of wage-dependence. As I noted in Chapter 4, this question was not particularly well-chosen as an indicator of workers' realisation of economic dependence, for it ignores the long-term economic benefits brought about by the company's high job security and generous fringe benefits. Nevertheless, even such an inadequate indicator of dependence did bring forth meaningful results in that those work-groups which were more objectively dependent upon the company were also more subjectively aware of their immediate wage-dependence. Let us see now whether this awareness also affected their relocation decisions. Table 23 analyses moving decisions by perception of immediate wage-dependence and by occupational groups. Unfortunately, small numbers (particularly of non-movers in higher level jobs) necessitates compression of the occupational groups into three job-grade groups. This table offers further indications of the influence of worker perceptions of economic dependence in relocation decisions. Ignoring the different worker-grades for the moment and considering only the column totals we can see that those who perceive difficulty in finding similar wages elsewhere in Birmingham are more likely to relocate. Turning to the occupational groups, this trend is more marked in the higher grades than the lower ones: once again we can explain the relocation decisions of the higher-level workers more easily in terms of job factors than we can the other workers. Nevertheless, even among the higher grades, the association in this table between moving decision and perceptions of wage dependence is not a strong one: for example, the χ^2 computed from the column totals is significant only at the 0.20 level. This may reflect simply the inadequacy of this particular measure of economic dependence. However, I think there are good grounds for believing that my treatment of dependence so far has been

Table 23: *Sample: moving decision by job grade and perception of difficulty in finding similar wages elsewhere in Birmingham – male manual workers (numbers)*

	Movers		Non-movers	
	Difficult to find similar wages	Not difficult	Difficult	Not difficult
Grades 50+	16	7	1	0
Grades 30–50	27	12	9	9
Grades below 30	7	16	3	12
	50	35	13	21

rather narrow in concentrating on the purely financial aspects of dependence. It would be foolish at this stage to deny the importance of economic dependence in helping to determine relocation decisions. However, there were indications in the response to the 'open-ended' questions of the first survey that dependence upon Birds was rather more diffuse in nature than has hitherto appeared. First, it is clear that many respondents were perceiving their dependence in a long-term manner from their responses to some of the open-ended questions. The key concepts behind their responses were time and again revealed as security and stability. These concepts, as they were used, were rather subtle. They did not appear to mean simply that they were in no fear of being dismissed, though this was a part of their thinking. But on top of that was often expressed a belief that Birds guaranteed the man a particular job status. Let me illustrate this with some examples of statements made by the workers.

From a middle-aged machine operator in Devonshire Works, doing only a Grade 20, but a specialised, job: 'For all its faults, this is a very steady place to work. I don't think they'd sack me without a good reason. Yes, I reckon I've got a good job here until I retire. That's why I'm moving.'

From a 35 year old coffee processor, Grade 50: 'You know where you are with this company. . . They leave you to get along with the job if you show you can do it.'

From a fitter's mate: 'I like the job because I can do it, and they all know it. I get along with . . . (the tradesmen) . . . and nobody's going to be poking their noses in.'

From a top-rated coffee processer: 'We don't see much of management where I work. Just the supervisors and they don't know much. Still, they leave it to us. They don't come running around at us just because someone in the offices over the road has had a new . . . and crazy . . . idea.'

All these statements contain the belief that the worker is to some extent in control of his own work, that management and supervisors know that he is a competent relief operator or fitter's mate and can be left on his own. 'You know where you are' is a crucial idea here: it was heard many times, and seemed to indicate a belief in a stable future at work. Moreover, it is no accident that such types of remark came almost exclusively from higher-graded men or from lower-graded men doing specialised work. These men had clearly demarcated work tasks which, they could reflect with natural exaggeration, nobody else could do. Such a sense of job-identity was reinforced by status satisfaction in the case of men whose 'security' was enhanced by their position up the internal promotion hierarchy.

It must be stressed that such conceptions of work are not unusual

140

among manual workers. In many studies the ideal supervisor has been described by the men as the one 'who lets you get on with the job on your own'.[9] And workers conceiving of themselves as having rights not just to a job with an employer but to their own particular job, i.e. a conception of 'job property rights', has been an important determinant of post-war British industrial relations.[10] These conceptions are heightened in companies like Birds which formally differentiate jobs into clear-cut hierarchical and functional types. They seem to have played an important role in the Birds relocation in giving work dependence its peculiar flavour. It is difficult to separate this dependence into economic and non-economic parts because the type of security and stability available for most workers at Birds guaranteed both at once. Thus the data presented in this section have tended to support the arguments advanced by Gladys Palmer and her associates. Where the keynote of employment involvement is 'steadiness' dependence can be unexpectedly high because of its diffuseness. But in the present sample this applied to skilled workers as well as unskilled. We have seen that the majority of manual workers were prepared to uproot themselves and their families and move over forty miles in order to keep a 'steady' job with a 'good' firm.

So far we have been looking at job dependence factors linked to the job structure of the company and have found them to be a very important influence on moving decisions. Can we add into the argument a similar prediction for the other type of job dependence factor, age? We would naturally expect older workers to be more dependent on the company than younger workers, and therefore to be more likely to relocate. But, in fact, it is not as simple as that. There is no linear correlation between age and moving propensity, as Table 24 shows. Those under 30 years of age and those over 50 are slightly more likely to relocate than the middle aged, but to interpret these trends we must introduce other factors into the analysis. We can obtain a clue for interpreting the trend by holding constant an indicator of the other kind of dependence, that deriving from the company's job structure. Accordingly, Table 24 correlates age with moving decision and also the learning period bonus.[11] In this table we catch glimpses of a correlation between age and moving decision in an unexpected direction, that is, where younger men are more likely to move. Men of over 50 are only more likely to move than the average when their

[9] See for example, Goldthorpe *et al.*, *The Affluent Worker: Industrial Attitudes* pp, 63–8.

[10] Turner *et al.*, *Labour Relations in the Motor Industry*, p. 337.

[11] It would naturally be more satisfactory to use the occupational groups separated in Table 20 as the indicator of dependence, but unfortunately small numbers prevent the use of anything more than a dichotomous variable. The two indicators of dependence are, of course, highly inter-correlated.

141

Workers on the Move

Table 23: Sample: moving decision by age and learning period bonus – male manual workers (numbers)

Age:	−30 yrs			31–40			41–50			51+			All		
Learning bonus:	−4 pts	4+ pts	All	−4 pts	4+ pts	All	−4 pts	4+ pts	All	−4 pts	4+ pts	All	−4 pts	4+ pts	All
Movers	11	4	15	10	15	25	8	18	26	10	14	24	39	51	90
Non-movers	3	0	3	14	1	15	7	3	10	7	2	9	31	6	37
All	14	4	18	24	16	40	15	21	36	17	16	33	70	57	127

142

learning period bonus is generally higher. But younger men are much more likely to move than their low bonuses would suggest. A further result in need of interpretation is that the least likely group of all to move is the middle-aged one with low bonuses.

We cannot yet interpret these findings because so far we have been concerned only to analyse the moving decisions of those men who were heavily dependent upon the company's job structure. In fact we had great success in explaining their decisions: virtually all those who were heavily dependent as a result relocated. But the reverse was not true, and Tables 20 and 21 showed that somewhere around one half of those who were not so dependent also relocated. Since this has not yet been explained, we cannot account for the first factor which cuts across the job structure, that of age.

Any interpretation of the moving decisions of those less dependent on the company's job structure is complicated by the fact that their reasons for their decisions were more varied. We have already glimpsed this in Table 22 where under one-half of those men in the Grades below 30 mentioned job factors as reasons for moving, while a third mentioned housing factors and half mentioned other factors. Yet age is one of the variables which helps us sort out these reasons, as Table 25 shows. The more important findings are to be found in the extreme age-columns. The eldest group almost all mention job factors and, as we have seen, this is largely because higher-rated workers predominate in this group. Among the youngest group we find, on the contrary, an even wider variety of reasons for moving, with housing factors mentioned by over a third (though the numbers involved here are rather small). So now non-work factors begin to exert some influence over moving decisions, and we must turn to analyse what these housing and 'other' factors are.[12]

Table 25: *Sample: reasons for moving by age – male manual workers movers only (percentages)*

	− 30 yrs	31–40	41–50	51+	N
Mentioning job factors	55%	87%	68%	95%	
Mentioning housing factors	36%	43%	42%	5%	
Mentioning other factors	55%	13%	16%	5%	
Number of respondents	11	23	19	21	74

[12] Before leaving job factors it is worth briefly noting two variables that were unrelated to moving propensity, namely the length of service of the worker and his disciplinary record (i.e. whether he had received official warnings from management for his conduct at work). From management's point of view, there might have been disadvantages involved if the workers transferred had been either inexperienced or unruly. This did not occur.

THE COMPARISON BETWEEN BIRMINGHAM AND BANBURY

As mentioned in the first section of this chapter, the relocation entailed four main choices, not just one. In addition to the job choice were the choices between Birmingham and Banbury, between maintaining or severing family and community ties, and between the company's relocation policies for movers and non-movers. Employees were conscious of these choices and normally they considered them all. The job choice was crucial for most of them but not for all.

Individual non-work factors were found at all levels within the plant. There was the highly-rated coffee process operator who stayed behind and took a cut in wages of about £3 per week which he had foreseen. He said he had stayed behind because he wanted to stay with his son whose apprenticeship could not be transferred. There was the long-service worker who stayed behind and took a far worse job in every respect (so he said) because his wife had not liked Banbury. There were a couple of coloured workers who were afraid of having to face racial prejudice in Banbury without the support of a coloured community. There was an enthusiastic fisherman who disliked Birds but thought Banbury was a good fishing centre. There was a man whose daughter lived in Hertfordshire and could visit him more easily in Banbury. These are idiosyncratic cases, but there were also exceptions which were more clearly structured.

The non-work factor which was best correlated with moving decision was the housing situation of the respondent. As a preliminary to analysis of the housing situation of the Birds employees let us consider what sort of a housing choice was presented to them by the move. Here we must introduce consideration of the company's relocation policy. As we have already seen, the relocation policy was generous in its provision of housing in the Banbury area. Council housing was available to all employees, and mortgages were also available on favourable terms for house-purchase. We might therefore assume that this would be a great incentive towards relocating with the company as has occurred in other relocations. In another company relocation described by one of its executives a large proportion of workers apparently relocated because their housing conditions prior to the move were atrocious.[13]

But in this case, the houses visited during the interviewing survey were in general clean, comfortable and well-equipped. The Banbury Borough Council Housing Manager was actually empowered to refuse to accept any Birds applicants for council house tenancies if the standard of main-

---

[13] The case is that reported by Cuttriss, *The Relocation of Industry*. See Chapter 2 above.

tenance of their previous homes seemed to indicate them unfit tenants – but in no case did he have to enforce his right.[14] Question 50 in the first survey asked 'Has this house/flat got an indoor toilet, a bathroom with hot and cold running water and an unshared garden?' Seventy per cent of respondents answered that it had all of them, and half the remainder lacked only an unshared garden. Figures are available from the 1961 Census for the City of Birmingham showing that 62.3 per cent of households in the City have exclusive use of hot and cold taps, a fixed bath and a toilet.[15] Of the sample who lived within the City 75 per cent had these fixtures. Of course, the sample, unlike the City's population, does not include households without a wage-earner (which will tend to lack more facilities), but this may be counteracted by the fact that the sample's toilets were required by the questionnaire to be indoors. If we look at the type of house tenure of the male sample living within the City, we find the proportions owner-occupying, renting from the council and with other tenures almost identical with those within the City as a whole, at 35 per cent, 35 per cent and 30 per cent respectively.[16] However, the whole sample (i.e. those living outside the City of Birmingham as well as inside) compares favourably with the English population as a whole in its housing tenure. Rather more (29 per cent as against 21 per cent or 24 per cent)[17] were renting council accommodation and fewer had other types of tenancy (26 per cent as against 34 per cent or 36 per cent)[18] – though, of course, these differences are not great.

So bad housing conditions did not 'push' the Birds labour force as a whole towards relocation.

But within the sample we find that housing conditions are related in the expected way with relocating propensity. Table 26 shows this for type of house tenure. Those renting council houses or flats were the least likely, while the house buyers were the most likely, to move.[19]

[14] Though two or three men not in the sample were only offered 're-let' accommodation by the Banbury Housing Department for this reason.
[15] *City of Birmingham Abstract of Statistics* (City of Birmingham Central Statistical Offices No. 9 (1964). Table 71, p. 109. By the 1966 Census, this figure had only marginally increased to 63.6 per cent: Sample Census 1966, England and Wales, *County Reports: Warwickshire* (H.M.S.O., 1967) p. 44. This datum in the present survey was collected at the end of 1964, i.e. between the two Censuses.
[16] Females in the sample have been excluded from this calculation because so many were not in fact household heads, whereas all the men save three were. Birmingham figure from *City of Birmingham Abstract of Statistics*, Table 69, p. 107.
[17] The first of these control percentages is taken from the 1961 Census. Housing Tables and the second from the 1962 Rowntree Survey. They are compared in J.B. Cullingworth, *English Housing Trends*, pp. 128–9.
[18] See note 17 above.
[19] Jansen (*Social Aspects of Internal Migration* p. 100) also found that council tenants were the least likely to be migrants, though he found private renters the most likely. He did not, however, control for occupation as is done here.

Table 26: *Sample: Moving decisions by type of house tenure in Birmingham – men only (percentages)*
Survey 1, question 52

	Buying	Renting from council	Other[a]	N
Movers	49	24	27	129
Non-movers	32	43	25	44
All	44	29	27	173

X^2 is significant at the 0.05 level.

a 'Other' is largely composed of persons renting from private landlords, but includes those paying board and lodging to a co-resident or living rent-free.

This might be explained by the likelihood that house tenure itself would be correlated with the level of job held by the respondent, and this is indeed the case, as can be seen from looking at the column sub-totals in Table 27. Perhaps, it is still the type of job held rather than the house tenure that is affecting the relocation decision. But Table 27 holds constant the effect of the department and shows that the housing tenure does exert an independent influence on relocation decisions. In this table, the maintenance and coffee process departments have been combined because of small numbers.

The explanation of table 27 is as follows. The large number of staff with 'other' types of tenancy are young men living alone or with a wife and possibly young children in 'digs' or flats. These men are slightly more ready to relocate than staff with other types of tenancy. Most of them used the terms of the company's relocation policy to buy their own houses for the first time. The tendency for an 'other' type of tenure to be associated with greater moving propensity is more marked among the manual workers, while among the unskilled 'other manual' group council tenure seems to be associated with staying behind in Birmingham. We have already seen that the sample as a whole did not lack adequate sanitation facilities. But the lack of facilities was most marked among those renting their accommodation privately (except in the case of gardens which were also lacking among the tenants in council flats), and all these were unskilled 'other manual' workers. If we turn to Table 18 we see that housing was mentioned as a reason for moving by 22 men. It was mentioned as the first reason by 14, 12 of whom were in the 'other manual' group. Of these 12, 11 were privately renting their Birmingham accommodation and 10 of them were lacking one of the sanitary facilities mentioned above. Most of these men were low-rated manual workers, renting

Table 27: *Sample: type of housing tenure by job groups and moving decision – men only (numbers)*

	Staff			Maintenance and coffee processing			Other manual			Total
	Movers	Non-movers	Total	Movers	Non-movers	Total	Movers	Non-movers	Total	Total
Buying	29	5	34	25	3	28	9	6	15	77
Council	4	1	5	16	4	20	13	14	27	52
Other	16	1	17	4	0	4	15	9	24	45
Total	49	7	56	45	7	52	37	29	66	174

privately and lacking at least one of the facilities. There is indeed a strong association between possession of these facilities and moving propensity. Considering only manual grades 10–40 (where four-fifths of those lacking at least one facility are concentrated) of those lacking at least one facility 72 per cent moved to Banbury compared to 57 per cent of those with all facilities. New houses were, of course, available to all the movers in Banbury. This group were quite clear about what was persuading them to move. Here are some of their comments:

> You can see for yourself this place [flat] isn't fit for human beings. It's not fit for my children, anyway.
> I'm very grateful to Birds for this chance of getting a new council house of my own. I would never have got one in Birmingham.
> I'm earning £17 a week. This is the only chance I'll ever have of owning my own house, and a new one at that.

Most of these men moved into new council houses in Banbury but a few were able to secure a mortgage for low-priced houses of their own. As the last man quoted said, such lower-paid workers would not have been able to do this without the relocation policy offered by Birds. Most of those who moved into council houses were on local authority housing waiting-lists in the Birmingham area but they were not optimistic as to their chances of actually being allocated a decent council property.

By contrast, those who already lived in council property in the Birmingham area were much more loth to move. The answers of these men showed a marked lack of further ambition, a strong sense of having already achieved life-goals in the sphere of the home. For example:

> There isn't much to move over there [to Banbury] for. I've got a good place to live, here.

or this comment about overtime working in a tape-recorded interview:

> Since we've had this [council] house I haven't had much call to do overtime. There's no point in working hard for ever you know.

or this from a non-moving shiftworker:

> I won't work shifts again, now, after Birds. I've got my home and my car.

Indeed even the council house tenants who moved to Banbury felt the counter-attraction of this security. They were less likely than movers with other types of tenancy to be pleased with the move.[20]

The house-buyers were in yet a third category. The generosity of the company's relocation policy towards those who were selling their

---

[20] χ^2 significant at the 0.05 level.

Birmingham houses meant that owner-occupation was not a disincentive to moving. The selling-price of the Birmingham house was guaranteed at the general market valuation; the legal and professional fees of buying and selling were paid by the company; and bridging loans and short term second mortgages at low interest rates were arranged by the company. Generally, the cash profits of house buying were somewhat illusory – the capital costs of buying and selling at least offset profits made through appreciation of prices. In this case, the capital costs were drastically lowered by the company's intervention. Of course, people still did not end the transaction with cash in hand – the lure of a better, more expensive, house in Banbury attracted practically everyone – but theoretically many of the house-buyers have a potential profit which could be realised by selling their Banbury house. Some men, particularly the managers more accustomed to the intricacies of the housing market thought that this was too much of a good thing to miss. As one man said:

> Yes I moved for the job – it's a progressive company. But even if I'd hated it I might still have moved with them, you know. The help they gave us with housing was too good to miss. This certainly made me *happier* about moving here. (his verbal emphasis)

Yet most of the owner-occupiers in Birmingham did not see the housing choice in these terms. These men did not see housing factors as being either an incentive or a disincentive to moving. One of them, when asked whether, from the point of view of his housing position, he welcomed the move or not, said:

> I can't say as it makes much difference one way or the other. I'm buying a better house there (in Banbury), I can't deny that, but we are quite happy in this one here. I suppose when you start buying a house you do expect to sell it at some point and move on, but to tell you the truth I think we had forgotten about moving on long since. Not that this move is a bad thing though – it's woken us up a bit.

This man pointed out both the theory and the practice of house-buying. A house is a disposable asset, to be traded in a favourable market situation. This relocation presented a clearly favourable market situation and a minority seized it wholeheartedly. But most house-buyers were not really viewing their home as a disposable asset and for them the relocation policy towards housing was viewed as minimising inconvenience rather than maximising profit.

Though the respondent's housing condition affected individual relocation decisions at all levels it is only among the 'other manual' group that it became a major determinant. The explanation for this must be that,

149

though not generally dissatisfied with employment, they seemed to be rather less enthusiastic about Birds than others, and though receiving good wages and conditions of employment at Birds, a move to another employer would not be as much of a step down as it would for others. In a company relocation there has to be strong motivation to move, not absence of motivation to stay behind. For unskilled manual workers at Birds outside of the coffee plant there were not compelling reasons at work motivating them to move, and so non-work factors could become crucial. If we look at their own reasons for their relocation decision this emerges quite clearly. The reasons given by those who moved are less likely to be job-related than are those of the other movers among the manual workers: 70 per cent compared to 90 per cent mention them at all and only 40 per cent compared to 80 per cent mention them as first reasons. The reasons substituted for work reasons by the movers from the 'other manual' group tend to be concerned with housing or with Banbury or Birmingham as places to live and work. The latter type of reason, those connected with Birmingham and Banbury, prove extremely interesting.

Tables 18 and 19 show that, among the men, 38 movers mentioned characteristics of Banbury and Birmingham as reasons for moving and 4 as reasons for staying behind. The numbers of mentions as first reasons declines to 16 and 1 respectively, and the persons giving them are disproportionately likely to be from the 'other manual' category. If we examine the reasons they give here, they seem to be rather vague, along the lines of 'Birmingham is going down the nick' or 'Banbury is a nice little place.' But if we turn to the responses given to the question 'Do you like the area where you are living now?'[21] we find interesting results. All these people dislike the area they live in now (or lived in prior to their move to Banbury), and they are concentrated in particular areas of Birmingham. Table 28 tabulates liking/disliking the area against the area lived in. It includes all respondents, not just men. These findings are of very general importance as regards women as well as men, and the differences between the sexes are negligible.

This table needs to be explained. The census ward in which the respondent lived was coded, and wards have been classified according to the percentage of private households in the whole ward having exclusive use of hot and cold water taps, a fixed bath and a w.c.[22] The first column of Table 28 comprises all wards where under 30 per cent of private households have all these fixtures; in column two are those where the proportion is 30–50 per cent; column three those where it is 50–75 per cent;

[21] Question 8, Survey 1.
[22] This information was obtained from the *City of Birmingham Abstract of Statistics* (1964). The map overleaf is to be found on p.3.

Table 28: *Sample: liking one's Birmingham area by classifica-*
tion of areas by proportion of dwellings having sanitary facilities
(percentages)

	Proportion of houses in census wards of respondents having sanitary facilities within Birmingham City					
	1 – 30%	2 30–50%	3 50–75%	4 75%+	5 Outside of Birmingham	All
Like area	43	55	85	84	74	71
Don't know	2	5	2	4	9	5
Dislike area	55	40	13	12	18	24
N	40	42	40	83	68	273

column four those where it is more than 75 per cent; and column five comprises the remainder, outside the City of Birmingham (whose proportion is mostly, but not entirely, over 75 per cent). Map 1, below shows the distribution of these census wards into the columns. The number contained within each ward on the map designates its column. Columns 1 and 2 are the central city areas. The residential areas they contain are overwhelmingly working class. If a worker has not been recently allocated a council house and if he cannot afford to buy a reasonably modern house, this is where he will most probably live. A few of these districts have something of a reputation for squalor and violence, but for the most part they are usually thought of as 'respectable' working class. But virtually half the sample living there do not like doing so, according to Table 28. Moreover, if we examine the reasons given for liking or disliking their area, we see that the other inhabitants of the area are more often mentioned as reasons for disliking the area than liking it. This hardly conforms to the picture of 'traditional' working-class life presented by many British sociologists, which I reviewed in Chapter 2. Yet there I also noted that sociologists were divided about the contemporary importance of these 'traditional' features. The authors of a recent study of Swansea claimed on the basis of rather poor evidence that many younger people were not at all attached to their traditional working-class communities but wished to leave to start a new way of life.[23] But rather more evidence on this point has recently emerged from the research studies of the Royal Commission on Local Government in England. Respondents were asked how pleased or sorry they would be

[23] See Chapter 2 above.

Map 1: City of Birmingham Ward Boundaries. Wards grouped by per cent of private house-holds having exclusive use of own sanitation facilities.

to leave their 'home area'. The general level of attachment to locality was quite high, with 41 per cent of the sample replying that they would be 'very sorry' to leave. But it is interesting that a correlation with socio-economic status in the unexpected direction is revealed: lower status respondents are less likely to reply 'very sorry' than higher status ones.[24] The correlation is actually rather slight, but conventional sociological

[24] Royal Commission on Local Government in England, *Research Studies*, No. 9 'Community Attitudes Survey: England' (H.M.S.O., 1969) pp. 26–7. Note also that those living in conurbations are slightly less attached to their 'home areas' than the rest.

wisdom would actually lead us to expect a strong correlation in the other direction, with lower status respondents more sorry to leave. The authors of the research report suggest that reluctance to leave is due to the desirability of 'select' or physically attractive neighbourhoods, bourgeois virtues far removed from the attractions of Bethnal Green! Perhaps then, these findings allied to my own suggest that there is a more uniform or less class-bound standard for judging localities than many sociologists have suggested. I will present further evidence to support this in the next chapter when discussing the type of housing and area which the movers chose in Banbury.

Returning to the sample, it is not difficult to guess what has so changed the working-class communities of Birmingham: immigration. After the initial hesitation characteristic of respondents faced with respectable middle-class interviewers many of the residents did make statements such as:

> This area was alright 'til the blacks started moving in, but once they start everything goes down right away.

or

> It's the coloureds who have done it all. I can remember the days when this was a nice area to live in, but that was before they came here.

But coloured people were not the only offenders, according to some respondents:

> It's dangerous to go out at night now on your own. It's not just the coloured people, it's the Irish too.

and

> First it was the Irish, now it's the blacks.

If happy long-settled working-class neighbourhoods did ever exist near the centre of Birmingham, successive waves of immigration seem to have destroyed them. The residents most satisfied in these areas were the Irish and coloured people in the sample – 11 of the 14 living there liked doing so. Apart from them, under half the residents liked their area – a striking contrast to the residents of other areas.

These findings confirm the more detailed study of Sparkbrook by Rex and Moore.[25] The English-born working class in Birmingham is being pushed outwards by its distaste for the recent immigrants to their old communities. As more obtain council houses on the fringe of Birmingham (and Rex and Moore show that their local political dominance enables many of them to do so) and as the more prosperous workers are able to afford to buy their own houses in the suburbs, the ones left are those

[25] J. Rex and R. Moore, *Race, Community and Conflict* (Oxford University Press, 1967).

who simply cannot move, because of the economics of housing. Feeling trapped, their hostility to the immigrants increases.

The Birds relocation offered a few more of them a chance to move out to a new house in a 'nice' area. There was in the sample a large measure of agreement as to what constituted a 'nice' area: it is a suburb containing fairly new, clean semi-detached (or detached if possible) houses with their own gardens. The houses need not be owner-occupied: a quarter of those living in the census wards of column 3 are council house tenants and they like their area as much as the owner-occupiers do. The relocation offered 'niceness' in both local authority and owner-occupied housing areas in and near Banbury. There is not a statistically significant relationship between residence in the areas separated in Table 28 and moving propensity. But what is sociologically significant is precisely the lack of statistical significance. Those residing in areas 3, 4 and 5 are disproportionately concentrated among the higher occupational groups who, other factors being equal, are much more likely to move. That those in the inner areas are as likely to move shows that there is a factor connected with residence near the centre of the city increasing moving propensity. This factor is recognised by residents themselves:

> I moved to Banbury because of the people moving into my old neighbourhood. I've got nothing to be ashamed of – they were West Indians.

Of course, residence near the centre of the city is more likely to be in sub-standard housing which has already been seen to be associated with greater moving propensity. The numbers involved here are too small to permit separation of the two interrelated factors of housing condition and character of neighbourhood. But in their reasons for moving central city residents mention both factors.

We have seen that some of those men who did not have compelling job reasons for moving, found equally compelling reasons outside work in poor housing conditions and in dislike of their neighbourhoods.

The moving decisions of the lower-rated, 'other manual' workers have now been largely explained. Among this group housing and community factors, not job factors, differentiated the movers from the non-movers. Those whose economic life-chances could be improved by the housing offered in Banbury tended to move; the others, particularly those already in council housing, were more divided. Reinforcing the housing factor was the surprising dislike shown by most of the residents of the inner working-class areas of Birmingham for those areas. Hence many of the lower-rated workers found a positive incentive toward relocation, and as job factors rarely constituted an actual disincentive to relocation, many of them accepted transfer. As those still in poor housing in the central areas tended to be younger than the others, the age problem has also been explained: age was not linearly related to moving propensity because, though older men tended to accept transfer for job reasons, this was counteracted by younger men moving to improve their housing.

Having largely explained the relocation decisions of the sample, I shall now change gear and turn to further hypotheses about moving propensity that were either rejected by my data or, although of interest, only add marginal improvements to the explanation.

OTHER FAMILY MEMBERS AND RELOCATION DECISIONS

Let us briefly consider role relationships within the nuclear family itself. This was not a central concern of the present study;[26] but it appeared that other family members played little part in determining relocation decisions. Though observers within the firm commented 'Of course, it's their wives who won't move, you know' or 'They're moving because they want their children to live a decent, healthy life', practically nobody made such comments about themselves.

The children of the sample did not exert much influence on relocation decisions. Those with children were neither more or less likely to move than those without. Nor did the number or age of the children discriminate movers from non-movers. Children were rarely mentioned by the sample in their own explanations of their decisions, and were not mentioned as the first reason for the decision except in the case of 4 non-moving men who said they did not wish to interrupt the careers (usually apprenticeships) of their sons – though three of these four also said that there was little to attract them to Birds in Banbury. Of course, when asked what sort of an effect a relocation would have on their children, the movers tended to answer that it would have a good effect and the non-movers a bad effect. (χ^2 significant at the 0.001 level.) But this appeared to be a rationalisation, rather than a determinant, of their actual moving decisions. There was no clear consensus as to the detailed effects Banbury would have on children. Movers were more likely to stress the healthy and clean surroundings of Banbury, while the non-movers recalled its poor social life, but there was division over the quality of the educational facilities of Banbury. And it was the education facilities which were the

---

[26] Jansen found that migrant husbands and wives were more likely than non-migrants to have conjugal roles (sharing in planning family budgets, sharing household tasks etc. pp. 159–60). But, as with many of his findings, it is difficult to separate the effects on marital roles of social class from those of migration.

most frequently mentioned effect of the town on children of all ages and both sexes.

The employment of other family members was related to relocation decisions (though only mentioned in the male sample by the four reported above). Fifteen out of 16 men with wives working at Birds before the move relocated, compared with 24 out of 36 of those whose wives worked elsewhere; 11 out of 13 with a child working at Birds relocated, compared with 18 out of 28 with one working elsewhere. But this was also related to the type of job held by the respondent: most of those with a wife and children working for the company were themselves in high status manual jobs, and several of these reported that they had actually encouraged their family to take the jobs because they themselves liked the company so much.

Thus, whether or not the wife or children actually participated in the relocation decision (and this was not discovered), the result would be the same. Virtually all respondents and their families recognised that their lives depended heavily on financial security. For most families this meant that the job situation of the household head determined their relocation decisions. And for a few, relocation decisions were affected by the financial aspects of their housing situation. Other family members, especially teenage children, did not usually welcome the prospect of moving to a small 'sleepy' market town like Banbury, but their objections were overruled. The primacy of economic considerations was assumed whatever the occupational status of the respondent.

FAMILY AND COMMUNITY TIES – TESTING THE MIDDLE-CLASS STEREOTYPE

In Chapter 2 we saw that mobility is often class-bound, and specifically that middle-class people are more mobile than working-class people. Moreover, sociologists have traditionally thought that being 'middle class' involved a great deal more than having a household head in a non-manual occupation – it involved a whole style of life very different from that of the manual worker. In particular, the relationships which the middle-class person has with his extended family and with his local community have been generally thought to differ from those of the working-class person. In this section, I will test the veracity of these differences by attempting to relate them to both the overall level of moving propensity and its variations within the sample. Thus a 'compound hypothesis' of middle classness is set up. The following are assumed to be some of the characteristics of the middle-class person which will be tested here:

1 more geographic mobility and over further distances;
2 more geographically-dispersed kinship grouping;
3 less contact with kin;
4 higher participation rates in voluntary associations and other formal settings of community relations;
5 more contact with non-kin friends, and over further distances.[27]

The occupational composition and the relocation decisions of the sample offer a convenient framework for testing these hypotheses. They give us a 'two-stage' test of the compound hypothesis. First, we can see whether the manual and non-manual groups in the sample are thus differentiated. This in itself constitutes a fairly tough test, for I have already demonstrated the heterogeneity of the manual workers in the company. If, nevertheless, they are easily distinguishable from the salaried staff this would be impressive support for traditional sociological theory in this area. Secondly, the relocation decisions give us a convenient test of the strength of ties to kin and community: did the ties present obstacles to relocation?

First, let us consider contact with kin. If mobility is part of a middle-class way of life we would expect relocation to be associated both with high occupational status and with infrequency of contact with widely-dispersed kin. In fact, high occupational status has already been shown to lead to a high relocation propensity. There is no significant tendency among men with parents alive for those who saw them in the previous week to move less frequently than those who did not. As I have noted, middle-class people are generally supposed to see their parents less often than do working-class people. And among manual workers, the maintenance and coffee workers were less likely to have seen a parent in the last week than were the 'other manual' workers – and, of course, more likely to move. Yet in this sample, the non-manual workers are no more 'middle class' in this respect, being as likely to have seen a parent in the previous week as the 'other manual' workers.

The 'middle-class' hypothesis is weakened even further when we consider the place of residence of these kin. In fact, as Table 29 shows, there is no relationship at all between relocation decision and the distance of residence of parents and children.

Turning to a consideration of the family's links with non-kin in the outside world, we can use the place of residence of friends as an indicator of 'middle classness', since it is assumed to be middle class for friends to

---

[27] These hypotheses are all derived from the writings of other sociologists. Some have already been discussed in Chapter 2. For an orthodox summary of the differences between working-class and middle-class styles of life see Josephine Klein, *Samples from English Cultures* (Routledge, 1965) I, chapts. 4, 5, and 6.

Table 29: *Sample: males with at least one parent, or one wife's parent, or one child, alive and not living in their own household*[a] *(percentages)*

Residence of parent or child by moving decision	Movers	Non-movers	All	N
With parent or child within 5 miles	42	42	42	72
Without parent or child within 5 miles	58	58	58	99
N	126	45		171

[a] This actually comprises the whole male sample responding to questions 29 and 35 except two single men (movers), living with their parents. Besides these, 5 other men also had a parent living with them – but this made them neither more or less likely to relocate than the sample average (three moved, two didn't).

reside some distance away from self.[28] Table 30 shows that the occupational status of the sample is related in this way to the residence of friends. The friends of the women and the 'other manual' group are the most localised, followed by those of the coffee processers with those of the maintenance workers close behind, and then finally come the friends of

Table 30: *Sample: location of named friends by job groups*[a] *(percentages)*

	−5 miles away[b]	Elsewhere in Birmingham or greater Birmingham	Further away	Total friends	Average no. of friends mentioned	No. of persons answering
Women	51	40	8	265	2.65	100
Staff	28	25	47	155	2.82	55
Maintenance	52	20	28	64	2.06	31
Coffee processing	38	34	28	58	2.76	21
Other manual	62	22	16	159	2.41	66
All	48	31	22	701	2.57	273

χ^2 is significant at the 0.01 level (average for all men only is 2.52)

[a] This table is based on responses to question 37, Survey 1. 'Where do your three best friends live? How far away is that?' A few residents failed to give three names, as can be seen from the fact that the total number of friends is less than three times the number of respondents.
[b] From the Birmingham Address of all respondents.

[28] See Klein, *Samples from English Culture*, p. 344.

the male staff, the only case where the largest number of friends is out-side Greater Birmingham. This ordering actually follows the hierarchical job-structure of the firm and was predicted by our 'compound hypo-thesis'. But when we look for the expected link between localism and non-moving we find only a very weak one, as Table 31 shows. The movers and non-movers have about the same average number of friends in the two divisions of the Greater Birmingham area. They therefore share what localism exists. In addition, the male staff have more friends living further away, which is responsible for the higher average in this category among movers.[29] It is worth noting that non-movers are rather less able to even name three friends than movers: the average number named by movers is 2.62 compared to the non-movers average of 2.24. This cannot be accounted for by the interference of the job-status factor. Table 30 shows that there are indeed inter-status differences in the ability to name

Table 31: *Sample: location of named friends by moving decision – men only (percentages)*

	−5 miles		Elsewhere in G. Birmingham		Further		Total	No. of
	%	Average number per person	%	Average number per person	%	Average number per person	no. of friends	respon-dents
Movers	44	1.14	22	0.57	35	0.91	335	128
Non-movers	51	1.13	33	0.73	17	0.38	101	45
All	45		24		31		436	173

friends but that the statuses more likely to name more friends are not simply those more likely to move as well. So there is a real connection between moving and having more friends.

Turning to the indicators used for community participation, we find little relationship between them and moving propensity. There is no dif-ference between movers and non-movers in their frequency of club-visiting[30], nor between manual and non-manual employees. The fre-

---

[29] See Jansen (*Social Aspects of Internal Migration*, p. 75) who also finds that migrants are less likely than non-migrants to have 'local' friends, but does not test for the effects of occupation (he has already shown that high-status groups were more likely to be migrants). These two correlations between the localism of friends and socio-economic status and length of residence are also found in the 'Community Attitudes Survey' of the Royal Commission on Local Govern-ment, pp. 43–4, but again there is no attempt to hold each factor constant.
[30] Measured by question 42, Survey 1.

quency of participation in 'other entertainment' activities[31] is related to job-status but in the unpredicted direction: recent participation was most frequent among the 'other manual' group and least frequent among staff males and coffee process workers. But there is not, as a result, an inverse relationship between this participation and relocation propensity. What is preventing this from emerging is the fact that within job-status groups those most likely to move were most likely to be involved in entertainment activities though the numbers are rather too small for statistical significance. It is clear then that in this case community ties played little part in moving decisions, and, as has been suggested by Wilensky,[32] those who were active in the community considered that their social life depended fundamentally on the enjoyment of a satisfactory employment relationship.

It seems therefore that the compound hypothesis relating mobility to 'middle-class' life-styles is not very helpful in predicting the relocation decisions of the sample. Some 'middle-class' indicators have been associated with propensity to move, but others not. We have seen that the manual workers in the sample were not much more embedded in localised kin relationships, nor were they less active in 'formal' community-wide activities, than the office workers. Nor was the social life of the movers particularly different from that of the non-movers. Indeed, the whole sample exhibited less variety in these aspects of social life than some previous sociologists have suggested exists.

However, the possibility remains that this is an untypical segment of the labour force. Indeed there are one or two indications that this is so. First, the employees of Alfred Bird and Sons Ltd were unusually mobile. Their length of residence in their Birmingham dwelling prior to the move is compared to data from the 1961 Census in Table 32.

It is possible that on the basis of their shorter duration of residence that the sample would have fewer contacts with their family of origin than would the population at large,[33] but there are no national statistics available to document this. The Bethnal Green, Dagenham and Woodford surveys found rather more frequent contacts than among my sample, if we control these for social class, but these surveys were conducted some

---

[31] Measured by question 43, Survey 1. 'Other' means any entertainment activity not classified under clubs', friends visiting, or church attendance.
[32] Wilensky, 'Orderly careers and social participation'. See above, Chapter 3.
[33] This is a frequently reported finding of previous research. See Young and Willmott, *Family and Kinship in East London*, chap. 11; Litwak, 'Geographic mobility and extended family cohesion'.

160

Table 32:   *Persons with residence duration of less than 5 years
in sample and in 1961 Census by sex[a] (percentages)*

	Men in sample	Whole sample	England and Wales economically active		All England and Wales adults	All Midland Region adults	All West Midlands conurbation adults
			Males	All			
Percentage of persons with residence duration of – 5 years	53	49	38	37	34	32	32

[a] See 1961 Census, England and Wales, *Migration: National Summary Tables* Part I, Table 1.

time ago.[34] We cannot be certain whether the difference reflects the untypicality of Birds or a post-war 'convergence' of life-styles toward the modified extended family. Unfortunately, the much larger, and more representative national sample of the Royal Commission on local Government was asked a non-comparable question on this issue, but the traditional occupational differences emerged, with manual workers likely to have more relatives nearby.[35]

We now begin to suspect that, in certain respects, the Birds sample was more 'middle class' than the population as a whole. This stereotype was certainly held by many within the company. Several workers made comments like.

> you get a good class of person working even on the shop floor in Birds.

or

> You don't find any roughs at Birds, that's one thing you can say. They're all nice people.

Recruitment of manual workers was based on criteria which supported these statements. Because the company offered good wages and conditions of employment it could exercise a great deal of choice in recruiting.

[34] The Birds sample also visited clubs more than their occupational counterparts in these surveys. Figures for Woodford are given in Willmott and Young, *Family and Class in a London Suburb*, pp. 29, 91.
Figures for Bethnal Green in Young and Willmott, *Family and Kinship in East London*, p. 21.
Figures for Dagenham in Peter Willmott, *The Evolution of a Community* (Routledge and Kegan Paul, 1963) pp. 35, 85.
[35] 'Community Attitudes Survey: England', p. 43.

Apart from the period beginning about a year after the move was first announced, the company had many more applicants than vacancies. Not surprisingly, its personnel managers chose 'responsible' persons with 'reliable' work-records and of 'good' family. One manufacturing manager said:

> They [Personnel] makes mistakes now and then but by and large they send us a good sort of worker with a responsible attitude. They [the workers] aren't tearaways – they're good family men, usually, buying their own houses or trying to buy them, trying to help their children get on. Oh yes, I suppose they aren't so very different to us, after all.

There is other suggestive evidence for this: in Chapter 4 we saw that the previous job histories of the coffee processors were by no means confined to the unskilled manual stratum. We will see in Chapter 8 that the non-movers found little difficulty in finding other employment partly because of the reputation for 'responsibility' of the Birds labour force.

These hints of atypicality must be balanced against the indications of support which the Birds data give to proponents of the modified extended family thesis. At this point I only wish to caution against relying too heavily on the sociological stereotypes of middle and working-class life-styles. In particular, we must remember that our cities are not static but in the process of great upheaval. Municipal housing has itself altered the pattern of working-class life: a much higher proportion of manual workers are living on the outskirts of towns in low-density developments than used to be the case. Central city areas – where the traditional working-class communities resided – are being left more and more to the unskilled grades of manual labour, and in particular to the immigrants, Irish and coloured. It is quite possible that the most settled and stable communities in our conurbations at this point in time are not the Bethnal Greens and Sparkbrooks but the Leytonstones and the Billesleys – the traditional lower-middle class areas.[36]

CONCLUSION

A large proportion of male employees relocated because of two mutually reinforcing facts:

(*a*) Alfred Bird and Sons Ltd provided for virtually every employee a favorable employment relationship,

[36] This could be tested on census ward data.

162

(*b*) The local non-work ties to the Birmingham community provided less of an obstacle to relocation than had been anticipated.[37]

Thus there were no generalised *obstacles* to moving and, even in the absence of the strong dispositions toward moving that will be discussed in a moment, the moving decisions made by employees could go either way. But, whereas the moving decisions of most of the movers have been thoroughly explained, those of a few movers, notably the lower-grade manual workers not in poor housing conditions, and most of the non-movers have not been thoroughly accounted for. This is fundamentally because their moving decisions were mostly finely-balanced and entering into their calculations were the kind of very detailed personal circumstances that cannot emerge as statistical trends. Among these people are found most of the idiosyncratic reasons for and against moving, and also those based on other family members. In fact, the sample possessed no general and strong objections to relocating, and if this finding can be generalised to the country at large, then the outlook for further industrial relocation is optimistic.

However, the really compelling factors for relocation were not found so widely. Leaving aside the predictable reasons of the women who moved and of the younger careerists among the salaried staff, there were two main inducements to move which did not affect everyone alike:

(*a*) ties of job dependence.

(*b*) housing need, often allied with a dislike of inner Birmingham (partly racial in tone).

The second of these is fairly straightforward. Because of the oddities of the British housing market, divided into non-competing public and private and rented and owned sectors, this relocation offered to many an improvement in economic (and also less tangible) status, through housing improvement. Many accepted the offer and some of these did so where there was no other major compulsion to relocate. This is found in most relocations, as we saw in Chapter 2. And on the contrary, among the small group with little to gain in terms of housing, those already in Birmingham council property, there was no such incentive to relocate. What was surprising, however, was that the housing incentive in the case of manual workers was reinforced by a positive dislike for the working-

---

[37] This would not be so, of course, in small isolated communities. Studies of the National Coal Board's transfer schemes have shown that local community ties in declining colliery areas do hinder relocation by miners. Those who do relocate tend to have fewer close ties with the community. See C. S. Smith, 'The Planned Transfer of Labour with Special Reference to the Coal Industry' (unpublished Ph. D. thesis, University of London, 1961) p. 60, and R. C. Taylor, *The Implications of Migration.*

class districts of Birmingham. As we saw, this was usually, overtly or covertly, a dislike of the racial groups moving into such districts. The implications of this finding are certainly worth discussing and I shall do so in Chapter 9.

The other main motivation for moving, ties of job dependence, was rather more complex and was discussed at length. Though one tie, that of age, was quite weak in this case, this was actually because it was counteracted by the other much more important tie deriving from the internal job structure of the company. Older, poorly-qualified salaried staff were quite predictably tied to the company for the preservation of their job-status, but what was unexpected was the extent to which many manual workers were also. The existence of an internal promotion hierarchy was the major factor here, so that the workers who had received some degree of promotion would probably have to start again at their approximate original level if they joined another company. But also worth noting was the specialised nature of much of the work done at Birds, for which the company was very careful to reward workers financially. Thus even the tradesman with full qualifications was to some extent financially dependent upon the company. Yet dependence had its non-economic aspects also. As well as providing a reasonable short and long-term wage, the company's job structure gave to the worker a sense of self-identity, a definable position in the functional and hierarchical structure of industry. Whether this kind of finding is typical of modern industry is of immense practical and theoretical importance and will be discussed in the concluding chapter.

7
The movers in Banbury

This chapter focusses on the post-move experiences of those employees who relocated to Banbury with the company. It is not my intention to give a comprehensive account of all the ramifications of the move for those living in Banbury,[1] but to concentrate on several particular issues which I have discussed earlier. Of these, the most important is the sample's degree of satisfaction with the move after the event. Whereas the previous chapter showed that most employees did accept transfer to Banbury, this one will establish whether they moved willingly and whether they were subsequently pleased with it. Obviously, this is of great importance in deciding whether this and other relocations can be considered as desirable. The first evidence presented, then, will bear upon the movers' overall level of satisfaction with their new life. In general, they will emerge as fairly satisfied with the relocation.

This will lead onto a discussion of the two most important possible disadvantages for the movers, namely the expense of the move and the social isolation and loneliness, particularly among manual workers. The latter of these problems – the social isolation – looms more importantly in previous research, as we saw in Chapter 2, and will be treated more fully. In general, the evidence presented does *not* support the hypothesis that the move would produce greater social isolation and loneliness. This reinforces the evidence contained in the previous chapter and leads me to doubt the usefulness of the simple class model of social relations which is apparent in much sociological writing.

Next, I turn to the after-effects of the move for the company's management structure, and relate this evidence to the brief earlier discussions of processes of managerial change within the company. Here, the relocation appeared at first to exacerbate the managerial conflicts described by the participants in 'thrusting–sleeping' terms.

Finally, I consider two peculiar advantages for the town of Banbury of this particular relocation. The first concerns the problem of maintaining

[1] Nor to describe the town of Banbury, of which an excellent sociological study already exists: Margaret Stacey, *Tradition and Change: a study of Banbury* (Oxford University Press, 1960). This study was completed over a decade ago, but Mrs Stacey and her associates have been engaged in a re-study of the town concurrently with my research. They intend to publish their results as M. Stacey, E. Batstone, C. Bell and A. Murcott, *Persistence and Change: a Second Study of Banbury*.

165

harmonious community relations in towns faced with extensive planned expansion. The second advantage (already apparent from the last few chapters) is that such a relocation brings in an immigrant group with a balanced age-structure.

All these issues obviously bear upon the overall desirability of relocation for the transferred workers, for the management of the relocating company, and for the reception area.

First, then, let us examine the overall reactions of the movers once in Banbury.

GENERAL REACTIONS IN BANBURY

In the previous chapter we saw that work-related factors dominated the relocation decisions of the sample. Most of the relocating employees moved in order to retain what they regarded as a highly favourable employment relationship. Thus, for them, the change of residence was a by-product of a desire for employment stability. Even if they had a clear prior conception of the advantages and disadvantages of living in the Banbury area, this played but a small part in their total relocation calculations. And when the Birmingham/Banbury comparison did enter into their calculations, we have seen – surprisingly – that most of the sample in Birmingham did not possess strong ties of affection for their city. In fact almost 60 per cent of the movers said in Survey 1 that they were 'pleased' about moving.[2] So we would expect them to be reasonably happy in their life in a new locality. How content were they?

The first, and most important, point to be made is that at the time of the second survey[3] the vast majority of the movers did appear to be well content with the move. When the sample was asked 'Are you pleased you moved with Birds?', seventy-five per cent of respondents replied that they were pleased, with the remainder split evenly into 'Not pleased' and 'Not sure'.[4] And asked 'Do you want to go back to the Birmingham area?' 75 per cent replied 'No'. But it is important to establish carefully the context of their answers. It may be that they were comparing their life in Banbury with a life in Birmingham which would include working for some employer other than Birds, and in this case we would expect them to reject this alternative and announce themselves to be 'pleased' in com-

[2] In response to question 98, Survey 1.
[3] At the time of the survey the movers had been living in the Banbury area between one and three years.
[4] In this chapter, men and women are treated together, except where their responses differ. Out of the 168 movers, 138 were men and 30 women. Throughout this section, the focus will be on the overall satisfaction of the movers rather than on inter-group differences.

parison with it. But futher evidence suggests that the comparison they were making was with their former life in Birmingham, of which working for Birds was a part.

The supporting evidence comes from the opinions of families of the respondents as reported by the respondents themselves. Table 33 shows that over twice as many husbands and wives were reported as thinking that they were better rather than worse off as a result of the move. This table is especially interesting as throughout the period of the fieldwork the comment was frequently made of other people 'It's their wives who don't like moving to Banbury'. Although no question designed to test this statement was inserted in the pre-move survey, the table shows that wives were apparently fairly happy about the move afterwards. Moreover, the married men rarely volunteered comments about their own wives' hostility to the move in the first survey. So probably the men used their wives as 'stalking horses' for their own doubts about their relocations when subjected to the cursory enquires of the company and fellow employees, but abandoned this tactic in the more thorough survey investigation.

The move was also considered beneficial for children by their parents. Parents were asked whether they thought their children under 15 were 'better off, worse off, or about the same', as a result of the move. To standardise for the number of children in each household, the answers were scored – 3 for 'better off' 2 for 'about the same', and 1 for 'worse' – and the total score for each household was divided by the number of children in it. Of the 86 parents with children under 15, the averages of 45 were above 2 (i.e. on average they thought their children better off as a result of the move), 20 were exactly 2 (i.e. 'about the same') and only 21 were less than 2 (i.e. 'worse').[5]

There was, however, a minority group who were not at all satisfied with the move. Seven of the sample, or 4 per cent of the movers, had al-

Table 33: *Sample: respondents' wives and husbands reported opinion of their own situation as a result of the move (percentages)*
Survey 2, Movers, question 13

	Better	Same	Worse	N
Wives	53	26	22	101
Husbands	45	36	18	11
All	52	27	21	112

[5] Even young people aged 15 and upwards were thought to be evenly divided on whether the move had been beneficial for them, and they were the group generally supposed to be the most discontented. (Survey 2, question 13)

167

ready returned to the Birmingham area;[6] a further 13 respondents, or 9 per cent of respondents said that they would like to go back. Throughout this chapter we will have to weigh the dissatisfaction of a minority against the satisfaction of the majority in drawing up a balance-sheet of the after-effects of the move.

In the remainder of the chapter I will examine the principal components of people's reactions to their move: their attitudes to their housing, their new community, and their employment.

HOUSING IN BANBURY

The vast majority of the Birds families moved into new houses. Though large numbers of them decided to live outside Banbury in the surrounding villages, a modern well-equipped house on a small new estate, and not a picturesque, rambling cottage was their most frequent goal. But what was even more interesting was that practically no-one moved into the older suburbs: a few bought 'period', the vast majority bought new, property, and practically no-one bought a house constructed between 1860 and 1960. Virtually all the council houses were brand-new, the only exceptions being those with tenants who had especially requested not to be put on the hilly Neithrop estate because of ailing physical strength.

'Period' and 'modern' are the twin housing ideals in Britain, and virtually everyone was well satisfied with his residence. A succession of proud residents showed the interviewers round their houses, making comments such as:

> We always wanted a bungalow but never expected to get one. And we never dreamed of getting one next to farms and open fields.

or

> This is John's bedroom. The children all have their own bedrooms now, you know.

or

> You can see the standard of workmanship is very high in these council houses. It's much better than in our old [Birmingham] flat.

or

> You didn't see many Tudor cottages in Solihull, did you?

---

[6] Though two had not returned voluntarily – they had been discharged from employment and had been forced to leave Banbury to find another job. Of the other 5, 2 had returned because they did not like the area, 1 because he grew disaffected from Birds, and 2 did not respond.

168

('Tudor' was actually an exaggeration of the age of his cottage).

Nevertheless, as we have seen, only a small minority had moved to Banbury in order to secure this improvement, and indeed for most of the sample housing improvement was a by-product, though a welcome one, of the relocation. Only 30 per cent of the movers gave housing improvement as the main advantage of having moved to Banbury in response to a question which invited non-work rather than work advantages.[7]

FINANCIAL HARDSHIP IN BANBURY

This universal improvement of housing conditions had to be paid for, and here we encounter a usual consequence of relocation–an increase in financial commitments. Though prices were slightly lower in Banbury than the Birmingham area for equivalent property, most employees paid more for their Banbury house than they received on the sale of their Birmingham property. The median difference was an increase of £300, financed mostly under the provisions of the company's loan schemes described in Chapter 5. Also, more people bought houses in the Banbury area than had done so previously – 83 compared to the previous 68 – and as 5 people had changed from buying to renting, 20 were now buying where previously they had rented. Some degree of financial strain was bound to result. The median change in regular mortgage outgoings was an increase of 30s per week.[8] Moreover, and this proved the greatest strain for some, new or period houses were felt to require new or antique fittings. The company's relocation allowance, intended to cover fittings such as carpets and curtains, did so in only a small minority of cases. After the move, in marked contrast to before it, was heard the grumble 'The company wasn't so generous with its allowances, you know.' Furniture was even more of an expense – even without the improvement in its quality which did occur, more of it was needed for the simple reason that most of the sample now had more rooms than they had previously. New expense did not stop here: 77 per cent now had cars, compared to 56 per cent before the move, and 65 per cent compared to 52 per cent before the move possessed a television, a washing machine and a refrigerator.[9]

---

[7] i.e. question 3 of Survey 2, Movers.
[8] There was only a very slight increase for those renting property before and after the move.
[9] Hammond also reports a great increase in car ownership among his Civil Service staff transferred from London to Durham. E. Hammond, *London to Durham* (University of Durham, Rowntree Research Unit, 1968) p. 68.

169

The sample was asked to estimate 'the actual cost to you and your family of your moving, including all expenses directly or indirectly involved, over the above what the company gave you'. The results are given in Table 34 below, subdivided into those renting council property and all others.[10] One man's refusal to answer this question was evidence for the problem of additional cost.

> It is impossible to estimate the cost of the move, for instance, considerable time and expense was involved in visiting Banbury to find a suitable home, and later to make arrangements with builders, decorators etc. In moving to a new area one paid more for a new property than one would have been paying perhaps in Birmingham. One's ideas progress. When one makes a change, then naturally you want it to be a change for the better.

Certainly the move involved most respondents in a lot of additional expense: only 9 per cent of respondents said that they had spent none of their own money on moving, compared to 15 per cent who claimed their moves had cost them over £500.[11] The average cost was no less than £250.[12]

It is not surprising, then, that the sample had to resort to new methods of raising money. Seventy-five per cent had to use savings possessed prior to the move (most of the remainder had not had such savings). Fifty-four per cent had to economise on their normal expenditures. Fifty per cent had to enter into more hire purchase agreements or into loans other than

Table 34: *Sample: estimate of total cost to whole family of the move by type of house tenure – movers (percentages)*
Survey 2, Movers, question 15

	Nothing	−£100	£100–200	£200–500	£500+	N
Council tenants	12	25	36	20	6	64
All others	6	17	29	26	22	72
All	9	21	32	23	15	136

[10] All but five of these 'others' were buying houses.
[11] This does not necessarily mean that the sums spent are lost to the respondents. If they had spent most of it on house-deposit or improvement, they could presumably recoup their expenditure later. Here, we are interested only in short-term financial outlay.
[12] Which seems slightly higher than the average cost reported by a sample of office workers relocated from London to Ashford, surveyed by the Location of Offices Bureau, *Relocation of Office Staff: a study of the reactions of office staff decentralised to Ashford* (L.O.B., 1969) pp. 7–8.

house loans.[13] Of course, people rarely admitted that they were actually in financial difficulties, but stories abounded of the straitened circumstances of other people. This was the most frequent theme of gossip heard by the interviewers. Respondents would make remarks such as:

> Some of these men in the factory went a bit mad with their new houses. Central heating, double-glazing, fitted carpets – the lot. They aren't so careful with their money as people like us and now they're regretting it, I can tell you.

or

> You know why old X is looking for another job. Oh yes, he is, no matter what he says. He's got to find a bit more in his wages to keep the wolf from the door.

But occasionally, people would admit to difficulties of their own:

> Not having had a house before, we find it very hard. There is so much to be done with a new house, and as we had no furniture at all before we moved it will be some time before we can afford things like carpets, bedroom furniture and a car. A car is really a must here for any family to be happy. (a written comment).

> The wife would be happier with more money as the strain since moving here has been terrific financial-wise. The cost of living is more, rents are higher, and we have to find school meals and bus fares to school and shops which we didn't before. £4 to £5 more a week are needed here compared to Birmingham.

One indicator of the financial difficulties faced by the movers was in the disadvantages they found in living in their new area. By far the most frequently mentioned important disadvantage was the cost of living and the price of shop goods in the area. Forty per cent named this, twice as many as those naming the next most frequent disadvantage (the lack of social facilities). A further 25 per cent mentioned it as a subsidiary disadvantage. It is perfectly true that goods were more expensive in Banbury than Birmingham, even in the case of meat which was often sent from the Banbury cattle market to Birmingham for distribution back to Banbury. The estimate of several housewives was that shopping cost between £1 and £3 per week more in Banbury. But it is significant that the worst disadvantage of Banbury had changed from lack of social facilities before the

---

[13] As people usually understate their degree of financial indebtedness, the true percentages may be somewhat higher. A possible indicator of the growing importance of debts to be paid off in regular instalments was the growing pressure from shift workers in Banbury for the fluctuations in their take-home pay to be reduced.

move,[14] to expense afterwards. The sample partly overcame the shortage of social facilities; they could not overcome the problems raised by the cost of living because they were already under financial stress from other sources.

Yet financial difficulties were usually seen as short-term ones:

> Well, I might as well be frank, we're in a bit of trouble now, but it will be over soon. These are once-for-all expenses we're paying for, and we'll be straight again in six months or a year.

One man commented on two of his neighbours, Birds employees, having just left the district:

> I think they must have had financial trouble. Well, everybody gets that in a new house. I'm just coming over it now.

Another said:

> There's only the shopping that'll cause us any bother after this year, and the wage-increase will take care of that.

Above all, and with the single exception of the cost of shopping, the additional expense was felt to be freely entered into and to be worth it. As one man said:

> Yes, it *is* costing me a lot, but I knew that when I came here. I'm buying the best house I've ever lived in – either I'll enjoy living in it, or I'll sell it and get my money back. Most of us knew what we were doing, we were buying ourselves *a better way of life*. (his emphasis)

Thus the financial strain caused by the relocation was considered to be an investment rather than a waste of money. So it was not a major undesirable consequence of relocation.

In other moves, financial hardship has sometimes been more severe where the housing improvement entailed has been greater. Thus Cullingworth found that among the overspill families he studied in Worsely and Swindon, the move from slum property to a new council house often involved a tripling of rent, usually where the move had been from a controlled tenancy under the 1957 Rent Act.[15] If slums are to be eliminated it is difficult to see how this rent increase can be avoided. Wherever possible, people should be given the choice as to whether they want a housing improvement involving a rent increase, but in large-scale social planning this will not always be possible. Thus a minority involved in relocations will regard an increase in financial commitment as being undesirable, even though the rest will regard it as being worthwhile. The question to be asked is 'are there other compensations found by the sample which

---

[14] See Chapter 6.
[15] See Chapter 2.

might outweigh any financial hardship?' Let us turn for a possible answer to the 'better way of life' mentioned by the last man quoted.

SOCIAL LIFE IN BANBURY

Asked 'Do you like the area where you live now?' no fewer than 81 per cent of respondents answered 'Yes'. Table 35 shows the responses to this question according to the area lived in. The table shows that only just over half the sample actually lived in Banbury, though most of the rest lived within five miles of the town. If we remember that all the council tenants on the Neithrop estate had no choice about area if they wanted to take a council property, it is clear that only just under a quarter of those who did 'choose' their place of residence chose the town of Banbury. And none of the remainder, living outside the town, disliked their area as Table 35 shows. Only on the Neithrop Estate itself is there any sizeable proportion (24 per cent) disliking the area, but even there it still remains a minority.

There are very specific reasons why some of the Neithrop Estate residents dislike their area. Half of this 14 were in fact thinking of leaving the estate[16]: they had mostly moved onto the estate as a temporary measure while they made up their minds whether they intended to stay in Banbury.[17] By the time of the second survey their minds were made up and, whatever their decision, they were likely to want to leave the estate, either to return to Birmingham or to start buying a house in the Banbury area. The remainder of the Neithrop tenants who disliked their area had local-

Table 35: *Sample: opinion of area of residence in Banbury by area. Movers (percentages)*
Survey 2, Movers, question 4

Do you like the area?	Area lived in					
	Neithrop estate	Elsewhere in Banbury	Within 5 miles of Banbury	5–15 miles	Further away	All
Yes	64	88	94	100	100	81
Not sure	12	0	6	0	0	7
No	24	12	0	0	0	12
N	59	17	33	17	4	130

[16] Three have subsequently done so.
[17] See Chapter 4.

ised grievances about the lack of public transport, shops and other amenities on the estate.

Those living outside the council estate found their environment as
they had expected it, and they were well contented as a result. New (or
period) houses in a country setting – but not too far from a town: this
seemed to them to constitute a highly attractive way of life. Why did so
many choose to live in the villages around Banbury? One man put it quite
well:

> Let's face it – Banbury is a potty little place. If you've got to
> move, you might as well go the whole way. It has no advan-
> tages over the villages in terms of amenities, so you might as
> well live in the real countryside.

In the first survey, those who intended to live outside Banbury had
been evenly divided between those who stressed housing factors and those
who stressed the 'real countryside' as reasons for choosing their place of
residence.[18] In the second survey we find the latter factor stressed much
more often. Asked to name the most important advantage of having
moved, 56 per cent of those living outside the estate mentioned 'environmental factors' of the countryside, and 20 per cent mentioned housing
factors (the proportions for all movers mentioning these were 47 per
cent and 30 per cent respectively).[19] Nobody was very eloquent about the
joys of living in the countryside, but the same key words kept re-occurring:
'pleasant', 'nice', 'clean', 'healthy', 'fresh', 'restful', 'relaxed'. Indeed, the
responses were usually no more than permutations on any combination of
these words: 'nice and clean', 'healthy but relaxed' etc. Nor were the responses of the Neithrop residents very different in this respect. However,
it is tempting to suggest that what these key-words denote is an entire
vision of life similar to the picture Dobriner has suggested is evoked by the
names given to their houses by residents in the American urban–rural
fringe:

> There are at least two promises that the names of suburban
> developments make to the city dweller – nature and com-
> munity. Cities conjure terrible visions of dirt, fumes and list-
> less settlements of foreigners in the ever present slums. But
> in suburbia there is nature: hills, woodland retreats, verdant
> hollows, rounded knolls – clean, green, and sweet. 'Five Oaks'
> are straight, tested, tall, and true. You can trust a tree, a hill,

---

[18] In response to question 7*b*, Survey 1.
[19] In response to question 3, Survey 2, Movers. Naturally, the response of the
London overspill tenants differed markedly here: all but one of the 32 respondents
to this question wrote that housing was the most important advantage, and also
the actual reason for their moving. Their London housing conditions were also
far worse than had been those of the transferred Birds employees in Birmingham.

if not a city. The names of suburbia say 'Come back!' Come back to the real things – the green mansions, the sylvan hollows and sun-sprayed meadows, the private small and uncorrupted little green places. Come back to the permanent, immutable and trusted forms of nature ... No great heaving city this, no paranoid bureaucracy, just a simple untroubled rural village where there is a family and 'roots' and friends.[20]

Such pretences were rather hollow in Solihull, but they could be indulged in the rural–urban fringe of North Oxfordshire. Yet most of the migrants were obtaining more from the move than this. In a sense, they were able to combine opposites: they had the impression of being rural dwellers (after all the countryside around Banbury is as 'rural' as can now be found in the south or the midlands of England), but they had the practical comforts of modern residences. As Pahl has shown, this is increasingly desirable in modern England.[21]

The attractiveness of a rural–urban way of life was already being suggested by the responses made in the first survey, but then it was restrained by a certain ambivalence on the part of the sample to the countryside and to Banbury. Then, Banbury was described in the same breath as 'a nice, pleasant relaxed country town' and as a place where 'there's nothing to do'. There was general agreement with both these statements and as a result people found it difficult to sum up their overall attitude to the area. Sometimes it was resolved, as it was by one man who had already moved, by saying, 'I like the peace and quiet here, but my wife wishes there was more to do', so that different members of the household were accredited with the different viewpoints. But often the individuals themselves would make both types of statement, and then laugh and say something like 'I don't know what I think about Banbury really. One thing's certain, though: it will be a new way of life for me.'

But by the time of the second survey this ambivalence was already resolving itself, because the surprising thing is that the movers found a lot to do in Banbury in their leisure-time as tables 36 and 37 show.

The responses contained in these two tables add up to a considerable amount of social activity on the part of the sample. In fact, further analysis of the responses contained in the first column of these tables reveals that no less than 90 per cent met socially with at least one person weekly and had taken part in one of the named activities in the previous week. The pattern of sociability clearly mixes up 'friends' and 'activities' and some social occasions are probably being counted more than once, but it is

---

[20] Dobriner, *Class in Suburbia*, p. 73.
[21] See also R. Pahl 'Urbs in Rure', *L.S.E. Geographical Papers*, No. 2 (1965).

Table 36: *Sample: % meeting socially certain groups of people in Banbury – movers*
Survey 2, Movers, question 6

	Weekly	Monthly	Less	Never	N
Other Birds employees from Birmingham[a]	40	17	28	15	138
Native Banburians[b]	31	11	22	38	138
Relatives[a]	18	44	34	4	138
Other recent immigrants[c]	18	9	25	48	138
London overspill tenants	15	2	13	70	138
Birmingham friends	7	30	46	17	138

[a] Unfortunately, these categories are not mutually exclusive: some respondents apparently included relatives as 'other Birds employees from Birmingham' (see below).
[b] 'Friends in this area who were born here or have lived most of their lives here.' Excludes relatives.
[c] 'Friends who have moved more recently into this area (and not with Birds)'. Excludes relatives and London overspill tenants.

still an impressive total, and represents more social activity than the probable average in New Towns. In Willmott's study, for example, 25 per cent of his Stevenage sample and 34 per cent of the East Kilbride sample had attended a club in the previous month, compared to the 48 per cent revealed here.[22]

Certain changes are evident since the move in the pattern of sociability. Fewer visits are actually exchanged with friends (i.e. excluding relatives) – 35 per cent did exchange visits in the previous week in Banbury, compared with 53 per cent prior to the move. But there is a large increase in other

Table 37: *Sample: % taking part in certain local activities in Banbury – movers*
Survey 2, Movers, question 8

	Last week	Last month	Less	Never	N
Exchanging visits with friends	35	29	16	20	137
Clubs	30	18	22	31	137
Other entertainment[a]	57	19	17	7	137
Church	18	9	27	46	137

[a] Including visits to pubs, cinemas, theatres and sporting activities.

[22] 'East Kilbride and Stevenage', p. 315.

social contacts made outside homes. Twenty-seven per cent of the movers had attended a club in the previous month in Birmingham before the move, compared to the 48 per cent who did so in Banbury; and 55 per cent had taken part in 'other entertainment' activities in the previous month in Birmingham, compared to 76 per cent in Banbury.[23]

In discussing the implications of these results, we must distinguish between those social activities which can be indulged in by 'privatised' families and those in which persons outside the nuclear family are encountered. The 'privatised' family is often described by sociologists as retreating into the home and abandoning all social life outside, but of course some other activities are congruent with a nuclear family-centred life: married couples going to the cinema together or taking their children out might still be leading privatised lives. My data do not discriminate perfectly between these two types of social activity, for 'other entertainments' includes both 'public' activities like playing sport and normally 'private' activities like going to the cinema (while going out to a pub might be either). Nevertheless, it is evident that privatisation has not occurred among this sample as a whole. The decline in exchanging visits with friends has been offset by the increase in club attendance, and my impression of the increase in 'other entertainments' is that it has mainly consisted in a greater frequency of going out to pubs. It seems plausible to interpret these results as indicating that the sample was successfully trying to maintain a fairly active social life by going out more frequently to clubs and pubs than in Birmingham. Usually friendships established were not yet at the Birmingham level of visiting each others homes, but then this is not very surprising given that the sample were newcomers to the Banbury area. In fact, this group of migrants seemed well on the way to establishing active and friendly ties with their new localities. This came out very strongly in the respondents' own comments:

> After two months I think I'd chatted with all the wives in the village, either at the shop or outside the school. (a respondent's wife).
> It may sound corny, but I think we've been made to feel as if we *belong* here. (his emphasis).
> I haven't found people at all standoffish. The Banbury people have quite taken to us, you know.
> Birmingham is so impersonal, but you only see that when you get into a community like this.

But at the time of the follow-up survey, the nature of these community

---

[23] This is despite the fact that there were considerably more 'other entertainment' activities to be undertaken in Birmingham than Banbury.

ties varied within the sample and it is to a consideration of these variations that we now turn.

Table 38 shows the main social activities of the respondents who lived
either on the Neithrop Estate or elsewhere. The Neithrop tenants exchanged visits with friends rather less frequently than did the others,
though their relative frequencies of visits to clubs and to other places of
entertainment are very similar. One obvious possible source of this difference is the social class composition of the two groups: while nearly all
those who live on the Neithrop estate are manual workers, only 40 per cent
of the other group are manual workers. Yet controlling for social class
does not affect this difference – indeed, it brings out further differences,
as Table 39 reveals. Thus, residents of the Neithrop estate are less likely
to exchange visits with friends whatever their social class.[24] They are also
slightly less likely to visit other places of entertainment besides clubs.[25]
But there are no significant differences in this table between manual
workers and staff as single groups, though at the beginning of the last two
rows, those who only rarely exchange visits with friends are disproportionately concentrated among manual workers.

Table 40 includes the surprising finding that the male manual workers
apparently meet more frequently with new local friends than do the male
staff (though Table 23 shows that they exchange visits with all friends
rather less frequently). So again we see that the social lives of the sample
are rather more complex, and less class-bound, than might have been predicted on the basis of much previous sociological research. Before turning
to the general reasons for this, there is one point relating to the particular
composition of the Neithrop Council Estate that must be dealt with.

The Neithrop Estate is a large housing complex and at the time of the
survey it possessed very few other amenities. The school, the shops and the
pubs catered for too many people to be themselves the instruments of
establishing relationships between strangers. But the residents were not
all strangers to each other. Three groups can be clearly distinguished
from each other by virtue of the location of their previous residence: the
native Banburians, the Londoners and the 'Brummies' (i.e. the Birds
families from Birmingham). These were not cohesive units as there were
many contacts between individuals in each group. The Banburians came
from all over the older parts of the town, the Londoners came from a
variety of places in south-east London and were mostly unknown to each
other on arrival, and the Birds employees had come from all over Birmingham also without strong ingroup ties. All three types were liable to

---

[24] These differences are significant at the 0.10 level.
[25] Though these differences are not at a sufficient significance level.

Table 38: *Sample: social activities in Banbury by area of residence – movers (percentages)*

Area of Residence	Exchanging visits with friends			Visiting Clubs			Visiting other places of entertainment			
	Weekly	Monthly	Less	Weekly	Monthly	Less	Weekly	Monthly	Less	N
Neithrop Estate	24	26	50	29	18	53	50	24	26	62
Elsewhere	44	28	28	31	13	57	65	15	18	72
All	35	28	38	30	15	55	58	19	22	134[a]
	x^2 significant at 0.10 level			x^2 not significant			x^2 not significant			

[a] Three council tenants not living on the Neithrop Estate have been excluded from this analysis.

Table 39: *Sample: social activities in Banbury by area of residence and by social class – male movers only (percentages)*[a]

	Exchanging visits with friends			Visiting clubs			Visiting other places of entertainment			
	Weekly	Monthly	Less	Weekly	Monthly	Less	Weekly	Monthly	Less	N
Neithrop Estate										
Manual workers	23	27	50	25	14	61	55	25	20	44
Staff[b]	17	33	50	17	33	50	50	17	33	6
Elsewhere										
Manual workers	53	17	30	26	17	57	70	17	13	30
Staff	40	37	23	20	9	71	71	17	12	35
All manual workers	35	23	42	26	15	59	61	21	18	74
All staff	37	37	26	19	12	69	68	17	15	41

[a] Women have been excluded from this table as their own occupations do not form as reliable a guide to the social class of their households. This does not affect the trend of results.

[b] Note that the percentages in this row are based on only 6 cases.

Table 40: *Sample: weekly meetings with friends in Banbury, by job-group – movers (percentages)*

Weekly social meetings in Banbury with at least one:	Women	Male staff	Maintenance workers	Coffee workers	Other manual workers	
Birds employee	37	39	27	33	49	
Other unrelated person	31	37	50	47	49	
N	19	41	26	15	33	134[a]

[a] Excludes the three persons promoted from manual to non-manual status between the first and second surveys.

meet on the shop-floor at Birds (there were, of course, very few non-manual workers on the estate), and the policy of the local housing department had ensured that the groups did not form residential clusters but were scattered throughout the newer parts of the estate. Thus, if we consider only the Neithrop residents in the sample we see that they have friendship ties with all three groups: 28 per cent meet other Birds employees each week, 29 per cent meet Banburians, and 27 per cent meet Londoners.[26] The Londoners and the transferred Birds employees had one thing in common – they were strangers to Banbury. This was perceived by the groups themselves as a factor bringing them together socially. A Birmingham man said:

> They're the same as us, actually. They came for the houses, we came for the jobs. None of us knew anything about Banbury when we came, so we had that in common, anyway.

If we analyse the responses of the London overspill employees, we find that they interact fairly frequently with the Birds employees: 55 per cent met socially with a Birds employee weekly, the same percentage as those meeting other Londoners on the estate. By contrast only 40 per cent met weekly with Banburians (combining 'natives' with 'recent immigrants'). As the overspill respondents say they meet more frequently with Birds transferred employees than the latter say they do with Londoners, and as there are more Birds employees than Londoners we may assume that the Londoners socially in demand are those working for Birds. This is not surprising and shows once again the importance of Birds factory floor as a prompter of friendships on the estate. Their principal localities

[26] Practically no-one living outside the estate had such contacts with London overspill tenants.

180

seemed to have been the pubs and the clubs of the Banbury area and these meetings cemented an acquaintance likely to have been begun already by the men at work and the women in the residential neighbourhood.

But the outgoing social lives of the movers are not to be solely accounted for by such specific factors. Nearly all the movers shared a desire and ability to establish new social contacts that is generally supposed to belong only to the middle class.[27] Once again, the manual workers in this sample do not conform to the working-class ideal-type: with a fairly active social life, they were probably not 'socially backward' and ill at ease in settings of formal social interaction. Of course, the nature of their relationships are different from those of the staff. Most of their friends and most of their clubs and pubs are working class – but then the sociability patterns of managers are class-bound, too. Given a common social experience, reinforced by common work experience, ties of friendship and of the secondary community have developed to a uniform extent which is surprising in view of previous research.

Thus we can partially explain the only moderate degree of contact maintained with relatives and friends in Birmingham, which is evident from Table 36. Many of the visits exchanged with relatives on a weekly and monthly basis were apparently with relatives who were also living in the Banbury area.[28] Indeed only 7 per cent of the sample said that they visited Birmingham weekly for any purpose, while another 48 per cent returned monthly.[29]

Greater contacts with Birmingham were apparently not desired. Nine persons (8 per cent of the respondents) said that being away from their friends and relatives was the most important disadvantage of the move, and only a further 6 gave this among the other disadvantages they listed (2 persons, however, put this among their other *advantages*). All but two of these 15 were without cars, which would significantly reduce their ease of visiting Birmingham. None of the London overspill employees responding in the survey complained of their lack of contact with relatives and friends in London. This comment may be taken as typical of their attitudes:

Banbury town itself is very nice and the people are friendly

---

[27] See Chapter 2.
[28] The existence of some kinship ties *within* the Birds migrants was another factor leading to cross-cutting friendship ties in Banbury. There were never enough relatives to form cohesive social groupings on their own, but relatives could introduce their neighbours, workmates etc. to each other. These are actually estimates derived from tape-recorded interviews with a sub-sample in Banbury, and should be treated with care.
[29] Among the unskilled manual workers, these proportions rise slightly to 11 per cent and 53 per cent respectively ($N = 35$). From Survey 2, Movers, question 5.

and help people, whether Londoners or Birmingham or
Banbury people – my wife and myself have got quite a few
friends here. We will never want to go back to London. It's
all right to go for a visit to see our relations but we are always
glad to get back to our place here.

And only 3 per cent (i.e. one) of the Londoners were seeing their relatives
weekly and 40 per cent monthly (less than the proportions of the Birmingham employees, with ease of access to London and Birmingham about
equal from Banbury).[30]

But this degree of contentment with separation from friends and relatives was not extended to all aspects of local community life. The most
frequently mentioned disadvantages of the Banbury area, after its expen-
siveness, all concerned the lack of community facilities: public transport,
shops, places of entertainment were most often considered lacking. This
discontent was overwhelmingly concentrated on the Neithrop estate –
only the lack of transport was complained of with any frequency outside
the estate. It also began to take a political slant, with the blame being
attributed to the Banbury town council. Indeed, a tenants association
was started on the estate in 1966 to contest local elections, the driving
force behind it being immigrants from Birmingham and London. Numerous written comments in the second survey gave support to this political
protest movement on the estate. This London overspill employee's view
may be taken as typical:

Birds is fine – a very good company. It's Banbury that's rotten.
No, even that's not true: Banbury is a nice little place, but
it's run by idiots. They promised us this, that, and the other
when they interviewed us for houses. There were going to be
shops, schools, a pub, garages, all on the estate. I was told
shops within six months – that's eighteen months ago and still
no shops. It's shopkeepers who run the council here and they
don't want any competition.

Complaints about the lack of public amenities are universal on new
estates and in new and expanded towns.[31] Cullingworth proposed an
interesting interpretation of this in Swindon, suggesting that their complaints seemed exaggerated:

the criticism often appeared to be a displacement of an
ill-defined, illusive feeling of unease on to easily identified

---

[30] Cf. Cullingworth, 'The Swindon Social Survey . . .', who also finds a low incidence
of returning to visit London from Swindon (which is rather further away from
London than Banbury is from Birmingham).
[31] Young and Willmott, *Family and Kinship in East London*, p. 143; G. B. Taylor,
'Social Problems of New Towns', pp. 53–4, 77; J. H. Nicholson, *New Communities
in Britain*, pp. 25–6.

scapegoats. The move to Swindon was, for many families, a major uprooting from a familiar, settled environment to one which was not only strikingly dissimilar but which was also rapidly changing ... It was all so different from London (or Liverpool or Stoke-on-Trent) ... By no means did all families regret this – indeed, to some it was instantly accepted – but usually 'it took some getting used to'.[32]

In this case-study it might be a plausible interpretation of the complaints about the entertainment facilities because, as we have seen, the sample were actually going out more frequently than they had in the Birmingham area.[33] But their complaints about shops, about public transport and about the provision of medical services seemed entirely reasonable, coming as they did from a large city generously provided with all these. The facilities eventually began to be provided and discontent diminished. The tenants association had a rather short political life,[34] and even at the time of the second survey, one man said that at last the local council was beginning to do something for them, while several would endorse the statement of a second who said that time was 'a great healer' of these particular wounds. Nevertheless, most of the sample seemed to draw a clear distinction between local people and institutions:

> The people here are very friendly to us – it's the bloody facilities they put up with that gets us down.

THE CONTRAST WITH PREVIOUS RESEARCH

The findings presented above have differed very greatly from those of Young and Willmott's survey of East Londoners moving to the overspill estate of Greenleigh, but in several respects are similar to the results of Cullingworth's two surveys. As in Cullingworth's studies, and unlike

---

[32] Cullingworth, 'The Swindon Social Survey', p. 157. Hall's psychiatric study of house movers also found evidence of their tendency to project their own psychiatric problems onto the move itself. He found little evidence that moving brought on psychiatric disorders – a corrective to the popularisers of 'New Town Blues'. Hall, 'Moving house in the aetiology of psychiatric symptoms'.

[33] Though an alternative explanation might be that the sample were more concerned about the standard of Banbury's entertainment facilities than they had been about Birmingham's. As this was poor in comparison they would naturally be very dissatisfied about it.

[34] 'The association has followed the usual history of tenants' associations, and has changed its function from a very militant quasi-political pressure group with short term aims to being a social club with very diffuse aims and functions. The membership now is almost exclusively drawn from one group: London overspill', from C. Bell, E. Batstone and A. Murcott. 'Voluntary Associations in Banbury' unpublished paper, *Banbury Social Survey* 1968.

Young and Willmott's survey, very little discontent was felt about the move. The principal component of the discontent found in Greenleigh was stated to be the migrants' separation from their extended families.[35] And Gavron states:

> a great deal of the distress amongst working-class couples who are rehoused in New Towns may be due to the fact that they have never learned the social skills involved in making new acquaintanceships and transforming these acquaintanceships into friendships.[36]

In the present survey the separation was not felt as a serious deprivation, and this is in agreement with Cullingworth's conclusion about the Worsley migrants:

> Separation from the 'extended family' was for over half the families a matter of no concern. For the majority of the others it was regarded as a minor incidental disadvantage of suburban life.[37]

Of course only a very few – as in Worsley – were actually pleased that the move had taken them away from most of their relations.[38] But the major advantages conferred by the move far outweighed this minor disadvantage. For the Swindon and Worsley sample (and the Greenleigh sample, too) the greatest advantage had been the tremendous improvement in housing condition;[39] for the present sample, it was usually the maintenance of a favourable employment relationship.

In the other surveys the extended family had played a great part in the lives of the migrants *before* the move. It is customary to divide into two types the principal functions of the extended family. First, its members can exchange services; mothers help their daughters bring up their young children, fathers help their sons to find jobs, parents accommodate young married children in their homes, and the children accommodate their parents when the latter retire from work. Secondly, its members share a sense of social solidarity which manifests itself both in day-to-day friendship ties and in occasional ritual occasions such as birthdays, weddings and Christmas. These are the characteristics of Bethnal Green and Cullingworth has not denied that they characterised the lives of his sample in Salford and London before they moved. Thus, when migration sepa-

[35] Young and Willmott, *Family and Kinship in East London, passim*. This is the argument of the authors, though they do not present any precise data on this point.
[36] H. Gavron, *The Captive Wife* (Penguin Books, 1966) p. 98.
[37] Cullingworth 'Overspill in South East Lancashire: The Salford–Worsley Scheme'. *Town Planning Review*, 30 (1959) p. 93
[38] *Ibid.* p. 84.
[39] *Ibid.* p. 79, and Cullingworth 'The Swindon Social Survey', p. 156.

rated them from their extended families the pattern of their lives necessarily changed profoundly. Kin could no longer provide regular friendship or services and these were not found elsewhere. The migrants withdrew into their homes and their nuclear families.

> the intimate social life of a working-class area has given way to the more reserved home-centred life of the typical middle class suburb. For the majority of families this change has been welcomed. The new house in clean and healthy surroundings has provided an impetus to achieve what is regarded as a better and higher standard of living. The house is now the centre of social life.[40]

Or, as a Greenleigh respondent put it:

> The tellie keeps the family together. None of us ever have to go out now.[41]

My findings differ from this in two respects. First, no such retreat into home-centredness was observed; indeed, rather the reverse occurred. Secondly, the contrast between 'middle-class' and 'working-class' lifestyles on which the work of these and other authors rests is not substantiated by my analysis of manual and non-manual respondents.

The sample reacted to their new environment by seeking more social activity outside of the home.[42] This was so for all the occupational strata represented in the sample. But then we had found in Chapter 6 that, already in Birmingham before the move, the social lives of the middle and the working-class respondents could barely be distinguished from each other and that very few respondents were in fact heavily dependent on their extended families.

However, some of the conclusions of Rosser and Harris are similar in these respects to mine. Rosser and Harris found a frequency of interaction between their sample and its extended families not far short of that found by Young and Willmott in Bethnal Green; these relatives also lived in

---

[40] Cullingworth, 'The Swindon Social Survey', p. 165.
[41] Young and Willmott, *Family and Kinship in East London*, p. 143. See also J. M. Mogey, *Family and Neighbourhood* (Oxford University Press, 1956); R. C. Taylor, *The Implications of Migration from the Durham Coalfield*, p. 191.
[42] It is worth noting that Hammond, with reservations, makes the same observation about his Civil Service sample moved from London to Durham:

> The writer's impression – and it is no more than an impression – is that overall there is no diminution, and there may have been a net increase, in the amount of social participation by the newcomers.

> Hammond, *London to Durham* p. 90. Hammond's sample is confined to office workers, of course. Another study of office workers finds a slight decline in social activity but notes that this tends to disappear fairly quickly on settling down: Location of Offices Bureau, *Relocation of Office Staff*, p. 13. Again we see that the whole of the present sample corresponds closely to 'middle-class' ways of life.

Swansea just as the Young and Willmott sample's relatives lived in Bethnal Green. But, they point out, Swansea has an area of 41 square miles as against the 1½ square miles of Bethnal Green, and in Swansea the frequency of visiting is maintained by good transport facilities. Despite this they do not see any great weakening of what they term the 'modified extended family' even where frequent visiting is not undertaken. This is because the 'modified extended family' fulfils two main functions, the provision of aid in times of crisis and the promotion of a feeling of social solidarity, neither of which depend on frequent interaction.[43]

My findings endorse this view of the 'modified extended family'. Kin are looked to on ritual occasions and in times of sudden need, and at both types of occasion their links with the respondents were seen as strong and enduring. Yet there was no apparent wish for day-to-day interaction, except among the group of families where the wives were enduring the most recurring 'crisis', the bearing and rearing of young children.

But there is another reason why the 'retreat into the house' of the overspill samples in Greenleigh, Worsley and Swindon should be treated as a special case, and again we return to the question of the peculiar age-structure of most overspill groups. These are overwhelmingly composed of young married couples with children – people at the point in the life-cycle where they need maximum help from others in order to lead an outgoing social life.[44] Young mothers in working and middle classes alike seek help from their mothers at this point.[45] In particular, mothers and other relatives are looked to for baby-sitting. Thus the absence of kin will prevent young married couples with children from going out together at all. This is pointed out by Cullingworth in his Swindon survey.[46] In the present sample, the few respondents who felt the absence of kin as a disadvantage of having moved were, all but one, in their twenties or early thirties and with young children.

Yet if we compare the amount of social activity of those with young children and those without we find little difference. The London overspill respondents, two-thirds of whom were young married couples with children at or below primary school level, actually enjoyed just as much social activity outside the home as did the transferred Birds employees. Moreover, 60 per cent of them,[47] compared to 35 per cent of those from

---

[43] See Chapter 2, for more details on the 'modified extended family'.
[44] See chapter 2 for the evidence on this point.
[45] Rosser and Harris, *The Family and Social Change*, p. 230, Litwak 'Geographic mobility and extended family cohesion'.
[46] Cullingworth 'The Swindon Social Survey', pp. 160–1.
[47] This figure does not change if we consider only the London overspill tenants with young children.

Birmingham, had exchanged a visit with friends in the previous week. Thus, their young children did not appear to prevent them from having social contacts, especially those brought into the home. The explanation, professed by several of them, is that sometimes they took children with them, and, where this was not possible, they arranged baby-sitting with friends. Thus the young mother found a certain amount of aid from other migrants, which might not have been forthcoming if the migrants had not met at the same place of work. For example, one girl, a Birds employee like her father,

> babysits for lots of them up the estate – she's practically a member of their families, they're so grateful to her for it.
> They can get off to the Club, or the Admiral Holland [a local pub] you see.

Thus we would predict that if migrant groups contained a balanced age-structure they would probably be both willing and able to enjoy an active social life in their new communities. The 'modified extended family' predominant in modern society no longer unfits its members for social contacts with persons other than kin. If migrants are not actually house-bound in virtue of their having young children and being in a community of complete strangers, we should not expect them to 'retreat into the home'. Overspill based on relocating jobs as well as people would seem to be the most effective way of ensuring that the retreat does not occur, first by ensuring a balanced age-structure among the migrants, secondly by ensuring that the migrants are not total strangers to each other and thirdly by putting the migrants, 'the outsiders', on an equal social footing with the locals, the 'established', at least in their place of employment.

WORK ATTITUDES

In the preceding section we saw that most of the movers settled down fairly contentedly in the Banbury area and that most of them were well satisfied by the residential change. Yet from the information in Chapter 6 we would expect the most significant component of their satisfaction to be located not in the local community but at work. It had been work factors which had persuaded most employees to relocate in the first place; if they were satisfied with their relocation afterwards we should expect them to be still perceiving their employment in a very favourable light.

This is indeed the case. Table 41 shows that just over two-thirds of the responding movers still thought Birds an excellent or a good company to work for. Another indication of this is found in the opinions of a group of newcomers to the company, the London overspill tenants. All thirty

Table 41: *Sample: opinion of Birds in survey 1 (Question 85) and survey 2 (Question 16) – movers*

		Survey 1				
		Excellent or good and without criticisms	Fair/ average	Bad	Total	%
Survey 2	Excellent	47	6	0	53	40
	Good but critical[a]	26	4	1	31	23
	Average	7	2	0	9	7
	'Worse than before the move'	29	4	2	35	26
	Bad	3	1	0	4	3
	Total	112	17	3	132	
	%	85	13	2		

[a] Responses in this category included two statements, taking the form: (1) 'It's a good company' *but* (2) 'the following is wrong with the company ...'.

respondents in this group thought that Birds was a 'good' company to work in[48] – the only grievances they had, as we shall see later, concerned the actual jobs they were performing. But the main factor revealed by this table is that there had been a decline in morale since the time of the first survey. In both surveys these were responses to open-ended questions, and the obvious categories into which they fell were not identical, but nevertheless the decline is still evident. The deterioration in morale is marked, but there is still a great reluctance to grade the company as 'bad' or even as 'average': almost all the downward movement has been into the two categories of 'good *but* ...' and 'worse than before the move'. It is quite clear that the company's position *vis-à-vis* other companies has remained virtually unchanged in the eyes of the sample. It is 'still one of the best you can find'. Only in comparison with its own past has it deteriorated.

Was this drop the result of the move or merely coincidental with it? One question in Survey 2 was designed to test this: 'Has your attitude to Birds become more or less favourable, or has it stayed the same, as a result of the move?'[49] Of the 141 respondents, 42 per cent replied 'worse',

[48] Though non-respondents, 21 per cent of this sub-sample, might be less favourably inclined toward the company. Five of the eight non-respondents had already returned to London, but in the three cases where their reasons are known they were all unconnected with their attitudes to Birds.
[49] Survey 2, Movers, question 17.

47 per cent replied 'the same' and 11 per cent replied 'better'. Obviously the sample was rather unsure as to whether the deterioration in the company could be attributed to the move itself; from the results of Table 47 we would not have expected nearly 60 per cent to say that the move had not worsened their attitude to the company. The drop in morale was probably caused not by the relocation itself but by factors changing at the same time as the relocation and loosely associated with it.

The economic conditions of employment cannot have been a cause.[50] Birds in Birmingham paid fairly high wages and salaries which, when allied to generous fringe benefits and high job security (for the manual workers), gave very favourable long-term financial rewards from employment. The wages and fringe benefits were maintained in Banbury. It was one of the surprises which Banbury held in store for the movers that local factory wage-rates were no lower than those prevailing in Birmingham factories.[51] Indeed, Birds on arrival found that the rates it had paid for female manual labour in Birmingham were actually lower than those operating in the two large Banbury factories (those owned by Alcan and Automotive Products), and a hasty upward revision of the Birds rates had to be made. General increases were also granted to all manual workers and to female clerical workers soon after arrival and, at the time of the second survey, the wages and salaries of the respondents had increased by an average of 15 per cent in just over two years. Not surprisingly, therefore, the sample declared itself well satisfied with pay in the second survey: 66 per cent considered their pay 'good', 31 per cent considered it 'average', and only 3 per cent 'bad' ($N = 127$).[52] These proportions are almost identical with those revealed in the responses to an identical question in Survey 1. Nor was there any relationship between attitude to pay, and general attitudes to the company.[53] Thus, the drop in morale had little to do with the economic conditions of work.

But the high level of satisfaction of manual workers in particular with the economic returns offered by Birds in Birmingham was due as much to the long-term security of employment, a near-guarantee of present wages, as to the level of the present wage itself. In Banbury the formal conditions of employment of manual employees actually improved. The

---

[50] The changes in *physical* conditions brought about by the new factory and new machinery actually occasioned very little comment, either favorable or unfavourable, on the part of the sample, and have not been treated here. There were grievances raised about shiftworking schemes in Banbury, however, but the complexity of these outweighed their long-term significance.

[51] Though, of course, factory employment constituted a smaller proportion of total employment.

[52] In response to question 19, Survey 2, Movers.

[53] That is to say between the responses to question 19 and questions 16 and 17.

institution of a system of 'Personal Grades' was the major improvement here. All hourly rated (manual) workers with five or more years service were given a Personal Grade, two grades lower than the job normally performed by a man and one lower for a woman. If the worker were transferred onto a job at a lower wage level than his (or her) Personal Grade, he (or she) would receive the wages due to his (or her) Grade for a period of three months. Thus, except in periods of long-term recession (unknown at Birds), or in cases of a very prolonged lowering of the worker's physical abilities (such as might occur in the last few years of the working life), the long-service worker was guaranteed a future wage of at worst only about £2 a week less than his present one. This new policy had arisen out of the controversy surrounding the arrangements made over job transfers in the short recession of 1964. It was a marked improvement in the conditions of employment of manual workers, and the manual workers in the sample were slightly more confident about their security of employment than they had been in Survey 1.

Among the salaried staff, however, the reverse was true, and there had been a slight drop in the confidence of their own security forecasts—whereas in Survey 1, 62 per cent of the movers had assessed their security as 'good', this had dropped in Survey 2 to 48 per cent. This was accompanied by a bigger shift in their attitudes to their supervisors – now only 30 per cent thought their supervisors were 'good' compared to 62 per cent in Survey 1 – and this was similar to the shift among manual workers (i.e. now 30 per cent, previously 46 per cent). Thus there are indications that the decline in morale may be attributable to the factors of job security among salaried staff and attitude to supervisors among all male employees. This is reinforced by both statistical and impressionistic evidence. Statistically, both attitudes toward job security and supervisors are positively correlated with both opinion of the company in general and of the company as a result of the move,[54] whereas no such correlations emerge in the case of attitudes toward pay and promotion prospects. The impressionistic evidence comes from the respondents' responses to the open-ended question 'What do you think of Birds as a company to work in?' Almost all of the criticisms made here concern the alleged decline in 'friendliness' within the company. The factors of security and supervision repeatedly enter them:

    'Through the move to Banbury the "family spirit" which was

---

[54] χ^2 is significant: at the 0.01 level for opinions of supervisors and of the company as a result of the move; at the 0.05 level for opinions of security and of the company as a result of the move; at the 0.05 level for opinions of security and of the company as a whole; at the 0.20 level for opinions of supervisors and of the company as a whole. The last of these must be rejected as not significant.

obvious in Birmingham has completely disappeared. This to a large extent has killed any team spirit and management is much to remote.'

'Birds is good. But since coming to Banbury it seems to have changed. It seems to be that everyone has gone selfish. It's more of a rat race.'

'The firm as a whole seems to be decaying rapidly in managerial–employee relations, the reason being that officialdom has taken over. This is mainly caused by over-supervision, therefore making employees feel they are not trusted at their jobs.'

'Moving from a large place like Birmingham to a town such as Banbury, with very little prospects of employment outside A B & S, has given the company power, which otherwise they wouldn't have obtained, so causing a feeling of insecurity among the staff who worked themselves up from the shop-floor.'

These two factors of job insecurity and criticism of supervisors are, of course, related. What is particularly interesting is that one – management insecurity – caused the other, spreading a problem which was entirely management in its origin to all levels of the company. And here we return to the intra-management rivalries mentioned in earlier chapters. There we saw that managers themselves were often aware of rivalry between those they tended to describe as 'thrusters' or 'paper qualified' men and those labelled as 'dependables' or 'sleepers' (the choice of label depending on where one's sympathies lay). As a company, Birds was clearly moving in the direction wanted by the 'thrusters', toward advanced management techniques necessitating more technical and professional managerial recruits. The relocation itself came in the middle of this process, raising for management the question of whether the emphasis should be on maintaining good general staff relations by encouraging everyone to relocate, or taking the opportunity to get rid of less qualified staff who might be unsuitable in the near future? The management took the first course of action but, unfortunately, they merely shelved the long-term problem of management structure, and judging by subsequent events top management was only too aware of this. For twelve months after the company relocated in January 1966 there was a 'purge', this time in the production planning department when three male clerical workers were dismissed. There were three important distinguishing factors about this particular incident. First, none had many 'paper qualifications'. Secondly, none of the three were in higher management levels, and none earned more than £2,200, though their ages were disparate (mid-twenties, thirty, and mid-forties). Thirdly, the men had only moved to Banbury about a year before.

All three men had difficulty finding another job in the Banbury area, especially the one in his mid-forties, and two had to move away from Banbury altogether. All three suffered financially as a result, though the actual terms of the dismissals were quite generous.[55] An acute, though partial, appraisal of this incident was made by a man whose own career benefited from the sackings:

> 'In any company there are a certain number of people who should not be in the job they are in, and some who should not be in the company. Frequently, it is not the fault of the individual, just as often it is a result of bad management. Nevertheless, there comes a time when these problems have to be faced and dealt with.
> Birds did not face up to these problems in Birmingham and offered all employees the opportunity to move to Banbury. However, since the move some of the problems have been faced. Some individuals had to change jobs and some to leave the company. Although the company were fair and even generous in dealing with these individuals when the time came ... (they) ... should never have been allowed to move to Banbury. A great deal of heartache would have been avoided if these problems had been handled before the move.'

This man implies that the situation in the production planning department was by no means unique. Indeed, one of the company's directors was quite frank at the time in stating to me that far too much 'deadwood' had been transferred with the company from Birmingham.

For a time, then, many managers' sense of uncertainty and insecurity was quite strong. Where supervisors and managers worried about their job security, their demands on subordinates seemed to increase in an effort to demonstrate their own competence. One manual worker noticed this:

> 'A lot of the friendly atmosphere has gone since being here. Too much of the 'Let's have more quantity' instead of quality, each supervisor trying to beat the other, regardless of how it is done.'

This sense of competition was confused and increased by the company's organisational difficulties immediately after the move. Two old factories had been replaced by one modern one, and this and other changes meant that the old administrative structure of the company was at first continually changing in Banbury, as the company strived to make its chain of

---

[55] All had been offered (and had refused) alternative jobs, at a lower authority level, within the company.

command fit in with the new physical and technological structure. Often supervisors were not sure whether activities on the fringe of their own were their responsibility or not, and direct competition between them over the same activities sometimes resulted. One of them said:

> Possibly as a result of the move there are frequent organisational changes, functions are not accurately defined and there is considerable overlapping of responsibilities. This results in red tape, frustration and sometimes a sense of insecurity.

The two factors of job insecurity and hostility to supervisors reinforced each other.

At about this point, when Survey 2 was being conducted, top management presumably began to realise the extent of the damage done by the 'purge'. One very tangible and, to them, disturbing sign was the fact that eighteen clerical and supervisory staff joined a trade union shortly afterwards – and 'the shop-floor union' at that![56] By late 1968 (i.e. at the end of my fieldwork period) a *modus vivendi* had clearly been reached. There had been no further dismissals, or threats of dismissals; 'shuffling sideways' occurred, but discretely, giving rise to few general fears. Hence, for example, trade union activity among the salaried staff was negligible and no further recruitment to the union occurred. Having possibly given way over dismissals and demotions, top management had its way over new recruitment and promotion and some younger managers and supervisors without 'paper qualifications' were already complaining by the time of the second survey that university and technical college graduates were being increasingly recruited and promoted over their heads. This, however, is the normal stuff of office politics. By late 1968 it seemed evident that a solution to the unusually high level of managerial conflict was well under way.

What conclusions do we draw from this particular process for the sociology of relocation? I have stressed that the managerial crisis was not caused by the relocation but antedated it by several years. The relocation had been only a part of the many changes which had taken place in the company within the prior five or ten years. In this respect Birds has shared the recent experience of the food industry in Britain. Process technology, chemical engineering, marketing and computing have all combined to change the character of the industry and the company. In the case of Birds, the contrast between the old and the new has been heightened by the relocation itself, from rather dilapidated to brand-new premises. Symbolic of the change in character has been the recent change

---

[56] That is, the N.A.C.S.S., the clerical section of the T and G.W.U. already organising most of the manual workers in the company.

in name, from Alfred Bird and Sons Ltd to General Foods Ltd. Such changes cannot avoid repercussions. The sample was unsure as to whether the deterioration they saw in the company could be attributed to the move from Birmingham. This was a reasonable reaction. The relocation was only one of a number of changes which together produced what many employees saw as a deterioration, but it did in its turn quicken up the effect of other changes. And the relocation produced one special problem by increasing the level of dependence upon the company of older, long-service staff. Thus their reaction to the Banbury 'purge' was far more extreme than it had been to such incidents in Birmingham. In fact there are two lessons to be drawn for relocations in general.

First, a relocation to a small country town (the typical destination of overspill) does increase the level of dependence of employees upon their company. This is not only because they are less able to find alternative employment, but also – and this will probably occur whatever the size of the town – because they feel that in relocating they have already put considerable trust in their company by putting their future in its hands. Both these facts mean that if there is trouble within the company after the relocation, it will loom larger for the employees than it would before the relocation. Thus, for example, those who reacted strongly to the 'purge' incident gave their reasons a moral as well as a calculative tint. Not only were they worried about difficulties in finding another job, but they also blamed the company for betraying them, for 'breaking its promise' (a phrase used by several of the critics).

The second lesson is the more specific one that a relocation may itself bring on a particular kind of trouble arising from changes in managerial structure. Companies that relocate are probably expanding and changing as was Birds and it is precisely this kind of situation in which 'thrusters' and 'sleepers' become ranged against each other. Thus relocating companies would do well to note the Birds' experience which I have chronicled here. It is, however, a story without an obvious moral: the company's dilemma was a genuine one, and it is far from clear whether the 'better' solution would have been to dismiss more staff before the move rather than to compromise after it.

We must keep the discontent in perspective, however. It severely affected only a minority of management, and its low salience is revealed by the fact that it did not 'spill over' into the family and community spheres of their lives in Banbury. This was tested by looking for correlations between opinion of the company, and opinions of the new area as a place to live and of the move as a whole. The correlations are indeed very low, and not at an acceptable level of significance. First, wanting to go back to Birmingham is not related to a worse opinion of the company at all. Secondly, there is only a slight tendency for those who say they are not pleased with the move to have worse opinions of the company (χ^2 only significant at the 0.30 level). And thirdly, there is also only a slight tendency for those disliking the area where they now live to have worse opinions of the company (χ^2 significant at the 0.20 level).[57] One reason for the lack of association is quite simple: whereas quite a number of employees voiced criticisms of the company, nearly everyone was pleased with the move, didn't want to go back and liked living where they did. Other reasons are more complicated. First, being displeased with the move and wanting to go back was in some cases caused by work dissatisfactions but in most cases it was caused by non-work grievances. Most of these concerned the shortcomings of the Neithrop Estate. The council tenants tended to be displeased for non-work, and the others for work, reasons and thus when we consider the sample as a whole the dissatisfactions of sub-groups within it tended to cancel each other out and minimise overall correlations. Thus, there is also only a very low correlation – and not a statistically significant one – between liking one's residential area, and being pleased with the move or wanting to go back to Birmingham.

From all this evidence we can conclude that work discontents were of relatively little importance for most of the sample.[58] For most of the movers, there was little of importance to detract from the 'success' of the relocation. And this, paradoxically, is why I have discussed at length such work discontent as there was. Because this particular relocation was successful, it has been harder to draw warning rather than encouraging lessons from it. Warnings may however be equally timely for other relocations.

THE IMPACT OF BIRDS ON BANBURY

In conclusion I will refer briefly to the way in which the Birds relocation affected Banbury. I will deal here with four main effects of Birds entry into Banbury.

The first impact was, of course, on the town's employment situation. Though Birds transferred much of its male labour force from Birmingham, female labour was recruited in large numbers from the town and its hinterland. By contrast, few male Banburians were employed in the

---

[57] There is a statistically significant correlation between the opinion of the company as a result of the move and being pleased with the move, but this statement is almost tautologous.

[58] One further instance of this is the complete absence of stoppages of work and industrial relations disputes among manual workers since the move.

company at the time of the case-study, though their numbers will obviously increase with time, particularly as Birds is an expanding company. But the company is attracting men from outside the region to live there, whether they are manual workers recruited through the London overspill scheme or managerial 'spiralists'. By attracting more women into the labour force and more mobile men into the area Birds is obviously aiding Banbury's gradual change from being a rural market town into becoming a part of the low-density, light-industry dominated trend of urbanisation reaching out from the conurbations to engulf most of the prosperous areas of modern Britain.

In this new pattern of urbanisation, town boundaries become increasingly meaningless as dividing lines between the urban and the rural. This is true in Banbury, where the development of many of the surrounding villages into modern suburbs of the town has been completed. But this brings with it a problem that has faced American towns for some time – the fact that, increasingly, the more prosperous occupational groups in the town do not reside there and do not therefore contribute to the local tax-revenue of the town. It is a worrying thought for the Banbury officials that their town is becoming increasingly a one-class town, and the Birds relocation actually fostered this trend. If in such relocations and town expansions the council housing is provided in the town and the private housing outside of it, then the trend towards a one-class town will be increased. Co-ordinated planning between the various local authorities serving the town and its hinterland will obviously be made more difficult by the growing divergence of interests between their inhabitants. In the Banbury area, there are three county authorities, besides Banbury itself, whose policies might be co-ordinated; this may be frustrated not by their urban–rural difference which is declining, but by a growing class distinction.

The third consequence for Banbury of the Birds relocation has been rather more pleasing for the local authorities, namely the age-structure of the migrants. There is very little difference in the age-structure of the movers and the non-movers, but the movers form a fairly balanced age-

Table 42: *Sample: moving decision by age – men (percentages)*

	Age unknown	– 30 years	30–40	40–50	50+	*N*
Movers	0	25	30	25	20	138
Non-movers	2	15	33	25	25	52
All	1	22	31	25	22	
N	1	42	58	48	41	190

group. This fact certainly struck local town planners very forcibly, because the local authorities of Banbury and Oxfordshire, having noted the contrast between this group of immigrants and normal migrants and overspill tenants, quickly produced fuller statistics on all immigrants to Banbury which bring out the contrast even more clearly. These are reproduced in Table 43.

Columns 2, 3 and 4 represent the three types of immigration received by Banbury and its hinterland: overspill from Birmingham (i.e. Birds) and from London, and private immigration mostly to areas outside the town itself.

All these immigrant populations have their age peculiarities, as can be seen from the table, but one of them – the London overspill tenants –

Table 43: *Age-structure of immigrant groups in Banbury and environs*

	Total population of Banbury 1961[a]	Birmingham overspill housed by L.A.[b] 1964–6	London overspill housed by L.A.[c] 1962–6	Immigrants in new private housing in Bodicote and Adderbury 1962–4[d]
0–4	8.5	9.1	23.6	11.4
5–9	6.8	8.8	11.2	9.6
10–14	8.3	11.0	5.9	8.3
15–19	7.2	11.0	4.8	7.2
20–4	6.9	9.9	12.0	3.5
25–9	6.7	6.9	15.6	8.0
30–4	6.5	7.3	8.8	11.0
35–9	6.9	7.3	6.9	8.6
40–4	6.6	9.3	4.0	9.7
45–9	7.2	5.5	2.1	4.1
50–4	7.0	5.6	1.9	4.9
55–9	5.9	5.1	1.2	3.4
60+	15.6	3.0	2.0	10.4
	100.1	99.8	100.0	100.0
N	21,004	736	2,144	889

[a] From 1961 Census, *Oxfordshire County Report*.
[b] I.e. all Birds employees and their families in council housing.
[c] Like column 2, virtually all housed on the Neithrop Estate in Banbury.
[d] Figures derived from a random sample of post-1961 private housing conducted by Oxfordshire County Council in two dormitory villages within 3 miles of Banbury where extensive speculative development has occurred. Includes many Birds employees.
My thanks are due to the Oxfordshire County Council, Town Development Group, for giving me access to the figures in columns 2, 3 and 4.

has the sort of age-structure dreaded by town planners. With a preponderance of young married couples with small children, the Londoners pose many problems for the local authority of Banbury – a present shortage of women workers; a present engulfing of primary school facilities, spreading subsequently to secondary education; future under-using of school facilities built up to cater for the immigrants' 'bulge'; and, possibly worse of all, an acute shortage of juvenile employment in ten to fifteen years time.[59] Many of the New and Expanded Towns have had their whole population dominated by the imbalance of the ages of overspill tenants, as was seen in Table 2. Their consequent planning problems have therefore been chronic. If their immigration could consist of columns 2 and 4 combined in table 43, instead of column 3, they would be greatly relieved.

This point has also been noted by Moss in an analysis of the age-structure of migrants to Stevenage in 1961–5. He concludes that his data 'confirm the view that "attracting" offices of a service kind, or other organisations with a pronounced career structure, can bring a far higher proportion of people over 30 to the town than other types of employment or people recruited individually'. He notes that the age-structure of migrants to Basildon in 1963–4 was also 'curiously balanced' and attributes this to the wholesale relocations of Standard Telephones and Her Majesty's Stationery Office. And finally he briefly notes the case of Banbury itself and rightly attributes the balanced age-structure of immigrants to the Birds relocation.[60] My detailed study of the relocation of Birds supports his argument. It is one of the principal conclusions of this case-study that New and Expanded Towns can receive a more balanced immigration by combining the flow of people with the flow of jobs, and by basing overspill on industrial relocation.

Finally, it is worth expanding on a feature of the responses to the second survey, namely the general consensus among the movers (and among the London overspill workers interviewed as well) about the friendliness of the residents in the Banbury area. Though I do not have the necessary data to analyse group relations from the point of view of all interested parties, the samples' view of interaction processes within the factory did emerge interestingly, and the following explanation is consistent with the statements volunteered on the subject. Elias and Scotson have described the interaction between an already-established large village and a new housing estate of strangers as the imposition by the former of an inferior

[59] See G. B. Taylor, *Social Problems of New Towns*, pp. 71–5 for the ill consequences for New Towns of their unbalanced age-structure.
[60] J. A. Moss 'New and Expanded Towns: a survey of the demographic characteristics of the movers', *Town Planning Review*, 39 (1968–9) p. 125.

status position on the latter.[61] This did not happen in the case of Banburians and Birds migrants nor could it because, although as newcomers in the local community the Birds migrants found it difficult at first to break into the community status system, it was the locals who were the newcomers to the factory. If the Birds employees wanted acceptance in the community, so too did some locals want acceptance in the factory. Though only the second largest employer in the town, the company was at first attracting the greatest local attention, being deluged with applications for employment from local people. A member of the personnel department described this:

> We have been overwhelmed with applications for
> employment. The large proportion of over 40's with 15 years
> service with other firms amongst them, means that we are
> really attractive. The recruitment of women is far better than
> we expected. This was obviously a previously untapped labour
> supply, as Birds are the only company to offer clean, light
> work, well paid. After every strike in Oxford we have a dozen
> BMC workers in here looking for jobs. We attract motor
> workers by offering stability. Averaged out over the years
> earnings here will be no less.

Thus both groups were involved in an exchange process, and according to some respondents 'a spirit of give-and-take' entered into their relationships after an initial period of mutual suspicion.[62] One supervisor said:

> At first I thought they weren't going to get along with each
> other at all, but they proved me wrong after about six months.
> It was quite peculiar to watch because what seemed to happen
> was that both sides realised at about the same time that the
> others wanted to be friendly.

And a worker said:

> I've no complaints about that, really – we all believe in 'live
> and let live' and I think they do too.

The London overspill employees were the only true outsiders to both work and community. To a limited extent a process of stereotyping,

[61] N. Elias and J. L. Scotson, *The Established and the Outsiders* (Frank Cass, 1965). For an account of a similar process, see R. N. Morris and J. Mogey, *The Sociology of Housing: Studies at Berinsfield* (Routledge and Kegan Paul, 1965) especially chap. 5.
[62] There was also a specific grievance held against the Londoners by the Birmingham employees, which was removed after about a year. At first, Birds were compelled under the overspill agreement to fill all vacancies from the London overspill register, if they could. Some of the employees transferred from Birmingham wanted jobs for other male members of their families, and this the company could not offer as long as there were suitably qualified Londoners. In fact, there were never many applicants forthcoming from London and the company was able to start recruiting locally in 1967.

similar to that described by Elias and Scotson, occurred on the estate with some of the newcomers from London being labelled as the 'averse elements'. But these were not identified as Birds employees. and the transferred employees on the council estate depended on the Londoners for many of their ties of friendship. Thus in the factory the London over-spill employees who filled in questionnaires did not once complain of an unfriendly reception. One of them, asked what the thought of Birds as a company to work in, wrote:

> Excellent! The most striking feature being the happy
> atmosphere prevalent at all times between workers in all
> departments. I was very impressed by the warm welcome
> extended to me by the people from Birmingham who made me
> feel as if I belonged as soon as I started working at Banbury.

(This man was one of the later arrivals among the overspill tenants and would have missed any initial period of unease.)

Finally, it should be noted that neither the Birds employees nor the Banburians were probably a cohesive group, able to keep out all outsiders from a place within their community. Margaret Stacey's earlier study of Banbury in the 1950s showed that the town was divided very greatly between the native Banburians and the 'immigrants' (who had moved in in the 1930s![63] and would be unlikely to present a united front against further immigrants. Had Birds been the first large-scale, modern industrial enterprise to enter the town, the Birds employees might have found them-selves faced with the hostility of almost the entire population as was the case with the Alcan employees described by Stacey. But Birds was the third such factory. Nor were the Birds employees a united group. In Birmingham there had not been one company but at least two insofar as the employees themselves were concerned. In Birmingham when the coffee process workers and managers talked of the 'family spirit' they often referred to Miller Works alone and not to the entire company. The same thing was true, though to a lesser extent, at Devonshire Works, while even the men at the Bradford St warehouse had derived satisfaction from being left on their own by the rest of the company. But in Banbury all these diverse groups were thrown together in one factory building, sharing the same services and facilities and with internal job transfers between work-ing areas becoming more frequent. One man wrote:

> I find that when men get together and talk is turned toward
> the move, among the older employees the feeling is that while
> they admit that it is a fine new building they all seem to say

[63] Stacey, *Tradition and Change*.

'it is not the same'. By that I think they mean that when at
Birmingham we were more or less two separate factories of a
smaller denomination and happier as such.

This forcible mixing may have been unpopular with some employees but
in all probability it greatly assisted the absorption of the migrants into
the local community, and is one of the social advantages of factory relocation as a form of overspill.

In this chapter, I have emphasised the advantages of the relocation for
the movers. To balance this, we turn now to an analysis of the group who
gained least from the relocation, the non-movers.

8
The experience of the non-movers

We have already seen that Birds enjoyed great success in its personnel relocation programme. Most male employees did move to Banbury. This success meant that few non-movers were represented in the random sample of employees chosen for this study. From the sample of 300, 132 persons did not accompany the company but 80 of these were women who are not the main focus of my study. The balance is too small for detailed statistical enquiry and this chapter contains only a rather summary discussion of the experience of the non-movers after they left the company. My aim is to outline only the few major consequences of staying behind in Birmingham, namely those connected with finding new employment.

The most obvious consequence of the relocation for the non-movers was the loss of their jobs.[1] At a time of very low unemployment in the region we might expect that those who actually wanted new jobs would have little difficulty finding them. But whether those new jobs would be viewed as favourably as the old ones at Birds is another matter, given the exceptionally good wages and conditions of employment at Birds. It is therefore possible that the non-movers might have suffered employment dislocation sufficient to outweigh in our balance-sheet of the entire move the undoubted successes from the company's point of view of the relocation. Let us examine this possibility.

Table 44 shows the employment situation of the sample at the time of Survey 2.[2]

The most striking result in this table is the difference between the men and the women. Forty-four per cent of the women were not in the labour force, compared to four per cent of the men. These men – two of them – had both retired, one before the usual retirement age. Only four of the women had actually reached retirement age. The other women not in the labour force had simply taken a free decision not to work again. Most had been married or had had children after the move, and made comments to the effect that their family commitments were now too great for them to go out to work. Several others showed that work was not very important to them by saying that they 'couldn't really be bothered' to go to the trouble of 'tramping round' looking for another job. But the remainder,

---

[1] One was actually still working for the company as one of the 'skeleton staff' manning the empty Birmingham factory (pending its sale) at the time of Survey 2.
[2] February-March 1967.

Table 44:   *Sample: employment status of non-movers after the move by sex (percentages).*
Survey 2, Non-movers, questions 2 and 3

	In employment	Involuntarily unemployed	Not in labour force	N
Men	83[a]	13	4	48
Women	44	11	44	72
All	60	12	28	120

[a] This includes 8 non-respondents who were known to have moved house again in order to work for a new employer. It is not, of course, absolutely certain that they were still in employment at the time of Survey 2. Also, one man and eight women in this column were actually in part-time employment, for voluntary personal reasons.

5 of this 32, said that they had given up work because no other place of employment would be as pleasant as Birds had been. One woman was typical of this group in saying:

I was only carrying on at Birds the last few years because it was so nice and friendly working there. Another place wouldn't be the same.

A few of the women not in the labour force mildly regretted the Birds relocation – not all of them would have chosen that particular moment to stop working – but this did not amount to hardship in their eyes.

Involuntarily unemployment is obviously a much more serious occurrence. Table 44 shows that 6 men and 8 women were involuntarily unemployed at the time of Survey 2. Two men and two women qualified this by saying that this was only a temporary matter, implying that they had future employment arranged, so this reduces the unrelieved unemployment to about 10 per cent. Of the remainder, two men were ill and so were not actually looking for employment at the time. It is worth noting that both were of fairly long-service at Birds and, had they remained there, would have been entitled to a long period of paid sick leave. Yet two women admitted that they were only looking for another job in a half-hearted way as they were not 'desperate' for work, and others may have been in the same position. Nevertheless, a degree of hardship clearly emerged from the responses of the remaining unemployed men, all manual workers. Three of them gave such details:

With the state the country is in its the devil trying to get a job. I worked in the motor industry for a bit but along with thousands of others I lost it in the redundancies. You get the impression that at 46 you are too old for new work, there's no doubt about it, and its scarce to get just now. Its a struggle for us just now.

I am not working because I am not a skilled man, only a driver. And with all the thousands out of work, with the situation the country is in, its quite a problem finding a job.

Shortage of work and the appearance that you are too old for work at the age of 61.

In fact, as these statements imply, the unemployment rate in Birmingham grew after most of the sample's initial attempt to find new jobs. In this situation there was a marked reluctance among the employed to attempt to leave their jobs:[3] length of service becomes crucial for manual workers where redundancies occur, and several respondents were well aware of this. These men expressed themselves as dissatisfied with their present employment but feared another move.

In Table 45 we see again that a minority of the non-movers had subsequently suffered considerable hardship.

Firstly, it should be explained that the responses of the women are undoubtedly biassed toward overstating the length of involuntary unemployment. A long period of voluntary unemployment between jobs–being actually out of the labour force – would here be classified as unemployment. Nevertheless, the responses of the men can be taken seriously. They reveal that 60 per cent of men had never been unemployed, had walked out of their Birds job and all subsequent jobs straight into another one. But 20 per cent had suffered unemployment of longer than one month and one unfortunate man had been (and still was at the time of the survey) unemployed for six months.

Table 45: *Sample: total length of unemployment of non-movers after the move, by sex (percentages)*
Survey 2, Non-movers, calculated from questions 6 and 13

	Length of unemployment					
	None	– 1 week	1–2 weeks	2–4 weeks	4+ weeks	N
Men	60	2	8	10	20	40
Women	54	1	11	7	26	72
All	56	2	10	8	24	112

[3] 66 per cent of the sample had only held one job since leaving Birds, 25 per cent had held two jobs, 8 per cent had held three jobs and 1 per cent (one person) four (N = 90).

We must remember however that all non-movers had received a 'termination allowance' from the company which had been partly designed to cushion the financial consequences of a period of unemployment. The termination allowances paid to the non-movers in the sample ranged between £68 and £250, the average allowance being about £95. These are quite substantial sums and sufficient to cover the financial hardships caused by unemployment of nearly all the sample. Only two of the men had not received the equivalent of their normal Birds wage out of their termination allowances for the duration of their period of unemployment. One of these was the man unemployed for six months. Of course Birds could do little to ease the non-financial hardships of unemployment, which other studies have shown to be very much disliked by unemployed men.[4] It is likely that they caused a certain degree of suffering among the minority who had endured a substantial period of unemployment.

Financial hardship would be at its severest in unemployment, but it might also occur when the respondents had taken a new job with a lower level of pay to their Birds job. This occurred quite frequently, as Table 46 shows. Non-movers were asked whether their present wage or salary was better, the same as, or worse than their last normal job at Birds.[5] The men divide almost equally into the three categories here, though twice as many women consider their present pay worse than that at Birds as consider it better. But very few of the sample's wages appeared to differ from that received at Birds by as much as £2 per week in either direction,[6] though over a long period of time the divergence would obviously mount

Table 46: *Sample: non-movers' comparisons of new job's pay and pay at Birds, by sex (percentages)*
Question 4a, Survey 2, Non-movers

	Better	Same	Worse	N
Men	32	32	35	31
Women	20	37	43	40
All	25	35	39	71

[4] See, for a review of this evidence, G. Friedmann, *The Anatomy of Work* (Heinemann, 1961) pp. 128–35. 'Men find the drop in status particular hard on personal morale – a man without work is no longer a man.'
[5] 'Question 4a Survey 2, Non-movers.'
[6] Estimated by comparing the responses to question 10, Survey 2, Non-movers to the actual Birds wages during November 1964 collected in Survey 1.

up. We also have to remember that over two years had elapsed since the Birds wage was calculated, and that the non-movers were not sharing in the income-increases secured nationally during that time, still less keeping pace with the increasing incomes of their former colleagues who had transferred to Banbury.

Thus we find evidence of mild financial retrenchment by many of the non-movers. Although only 2 per cent (2 respondents) said they had been forced to take the serious step of selling property as a result of leaving Birds, about 40 per cent of the men and 60 per cent of the women stated that they had to use savings owned on leaving Birds, and similar proportions stated that they had economised on their expenses or postponed intended purchases.[7] Naturally, the proportion of retrenchers is higher among women because so many of them had given up work completely.

Moreover a few of the non-movers had lost financially in the long-run as well, by withdrawing their own contribution from the Birds pension fund. Though this gave them an additional amount of cash in hand, it deprived them of the company's contributions in the long-run. However, most of the non-movers, and particularly the long-service employees, were cautious enough to 'freeze' their pension fund. Of course, the long-service employee by adding his cashed pension rights to his termination allowance could leave Birds with a substantial 'golden handshake' of £500 or more.[8] Two or three of these employees did this in order to start businesses of their own – with very mixed results. Only one of these, a manual worker, was actually in the sample. He had bought a green-grocer's shop, which he said he had always wanted to do, and at the time of the second survey was quite optimistic about his prospects.

In general, then, there was very little severe financial hardship imposed on the non-movers by the relocation. One or two did suffer considerably by virtue of their late middle age or ill-health, and up to half the non-movers had to retrench slightly in their expenditure principally as a result of the difficulties in finding employment as well-paid as at Birds. Though, of course, there were very few non-manual male workers in this sample of non-movers, there was no evidence at all of any hardship among them. This corroborates the findings from Dorothy Wedderburn's rather larger sample of white-collar workers made redundant in Stevenage and Luton by the English Electric Company in 1962. Seven-tenths of them were in other employment within two weeks, while 'financial hardship arising from being without a job was negligible'.[9]

[7] Responses to Survey 2, Non-movers, question 5.
[8] Of course, this was only a pittance compared to the 'golden handshakes' rumoured to have been given to the two non-moving directors of the company.
[9] Dr Wedderburn, *White-Collar Redundancy: A Case Study*, pp. 26–8.

As we have seen, the vast majority of Birds employees before the move also considered the non-wage aspects of their employment as being extremely favourable. We might suppose, then, that the non-movers would have difficulty in finding subsequent employment comparable in these respects too. We can analyse the non-movers' general estimate of their new employer compared to Birds.[10] Table 47 shows that half of them thought their present employer worse than Birds and only a third better. This is not a dramatic difference but most of the respondents had worked for their new employers for over a year at the time of the survey, and what is absent is the overwhelming approval usually found among members of organisations after they have remained within them for some time. Indeed, in Dorothy Wedderburn's survey of workers made redundant from railway workshops in Darlington and Manchester, rather different attitudes to those of the Birds' workers emerge. There, 52 per cent of workers thought their new employment clearly better than their old, 20 per cent thought them roughly equivalent, while only 28 per cent thought the new employment was worse.[11] Moreover, most of the 51 per cent of former Birds employees who thought their new employment worse than that at Birds appended fulsome testimonials to the company such as:

> I would like to pay my best tribute to Birds as it was the best firm I have ever worked for. I still work in Birmingham but my heart is at Birds in Banbury and always will be.

or

> The move was quite a blow to me. I was happy at Birds. As I said to them, it wasn't me leaving Birds, but Birds leaving me.

Table 47: *Sample: non-movers' general comparison of new employment and that at Birds, by sex (percentages)*
Survey 2, Non-movers, question 4*b*

	Better	Same	Worse	N
Men	38	13	50	32
Women	30	18	53	40
All	33	15	51	72

[10] Respondents were asked to make other specific comparisons between Birds and their present employment, but their answers are, unfortunately, not usable. For, when estimating their security and their promotion chances at Birds, some of them were referring to the period just before they left, when, as non-movers, their insecurity and ineligibility for promotion were evident. These were poorly-chosen questions.
[11] Wedderburn, *Redundancy and the Railwaymen*, p. 112.

The long-service employees found it more difficult to settle down in a new company's 'atmosphere': even where their wages were not worse, the way that they were earned was often rather different from that at Birds. In particular the car factories came in for criticism. Most of this was vague, along the lines of this comment:

> I went into Austin but I didn't like it. Its the atmosphere there, and its dirty too. It was a tremendous difference.

But, significantly, he ended up quite happily in a leading food company:

> That's why I went into Cadbury's. Its a food factory. I like it very much: its as good as Birds – just as friendly.

Another man was rather more explicit about what he disliked at the Austin works:

> Its a different world at Longbridge. The car-workers are different altogether. Its a rat race: everyone for himself. The ordinary happy-go-lucky bloke like myself gets cut right out. I left it because there was no work guaranteed. You never know whether you were in or out when you went down there.

This was stated, in an informal discussion, after he had been persistently questioned about why he missed Birds for its 'friendliness'. It is reinforcement of the argument that employees' apparently vague stereotype of Birds as being 'friendly' was in reality a shorthand way of describing quite specific advantages of working there: the operating of informal channels of communication between superiors and subordinates, confidence in predicting future events, *security*. These were obviously missing at Longbridge and the man quoted above was unwilling to appreciate the rather different advantage of working there – high immediate wages. Another man, this time a young married man with a baby and in need (as he said) of money quickly, saw Longbridge and Birds in a different light:

> Blokes who have worked in Birds 5–6 years tend to give the impression that Birds is the only company in Birmingham. I wouldn't say Birds is the best in Birmingham. They pay good money. A lot of jobs there are unskilled and its damned good money for unskilled work, but anyone at Birds could work on the track here and get £20 to £30 a week. I suppose, though, that the security is good at Birds. In the motor industry there is a chance you'll get laid off all the while, but you accept that when you accept the job. The money's good enough to risk it.

Problems of adaptation were sometimes rather more idiosyncratic than this. One man said he could only find work doing much heavier tasks than at Birds, and the sheer physical strain was taxing him. One office worker said she couldn't understand the filing system of her new employer, though she had worked there nine months. Another said that nobody would talk to her at work.

Those who said their present employment was better than that at Birds were mostly officer workers, male and female, while those holding the opposite view were mostly manual workers. The few managers were quite content with their new jobs and considered that their careers had been advanced by leaving Birds. But only one of them expressed retrospective hostility to Birds: he said he was very glad to get away from its intense politicking! One manual worker who said he was glad he had left Birds made an interesting – though unique – written comment:

> The move proved to me that you can stop at one particular job or firm too long, and so get yourself into a rut, and it takes something pretty drastic to shake oneself from it. Its up to you. (As thou sow, so shall thou reap).

Thus, the experiences of the non-movers after the relocation were, for the most part, neither highly unpleasant nor highly rewarding. A small minority appeared to have suffered, a few said that they had gained greatly. But nearly all thought that they had made the right decision, as Table 48 shows, 87 per cent thought they had been correct to stay behind in Birmingham.

Of course, very few of the non-movers had been pleased about the relocation.[12] Obviously, even if employees were actually thinking of leaving the company they would rather choose their leaving date themselves. Though the termination allowance was a welcome sum of money for many of the non-movers, in most cases it was only slightly more than they were legally entitled to.

Table 48: *Sample: non-movers wishing that they had moved, by sex (percentages)*
Survey 2, Non-movers, question 1

	Wish had moved	Not sure[a]	Did not wish had moved	N
Men	10	10	80	40
Women	8	1	90	72
All	9	4	87	112

[a] This was a fixed-choice, yes or no, question. 'Don't knows' were written in by respondents themselves.

[12] In response to Survey 1, question 98.

The experiences of the non-movers after the relocation can be rather interestingly compared to those of the car-workers made redundant in Birmingham by B.M.C. in 1956 and studied by Hilda Kahn.[13] Her sample found rather greater difficulty in finding comparable employment than did the Birds workers – indeed, the majority did not find such employment. She found a higher duration of unemployment between being discharged and entering the first subsequent job than I found altogether in a similar period of time. Also, a slightly higher proportion (47 per cent compared to 40 per cent among the Birds men) had used savings to cover their difficulties. And she concludes that 'even a comparatively mild redundancy causes a not inconsiderable degree of hardship'.[14]

There seem to be four main reasons why the B.M.C. workers suffered greater hardship than the Birds workers. First, about 5,000 of them were suddenly discharged on one day, just before the local holiday period when they would, at least temporarily, 'flood' the labour market. By contrast, the 400 or so Birds workers had had two years warning of their discharges which in any case were spaced out over a period of twelve months.

Secondly, while the Birds workers received considerable help from the company in finding new employment, the B.M.C. workers received none at all. The Birds' Relocation Services Manager spent about nine months of his time helping non-movers, mostly the male manual workers among them, to find new jobs. His help can be classified as being of three sorts. Fourteen per cent of the male non-moving sample (and 25 per cent of the male manual workers) said they actually obtained their first jobs through his contacts with other employers, and just over half of these (and of the manual workers) were still in those jobs at the time of the second survey. Secondly, virtually all of the non-movers were interviewed by him and given advice in general terms about where they probably could and could not find employment. And finally, nearly all of them could secure a favourable reference through him from the company for a new employer. This last point is worth dwelling upon. Hilda Kahn had found that some of the difficulties faced by the B.M.C. workers in finding other employment stemmed from their being labelled as 'irresponsible car-workers' by potential employers. By contrast, the Birds workers were regarded favourably by other employers. In Chapter 4, we saw that management at Birds thought its workers were in general 'a better sort of person', more 'responsible' and co-operative than the average; employers would probably have shared this belief. The Birds workers, unlike the workers they were probably competing for jobs with, could usually bring a reference with them

---

[13] Hilda R. Kahn, *Repercussions of Redundancy* (Allen and Unwin, 1964).
[14] *Ibid.* p. 236.

stating that they had a long proven history of steadiness and co-operation[15] and were now unemployed through no fault of their own. Several workers themselves stated that they owed their new jobs to a strong recommendation from Birds. The effort put into this assistance by the company was well rewarded both by the gratitude of the non-movers and by the favourable impression of 'fairness to all' that it created among the movers.[16]

Thirdly, the redundancy compensation paid by Birds was always twice and usually four times that paid by B.M.C. We have already seen that it was sufficient to cover the financial losses caused by unemployment itself of all but two of the sample.

Finally, it must be pointed out that the immediate wages paid by B.M.C. are reputed to be the highest in the area, and certainly higher than the Birds wages. Though both B.M.C. and Birds workers would have difficulty finding comparable wages elsewhere, the former would normally have to settle for a larger wage-cut than the latter.

There is good reason to believe that the experience of the Birds workers, as regards the first and third of these points, might be fairly typical of most relocation situations where redundancies are usually planned well in advance and staggered over a period of time, and where redundancy payments on the Birds scale are now legally required. As for the last point, B.M.C. rather than Birds is the anomaly. And if the relocating company is at all concerned with its image as a fair employer, it may feel inclined to follow Birds' example on the second point as well. Also we should not forget that the other relocations we are hypothesising will be largely from the conurbations of Birmingham and London, where labour shortages are acute. Provided that redundancies are administered according to the conditions specified above, most employees should have little difficulty finding other employment. This is indeed the conclusion to be drawn from a wide-ranging Ministry of Labour survey of redundancies. In most of the cases listed 80–90 per cent of the men had found another job within six weeks of being made redundant (a similar proportion to that in the present study), and the report concludes:

> experience demonstrates very clearly that the effect of major
> redundancies is considerably eased by ample warning in
> advance and the phasing of dismissals.[17]

[15] The majority of people in the labour market have usually stayed with their previous employer for only a short period of time, and many will have been discharged by him. See Jefferys, *Mobility in the Labour Market*, pp. 55–7.

[16] See Chapter 9 for the importance of this point in relation to the concept of 'job property rights'.

[17] *Ministry of Labour Gazette*, February 1963, pp. 53–4. Note, however, that not *all* redundancies pass so smoothly. Among Wedderburn's railwaymen, for example, 21 per cent had experienced 37 weeks or more of unemployment and were still unemployed (p. 71).

Yet the problem of 'hard core' redundancy is encountered in all redundancy situations. Though they are certainly not 'work-shy', the minority who remain unemployed for some length of time are often, from the
point of view of industry, 'unemployable'; that is, elderly (and therefore
neither strong nor flexible in responses) or in bad health.[18]

Fox, after describing hardships caused by the B.A.C. relocation, makes
a reasonable suggestion for dealing with it:

> It would be wrong to gloss over these personal misfortunes or to
> burke the fact that, when industry has gone as far as possible in
> discharging its own responsibilities, there may still be an
> obligation bearing upon society as a whole – which does after all
> derive the benefit from greater industrial efficiency.
> It is worth drawing attention to an agreement in a nationalised
> industry which provides flexibly for continuing hardship from
> unemployment, and at the same time gives special attention to
> the older worker.[19]

In the case of relocation from a conurbation, the public benefit is increased not only by an increase in industrial efficiency but by a relief of
urban congestion and living standards. Surely here the case for cushioning
the effects of attendant hardship is even stronger?

---

[18] Wedderburn, *Redundancy and the Railway Men*, pp. 75–86.
[19] Fox, *The Milton Plan*, p. 58.

9
Conclusions

Many of the results presented in this study have been rather surprising. Not least, to the outsider, is the ease with which Alfred Bird and Sons Ltd persuaded the majority of its male labour force to relocate with it 42 miles from Birmingham to Banbury. The response of both the sociologist and the practitioner to this and other findings is probably 'How typical are they, can they occur again?' In this chapter I hope to generalise from the case-study and help resolve some general sociological and practical issues presented earlier in Chapters 1, 2 and 3.

THE SOCIOLOGY OF WORK AND NON-WORK

Throughout this study I have shown how worked-related factors dictated the vast majority of relocation decisions made by the sample of Birds employees. Most of them moved with the company to Banbury because they thought that at Birds they had found a better job than they could find elsewhere in Birmingham if they left the company. Most of those who did not relocate (and nearly all the managers who did not relocate) stayed behind because they disagreed with this assessment. Only a minority appeared to base their relocation decisions on non-work factors, and very few indeed made their decision despite work factors. Yet many moved to Banbury despite non-work factors: only half the movers would rather have done so than continue to work for the company in Birmingham.[1]

As far as the salaried staff of the company are concerned, these results are not very surprising, for the centrality of work in the lives of non-manual workers has been well-documented by previous research. The word career is the key one here. Nearly all the moving decisions of the younger staff were dominated by one thought: was the company offering a more progressive career in Banbury than could be obtained by finding other employment? Nor was attachment to the local community a significant factor in the decisions of the older salaried staff. They, too, gave priority to thoughts of their future work-life in Banbury, although they

---

[1] This was in response to a purely hypothetical question (Survey 1, question 99), of course. No-one was presented with this actual alternative.

were less concerned about future promotion and more about security. All this was predictable enough, especially given the bias in the sample which possibly removed 'deviant' managers from the study, and I do not place great emphasis upon these results.

But for the manual workers the situation is different, for the results I obtained here are strikingly at odds with traditional thinking in sociology. Neither from British 'family and community sociology' nor from much of Anglo-American industrial sociology would we have predicted the importance of present employment in the total life experiences of the manual workers, particularly the skilled workers, in the sample. This is because both traditions have concentrated largely on intrinsic aspects of work to the neglect of extrinsic ones.

Intrinsically, the Birds manual workers were not highly involved in their work. True, there was a great deal of praise for the company. Many of the criteria on which praise was based appeared, at first, to be intrinsic to the work environment: workers said that Birds was a 'friendly' company, that it was a 'relaxed atmosphere', that the employees were a 'good set of people'. But in fact they were talking primarily of the consequences that followed from the satisfactory state of the extrinsic economic rewards offered by the company. High wage-rates on their own do not necessarily lead to such consequences.[2] But we have seen that the peculiar economic attractiveness of Birds lay in its near-guarantee of high earnings in the future. It was the perception of a predictable and economically favourable future led to the atmosphere of relaxed friendliness in the company, remarked by all including the present investigator. 'You knew where you stood, and you stood well'; this rueful comment on the company by one of the non-movers is the key to what made Birds a 'good company' for the manual worker. Some intrinsic aspects of work are not connected with the level of economic rewards obtained, and these are the aspects which were only very rarely mentioned with approval. Thus, the level of meaningful intrinsic job satisfaction seemed as low as among manual workers generally[3] and thus, although other employees were seen

---

[2] As the numerous studies of labour relations in the motor industry show. See in Britain the studies by Goldthorpe *et al.*, *The Affluent Worker*, and Turner *et al.*, *Labour relations in the Motor Industry*, and, for a French study, A. Touraine, *L'évolution du travail*.

[3] By this is meant that although, as usual, about three-quarters of the sample said they were 'satisfied' with the job they did, the *salience* of this satisfaction was very low when compared to that of other satisfactions: for example, there were very few spontaneous comments of approval for the job itself, when compared for example to the 'friendliness' of the company, or the way it 'looked after you'.

as 'friendly', their friendship was not highly valued.[4] So the activities and relationships taking place within the factory itself were not important as ends in themselves, but were subordinated to the material and extrinsic rewards of work. In this sense, they are 'instrumentally involved' in their work, to follow the terminology used by Etzioni and Goldthorpe *et al.*

Furthermore, we saw that when confronted with a really important decision about their working and non-working life job satisfaction – indeed all kinds of satisfaction – played very little part in their thinking. Satisfaction proved to be virtually useless as an explanatory factor in relocation decisions. As I have argued throughout, satisfaction with employment is a very poor indicator of the nature of an employment relationship. What I have termed employment *dependence* is of much greater importance. And if we seek to analyse what type of dependence dominated this relocation, we conclude that it was a very diffuse kind of economic dependence.

The quality of life which the Birds employees enjoyed in their family and community relations depended to a very large extent on their being able to maintain their exact material standard of living. As expected, the aspirations of the salaried staff who might be termed 'spiralists' actually depended for their fulfilment on their increasing this material standard of living. As the financial rewards offered by Birds seemed to guarantee both of these – a secure and high standard of living for manual workers and less ambitious salaried staff, and a progressive career for the managers — most employees did move with the company to Banbury. Hence the primacy of work in their lives was shown by their relocating behaviour.

Yet this distinction between intrinsic rewards of low importance and extrinsic ones of high importance is not wholly satisfactory, because of the diffuseness of the economic ties to the company. This is obvious in the case of the managerial career, where promotion brings an increase in almost all rewards because of the wide span of the managerial hierarchy. Here I must confess that my data are not sufficient to analyse this problem in any detail. For the manual workers, however, sufficient evidence has been presented to show the importance of the hierarchy constituted by the internal labour market. This hierarchy renders more diffuse the economic ties of the manual worker to his firm. In this technology plays

---

[4] For example, only 20 per cent of the male manual sample said it would be an advantage to have Birds employees as neighbours, compared to the 60 per cent who said it would be a disadvantage. (In response to Survey 1, question 14.) Or again, there was virtually no support for the idea that the company should provide a social and sports club in Banbury.

an important part, and here we return to the theme of technological determinism.

The effects of technology on manual workers have been described by the 'technological determinists'. The introduction of *Phase C* technologies has been claimed to raise work satisfaction levels among manual workers and to socially re-integrate them into the enterprise. But in this case-study, the crucial point about the Birds labour force was not that it tended to be satisfied, nor that the workers described the company as a 'happy family', but that the workers were heavily dependent on the company in an economic sense.

The most important feature of the continuous process plant for the worker seems to be *the security of employment it gives him at a high level of earnings*. This is primarily a question of industrial economics: an employer with a continuous-process plant cannot generally afford to have it stopped. The machinery is so expensive that he cannot let it lie idle other than for maintenance purposes. The immediate contract of employment he offers to the worker is likely to have two main features: shift-working and high wages. The shift-working is intended to keep the plant continually in operation and is often therefore worked on a continuous, rotating system. The consequences of operator error are so costly to the employer that he is willing to pay high wages to attract and retain 'steady', 'responsible' workers. But these workers were usually recruited from the general un-skilled and semi-skilled pool, because traditional manual skills are not required for job.[5] Thus the unskilled or semi-skilled worker usually has his wages boosted by responsibility bonuses and shift bonuses. More-over, the fact that the employer cannot generally afford to run the plant intermittently means that the worker's earnings will be less likely to fluctuate than will those of workers in less capital-intensive working areas of factories.[6]

The employer's usual need for labour stability increases the worker's actual security in other ways, too. The employer is likely, as Birds did, to secure the long-term allegiance of workers with the 'golden chains' of generous fringe benefits: pensions, sick pay, paid holidays – all increasing with basic pay and with length of service.[7] We can trace back much of the 'fairness' of Birds, much appreciated (as we have seen) by the workers, to this emphasis on labour stability.

[5] Both at Birds and in general, these points are upheld. See Crossman, *Automation and Skill*, for British evidence; Bright, *Automation and Management*, for American; and Naville, *L'Automation et le Travail Humain*, for French.
[6] See Crossman, *Automation and Skill*.
[7] See Dorothy Wedderburn, 'The Conditions of Employment of Manual and Non-Manual Workers', pp. 14–15 on the relationship between technology, fringe benefits, and stability.

But there is one other important effect on manual occupations, stressed by other writers, which seems typical of the highly-automated plant and that is the diversification in the labour force. This does not mean simply that there are fewer workers in the same factory area, but also that their jobs are more diversified. At Birds in the coffee plant we saw that the process workers were spread fairly equally between many job-grades, in fact between grades 30 and 110, and that, correspondingly, their wage-range was a very wide one. The top-rated men earned half as much again as the bottom-rated,[8] and again let it be stressed that these jobs are all without traditional manual skills. This phenomenon has been noted before and so have its consequence: that there usually exist in highly-automated factories, 'career' ladders remaining within the manual worker stratum but offering considerable advancement in wages, status, and responsibility throughout the working-life.[9] As we saw, the presence of such promotion ladders was an inducement for the manual worker to move with Birds to Banbury. Thus the importance of what labour economists have termed the internal labour market played a major part in increasing the mutual ties of dependence between managers and workers at Birds, and in compelling so many manual workers to relocate. As internal labour markets are increasing in importance in modern industry, particularly in industries with advanced technologies, such ties of interdependence are probably becoming more typical in modern societies.[10]

Thus I would emphasise the economic basis of the level of work satisfaction found among the Birds workers. The Birds coffee processors had dirtier jobs in more unpleasant surroundings than did Blauner's chemical operators. Indeed there seems little reason why process plants should all resemble the gleaming antiseptic plant pictured by Blauner. Nor was the intrinsic job satisfaction of the coffee processers any higher than that of other workers in the company; the 'responsibility' of the jobs, though always important from management's point of view, was only seen as a major improvement by the few top-rated processers. Indeed, the intermittent, though normally highly predictable, work-routines of most processers introduced a boredom element into the job.[11] Moreover we saw that job satisfaction – being *un*correlated with relocation decisions – was of little importance in determining the overall employment depen-

---

[8] At 1964 wage-rates, this represented a range of about £30 to £20 (on continuous shift work).
[9] E.g. by Blauner, *Alienation and Freedom*, p. 149.
[10] For a discussion of internal labour markets from the point of view of a labour economist, see Doeringer 'Determinants of the structure of industrial-type internal labor markets'.
[11] This has also been stressed by Naville, 'The Structure of Employment and Automation'.

dence of the sample. Now it is true that social relations on the process plant were perceived as being better than elsewhere. The processers often said that they felt close to management; in Touraine's terms there existed a certain measure of 'social integration' usually absent in mass assembly-line production, for example.[12] But whereas Touraine and Blauner both stress the interdependence of the work roles of worker and employer as the cause of this, I would stress their economic interdependence. Both need the other to an extent which is unusual in labour relations: the employer cannot afford operator error and the cost of training replacements, the worker cannot afford to return to the unskilled and semi-skilled labour pool outside the factory. We saw the intensity of this interdependence revealed in the reactions of both management and coffee processers to the short coffee recession of 1964. There the company was willing to guarantee their wages for its duration, with very little prompting, in order to keep them 'loyal', while the processers realised that, recession or no recession, they could not leave the company.

To summarise, it seems that most of the characteristics of the 'good employer', which all admitted Birds possessed, can be reduced to the dual factors of high wages plus security and, for some, career advancement. Bird's favourable long-term, contract of employment spilled over into many of the intrinsic aspects of work. Workers felt 'close to' the company because they thought that their security gave them a certain amount of control over future management plans. In one sense, of course, they were dramatically wrong. In 1962 a total company relocation burst on them with very little warning and they were suddenly confronted with the choice of losing their jobs or uprooting themselves and their families and moving to a strange, very different area. But in another sense, their faith in the company was vindicated, because throughout the relocation Birds behaved with consciousness of its economic need to retain a stable, fairly contented work-force.

Nevertheless, we saw elements of other work rewards besides wages entering into the relocation decisions of the manual workers, particularly those in higher grades. These are summed up in the concept of 'status'. We saw that men doing fairly specialised work derived considerable satisfaction from the knowledge that they were occupying a special position in the company. The knowledge that they were able to perform satisfactorily a specialised function gave them a sense of their own 'territory'. As long as they performed adequately, management would not interfere but would respect their abilities. Their territory was located not only

---

[12] Touraine, *L'évolution du travail*, pp. 173–83. See also Blauner, *Alienation and Freedom*, pp. 146–8.

geographically in the factory but also hierarchically in the internal labour market, thereby conferring status upon them. This was obviously important in a company whose management perceived that technology would need a considerable hierarchical span at the manual level. Indeed, in the concern of the workers with promotion issues in industrial relations and in the fact that concern with promotion was related (though weakly) to relocation decisions, we can perceive the emergence of manual careers in the company's hierarchy. It is worth recalling in this connection Wilensky's article. In 'Orderly Careers and Social Participation' Wilensky found that among a sample of American upper manual and lower white-collar workers (whom he termed the 'middle mass') orderly, progressive work careers determined the nature of community social relations. This is strikingly similar to my results: many manual workers as well as salaried staff relocated (thereby disrupting their community relations) in order to maintain their career position within the company.

However, there may be situations in which the mechanisms of 'techno-logical determinism' would not affect worker satisfaction in the ways specified. The usually high levels of satisfaction found at present among most process workers probably occurs because they are comparing their present terms of employment with either other present types of employ-ment or with their own past job experiences. Once their frame of reference for comparisons became limited to process situations only (or to even more advanced work environments as yet undeveloped), we would no longer expect automatically high work satisfaction. We have seen some evidence that the Birds process workers were taking their employment advantages a little for granted after about 1963. Thus it would be quite premature to state that automation will inaugurate a new era of higher work satisfaction and harmonious industrial relations, as Blauner argues.

However, it does seem reasonable to suggest that a new era of work dependence might be ushered in by automation for the manual worker. On the highly-automated plant a widening hierarchy of manual jobs develops, offering promotion channels and even a doubling of earnings within the individual's work-life. As yet the principal criteria for promo-tion seem to be 'responsibility' and 'experience'. Management stress both, but trade unions, fearing favouritism on the former, press for seniority which embodies the latter. The result of their conflict is certainly to put greater reliance on internal promotion ladders within the automated factory. Thus if the worker advances up these ladders he is less likely to want to move out to another company where he will be forced to start at the bottom of its ladder. His dependence on the company is therefore increased to match its greater dependence on him. Such a trend could be stopped by the development of generally-recognised and trainable skills for these new automated jobs, and in this case new craft occupations might develop with attachments to occupation and not to industry. But without such a development the intensity of the worker-employer ties will probably grow stronger, at least in the short-run.

What are the implications of this for industrial conflict? French sociologists have been speculating on this subject in recent years, and Touraine's notion of 'conflictual participation' receives some support from my data. In *Phase C* technologies workers must commit more of their lives to the industrial enterprise, and this may well increase their level of interest in the enterprise. But conflict will also be of greater intensity if this happens because more will be at stake for the worker. As there are still many conflicts of interest dividing workers from employers, it may be appropriate to label the worker's changed situation as conflictual participation. As Touraine observes, this is not at all the same as classic working-class consciousness, for now the worker no longer regards himself as being outside of the enterprise. And if such changes are accompanied by a decline in traditional working-class communities – as both Touraine's and my own data suggest – he may be brought increasingly into modern industrial society itself. [13]

This is, of course, highly speculative. What is more certain is that the high level of employment dependence found in this company and in advanced technologies generally lends support to the hierarchical rather than the compensatory model of the labour market. In their comparisons between this company and the external labour market, most of the workers could see that in the internal labour market they had reached a hierarchical level above that available to them outside the company. If they left the company, they did not envisage themselves 'trading off' the costs and benefits of Birds versus alternative employment, but falling down the hierarchy. This was sometimes even true in the case of wages, where the belief persisted among them that though 'the car firms' offered higher immediate wages than Birds their annual earnings might be no higher there, and possibly even less. Wages, security and status seemed to them to be distributed hierarchically both within Birds and between Birds and other firms. Thus the question of whether there were differential work orientations and involvements among these manual workers (on which I have no data) is largely irrelevant, because these workers were not placed in a situation where they would have been able to exercise any they might

---

[13] *La Conscience Ouvrière.* See also, for a rather simpler view of an increase in conflict, S. Mallet, *La Nouvelle Classe Ouvrière* (Editions du Seuil, 1966). I discuss these theories of the 'new working class' in my *Consciousness and Action in the Western Working Class.*

possess. But this case-study cannot lead us to reject the compensatory model of orientations and the labour market. It is simply that it did not apply in this particular case. If we wish to come to some conclusions as to the relative importance of the two rival models, we must discuss the problem of the typicality of this situation.

Before leaving the case-study, however, I wish to discuss why technology did play such an important role in this company and in the others studied by the 'technological determinists'. This becomes an interesting question as soon as we perceive that almost all companies and industries actually possess very mixed technologies. It is useful to assume that the typical car worker is an assembler on a line and the typical chemical worker a process operator, but in fact these form only a minority of the total manual labour force in any firm. The majority will be a heterogeneous collection of craftsmen, their mates, labourers, storemen, drivers, machinists and many other different job groups. So why should we find that assemblers and processers are 'typical' in many ways of their firms and industries? the answer lies in the 'generalising effects' of certain technologies. Let me illustrate this point from the case-study.

Although the same conditions of employment existed for the whole labour force, the intense economic interdependence existed only with regard to the coffee process plant. In 1961–2 the company took a conscious decision to avoid further labour trouble by extending some of the favourable terms of employment (the high wages) enjoyed by coffee workers to all manual workers. This was partly because it regarded these other categories of manual labour as recruiting ground for coffee operators, but also because it was 'buying off' discontent to enjoy peaceful industrial relations. Many employees of the company complained that the coffee plant dominated the company, but this brought them benefits as well as costs. And the case of the skilled maintenance workers at Birds is one where management has both given and taken. It took away traditional status prerogatives and introduced specialised training because of what it felt to be technological pressures, and yielded to social pressures from the men in granting the large wage increases described in Chapter 4. Both factors increased the employment dependence of the skilled men and made them very unlike the traditional stereotype of the tradesman described in Chapter 3.

This illustrates the uniformity of treatment which employers typically meet out to their heterogeneous manual labour forces. If the employer feels forced to treat his operators on automated plant in a certain way by economic pressures, it may be social pressure which can force him to

221

treat workers in other technological situations in a similar way. The nature of the employment relationship in companies depends on other factors as well as technology.

In the Birds case there were three major determinants besides the dominating presence of coffee processing within the company. First, there was the pressure exerted by employees, mainly through the trade union, for uniformity of treatment, particularly over the promotion issue. Secondly, there was the self-image of a benevolent employer held by top management which made the company so quick to respond to this pressure. We should not put too much emphasis on the structural determinants of industrial relations: in 1962 Birds made a quite conscious decision to buy off employee discontent, a decision quite consonant with the strategy of American management. Many firms would have chosen otherwise, preferring to risk discontent to keep labour costs down. The third factor is also located in management attitudes. It is the positive obsession of managements with their most advanced sections of technology. This was most evident at Birds where throughout the fieldwork I was repeatedly struck by the tendency of managers to generalise about the company on the basis of the coffee plant alone. This is understandable. Management hopes future progress in sales and profits will come from new technologies. They are also the problematic part of the company: whereas most managers think they know how to run the traditional sections, they must spend a considerable part of their time worrying about the organisation of the new ones. This factor and the first one mentioned (employee pressure for uniformity) are probably general throughout modernising industry. How else can we explain, for example, the growth of fringe benefits in the advanced technology firms and industries? As at Birds, managements, in trying to retain their specialised operators, grant benefits to their factory labourers as well. It is not just sociologists, but managements and workers as well, who exaggerate the typicality of advanced technologies.

This raises the important question of how deterministic can 'technological determinism' be. Technology can only influence workers' situations through the actions of management: it is management that introduces technological innovations and decides how new machinery shall be manned. And management is not simply the passive translator of techno-economic pressures into new industrial structures. At the very least, management may mis-interpret those pressures and introduce inefficient working practices; and normally they are also influenced by non-technical pressures such as the type of employee and trade union pressures which affected events at Birds. Hence both management and worker strategies intervene in the causal link between technology and work involvement.

If I have been able to use a model of 'technological determinism' to pre-dict from technology to involvement, this is only because I have assumed that the strategies of the principal parties were constant. Empirically, this has appeared a useful working assumption. Most managements have in-deed reacted to automation with the same perceptions of what efficient working practices should be, and have fostered the development of shift-working and the internal labour market. Most workers have reacted to the latter in terms of a work orientation dominated by a desire for high but stable economic rewards. The assumption about the efficiency model of managements is exactly the same as the one I attributed to one of the 'technological determinists', Joan Woodward; the assumption about 'universal' worker orientations is actually the reverse of that of Robert Blauner, another of the 'determinists', stressing extrinsic and not intrinsic rewards. Both assumptions should be tested against the data.

THE TYPICALITY OF THIS CASE-STUDY

I now want to confront the issue of how representative the results of this case-study might be of national trends.

It cannot be said that the Birds employees constitute a completely typical cross-section of the working population. Their incomes are greater than that of the population as a whole, and they had previously been rather more geographically mobile than the population at large, and also the manual labour force was more 'middle class' in certain respects than workers are usually conceived of as being. But there are major methodo-logical difficulties to be surmounted before these statements can be accepted as proved. Many comparisons made here have been with groups studied some years ago, while some of them have been with groups which, even then, were probably rather untypical of the whole country (the Bethnal Green residents, for example). So even if we find that the Birds employees are unlike these other groups, what is our conclusion to be? Is this sample untypical, or are the others?

I think the correct conclusion lies somewhere between these two ex-tremes. Certainly, the family and community lives of the Birds employees are not very dissimilar to the respondents in some other recent surveys, particularly that of Rosser and Harris. Changing patterns of land use, particularly as it affects the housing market, coupled with urban and conurban transportation facilities and the private motor-car, have pro-bably made the 'modified extended family' more typical of modern Britain – and, indeed, of most industrialised societies – than the 'tradi-tional extended family'. In certain respects, this indicates that a convergence in life – styles is taking place, at least among white, native urban dwellers.[14] This does not mean that we cannot distinguish between the life-styles of different strata in society, but simply that the old ways of distinguishing them are no longer appropriate. Simple survey indices of life-styles, such as the geographical distribution of kin and frequency of contact with them, or frequency of participation in voluntary associations and other formal social activities – these may not always enable us to discriminate between the life-styles of various classes. What is now becoming apparent is that there are not nation-wide patterns of social life for either the middle or the working class. Surveys undertaken in different places emerge with different findings. Two recent studies have, presented results which are opposed to my own. Dennis' study of Sunderland has shown a considerable degree of attachment by the working class to the old inner areas of the city.[15] It is fairly easy to perceive that Sunderland, with a very stable and predominantly working-class population, negligible coloured immigration, and an active, civic-conscious local authority, exists as a civic unit in a way that Birmingham does not. But the problem is, how many conurbations and cities resemble the one rather than the other? The second study is the latest volume of the *Affluent Worker* in which the manual workers generally lead 'privatised' social lives, very different from those of the present study.[16] With a past history of geographical movement, the affluent workers have in all probability 'retreated into the home' (though the authors of the study present no historical data). The argument I put forward in Chapter 7 concerning cross-cutting ties might account for this difference: if migrants and natives both constitute social groups with insufficient exclusivity to outsiders, and with cross-cutting ties of dependence at work and in the community, then the migrants will establish an outgoing social life. This situation is only found in factory relocations such as the present case-study. But Clearly more research on these points is needed.

Given the diversity of recent research findings,[17] more account must now be taken of the character of particular districts, their provision of housing, entertainment, employment and other facilities when attempting

[14] I use the term 'convergence' because it has been traditionally used by sociologists in this context. Strictly speaking, however, we would need to know considerably more about social structure in the past than we do, before we could assert that this kind of change was occurring.
[15] Dennis, *People and Planning*. His data are, however, presented in a piece-meal way which make it difficult to estimate the precise level of this attachment.
[16] Goldthorpe *et al.*, *The Affluent Worker in the Class Structure*, chap. 4.
[17] For example, Gavron's St Pancras study of working-class 'house-bound' wives found yet another pattern of social life: 'a rather isolated, extremely family-centred existence, with the focus not on the extended family but on the nuclear family', despite the fact that the vast majority lived very close to their extended families (pp. 95–100).

to generalise about life-styles. It may be that there is scope for secondary analysis of published surveys, taking into account such variations, but this is an area where the sociologist's traditional plea for 'further research' is justified. At the moment we can only make tentative suggestions as to the nature of the 'convergence' process which might be perceptible even through these local and regional variations. Let us examine my research findings to see what these might be.

First, the extended families of nearly all the Birds manual workers were spread out over quite a wide area, though they were not so dispersed as were the families of the salaried staff.[18] The crucial point is that in modern towns and with modern means of communication, once kin are removed from the day-to-day contact that stems from living within a few hundred yards of each other, then the exact distance between them does not greatly affect the nature of their contacts. Regardless of whether the distance is 1 mile or 50 miles, cars and telephones increasingly enable what Rosser and Harris (and Litwak) have termed the 'modified extended family' to perform its two main functions: aid in times of crisis, and the enjoyment of a sense of social solidarity at occasional festivities. Thus a move to Banbury was seen as a serious disruption to the life of their extended family by only a very few respondents.

Secondly, it was quite difficult to distinguish the manual workers from the salaried staff in terms of the extent of their social activities outside their extended family. Of course, the nature of the activity was very different. Managers did not attend working-mens clubs, nor their wives bingo halls. But on a crude measure of formal secondary relations – the frequency of club visiting – the manual and the non-manual respondents behaved similarly. Nor was there any difference at all in the extent to which manual and non-manual workers exchanged visits with friends in Birmingham.

The third result of this nature is actually new, though it might be predicted from knowledge of the first two. It is that when such people, manual or non-manual, are relocated they are not socially helpless, pining for their lost mothers-in-law and unable or unwilling to make new friends. In Chapter 7 we saw that, if anything, the reverse happened, and that in an attempt to 'strike new roots' the transferred workers probably indulged in more social activities than they had previously in Birmingham, despite the fact that Banbury offered far less in the way of social amenities than Birmingham had done.

These three groups of results point towards a similarity of life-styles

[18] This occupational difference usually emerges in surveys, e.g. the Royal Commission on Local Government, 'Community Attitudes Survey . . .', p. 43.

among the present sample, manual and non-manual alike. In particular, the manual workers' social lives seem much more outgoing and much less cut-off from the wider society of modern urban Britain than some sociologists had led us to expect.

If the sample had been deeply embedded in a network of local kin relationships we might have expected these to have restrained them from relocating. In such networks, the most meaningful life experiences are found in close-knit interactional systems which, because they are kin-dominated, cannot be replaced by social relations with other people. But in fact, the present sample were involved more in what Plowman *et al.* would term an 'attributional' status-system, linking up with selected relatives and friends, meeting them in semi-formal settings like clubs and associations, and participating in a mass, not a local, culture.[19] In an attributional system, status is allocated according to external criteria of worth and not inherited kin relationships. The most important external criterion seems to be the housing situation of the individual.

Rex and Moore have argued this case even more strongly. They see elements of a new class structure emerging from the emphasis which city residents give to their housing situation. They state:

> there is a class struggle over the use of houses and .. this class struggle is the central process of the city as a social unit.[20]

We could, of course, argue over the use of the term 'class' here. Rex and Moore's usage seems to differentiate social groups by their access to economic life-chances (the Weberian definition) rather than their relation to the means of production (the Marxist one). And obviously Rex and Moore's new housing 'classes' are not completely different from existing classes in the sphere of production. Nevertheless, it is an interesting argument that access to the means of consumption, as well as those of production, are increasingly helping to determine economic life-chances. I noted evidence to support this argument in relation to general urban structure in Chapter 2. I have also produced supporting evidence from this case-study. A satisfactory housing situation appeared as one of the major life-

[19] D. E. G. Plowman, *et al.*, 'Local social status in England and Wales', *Sociological Review*, 10 (1962).
[20] Rex and Moore, *Race, Community and Conflict*, p. 273. It may be more than mere coincidence that Rex and Moore and myself have been forcibly struck by the class struggle over houses. After all, we studied the same town (Birmingham), which has indeed received more unpopular immigration than most others in Britain. It seems then that part of the housing struggle we observed is a consequence of the phenomena of immigrant 'invasion and succession' noted by the Chicago sociologists of the 1920s. See R.E. Park *et al.*, *The City* (University of Chicago Press, 1923).

goals of the sample.[21] There was also remarkable unanimity as to what constituted a satisfactory housing condition: it was a new, or period, house, detached or semi-detached with its own garden. Private ownership of it was the ideal, but renting from a local authority was, for many of the manual workers, an adequate substitute. It followed, therefore, that the 'nice area' to live was defined as a low-density, suburban or rural setting. There was near unanimity on this point and the only areas disliked by a majority of their residents were the inner parts of Birmingham which did not conform to this ideal. These unpopular areas are precisely the 'traditional working-class communities'.

Again we must be wary not to confuse demand with choice. It is still a possibility that if the conurbation inner areas were rebuilt to very high standards, most residents would prefer to remain there. We have seen, for example, that those already in adequate council houses and flats in Birmingham were less likely to move than the others. As against this, however, we must set the facts that immigration had destroyed for many the social desirability of the inner areas, and that housing preferences did seem for most people to be hierarchically arranged. This hierarchy corresponds closely to that of the class structure and it is certainly worth investigating further the possibility that each stratum wishes for the housing standards of the next higher one – manual workers for suburban estates, managers for the country houses of the (ideal-typical) gentry!

Conurbations in their present state are clearly unpopular. More people are wishing to move out of them, and more are doing so. Flight from them is possible even on the wages of the unskilled worker. The younger worker earning £25 a week has a fair chance of obtaining a mortgage on a low-period suburban house, while those who live in the city for several years will eventually qualify for a council tenancy, which might be a tower-flat in inner Birmingham, but for the man with a family would probably be a suburban council house. The Birds relocation contained a better mortgage offer than is usually found on the open market, especially for the lower-paid worker, and an offer of a council house even for those with the briefest of residence in Birmingham. Also, like most house-buyers, the Birds employees with house-mortgages before the move depended on the continuance of their income to pay off their mortgages while retaining their general standard of living. So, given the importance of the housing-ideal, the relocation offered a chance of advancement in life-style to most employees. And we saw in Chapter 6 that those already renting council

[21] See Chapter 7.

houses were much less likely to move than others. This study offers no explanation of why the British are so housing-conscious, but this characteristic seems to be eroding the appeal of the traditional, working-class community.[22] I have suggested that there are no such communities now left in Birmingham at least.[23]

Yet we must not generalise too far from the experience of this sample. The Birds sample was at least more geographically mobile, more prosperous, and in better housing conditions, than fairly accurate national averages. All this probably stems from the industrial structure of the company.

Not unexpectedly, we return to the subject of the effects of technology and modernisation on employee attitudes. Birds is a progressive company, with above-average profits, above-average growth, above-average wages. It uses modern methods of marketing, computing, personnel management and chemical engineering. It is part of an American-owned international corporation.[24] It possesses two sections of continuous-process plant technology.[25] In all these respects, more companies will probably come to resemble it in the future, though this is not an argument to be pressed far: there are almost as many different firms and workers 'of the future' as there are types of firms and workers! But a much stronger argument, and one that brings us back to the practical aspects of relocation, is that Birds is certainly more typical of the companies contemplating relocation. Most relocating companies – other than those moving to Development Districts because of labour shortages – are seeking more space. They are the expanding, modernising companies which disproportionately fill the new and expanded towns of Britain.[26] I have argued that this sort of company is likely to have on its payroll a disproportionate number of 'spiralists' among its managers, and a disproportionate number of manual workers held by strong economic ties of interdependence to the company. Both these groups are very likely to accept the offer of a relocation transfer, the managers as a temporary phase in their work-lives, the

[22] Of course, if land-use patterns settle down again in the future, then common long-residence may recreate them – though this is rather less likely in privately-owned housing areas.

[23] See Chapter 6.

[24] This enables it to draw on large reserves for new capitalisation. General Foods' interest in further expansion in Britain is evidenced by its unsuccessful take-over bid for Rowntree's in January 1969.

[25] The second, 'Dream-Topping', section was not opened in Banbury until this study was virtually completed.

[26] See J. H. Dunning, 'Manufacturing industries in the new towns', and G. F. Everitt (Chairman, Greater London Council New and Expanding Towns Committee) 'The First Report of the East Anglia Economic Planning Council seen in relation to the London Town Development Programme' *Town and Country Planning Association*, Conference on 'East Anglia a Study', Bury St Edmunds, February 1969.

workers as a permanent one. This is a very general answer to the important practical question, can other firms too be successful in relocating their labour forces? Let us examine this question in rather more detail.

From this sociological analysis came several conclusions of very great practical importance about industrial relocation. They turn on the question of the practicability of such relocation. Birds and doubtless other, less-publicised companies have shown that personnel can be transferred *en masse* in relocations. The conclusions of this chapter so far have been that other companies in other situations can do it also. Put very baldly, the 'good' company, from the point of view of its employees, will be able to persuade a good proportion of them to relocate and the 'bad' one will not.

Certain assumptions underlie this statement, however. In the present study, it was work-related factors of a basically economic character which determined the sample's relocation decisions, but that was because some other, potentially important, factors were held constant. The most important of these is housing. Only a minority of the sample relocated to Banbury primarily because of the lure of attractive housing there, but we have to remember that for the rest of the sample, too, good housing was provided (and taken for granted) in the Banbury area. If it had not been, perhaps fewer would have relocated. Indeed, it is difficult to see how many lower-paid workers, ineligible for mortgages, could have done so without the provision of council housing. Yet, in the context of British relocation policies, it is permissible to ignore this complicating factor because such housing always is provided in New and Expanded Towns for all transferring workers. In other circumstances, housing factors are usually treated as barriers to long-distance mobility, but this is not so in the special type of mobility discussed here.[27]

The attraction of the exporting and importing locality may also affect the numbers moving. In the present case-study, for example, only about half the proportion in the sample who relocated to Banbury said that they would also have moved to Liverpool if that had been the destination. But Liverpool and Banbury are very different places, and the likely destination of the relocating company is more likely to be a Banbury than a Liverpool if it seeks to transfer most of its labour force. And the proportion in the sample who said they would have moved with the company to Glou-

[27] See J. B. Cullingworth, *Housing and Labour Mobility* (O.E.C.D., 1969).

cester and Cardiff – two of the destinations rumoured in the early stages – was very similar to that which actually moved to Banbury.[28] One might expect that a planned, large-scale expansion of towns in the Midlands and the South of England[29] would attract a few more movers, but the differential lure of the importing town would probably make little overall difference. It is worth noting here a point made by Hammond, that the population of London (and also Birmingham) contains a large number of immigrants from most regions of Britain. These will usually be willing to move back to their original region if presented by a relocation with an opportunity to do so.[30] Thus the differential lure of various regions may vary to the degree that they supply the conurbation with population.

Only in unusual circumstances can it be expected that large numbers of employees involved in British relocations to New or Expanded Towns would eagerly move for reasons unconnected with their work. Take away the lure of the new council house for the slum-dweller, and non-work factors would dwindle even more. Though I have emphasised that the recent development of urban land-use patterns and of private transportation remove many of the traditional disincentives to relocation, people only rarely want to move to another place. This seems borne out by the findings of a recent study of the move from London to Durham of the Post Office Savings Certificate Division. There the movers were 'volunteers', that is the non-movers were not made redundant in London. Of the 2,046 staff asked to move, and responding in the survey, only 180 freely volunteered for permanent transfer, though a further 240 said they would move if transfer to another Civil Service department in London could not be arranged.[31]

It is one of the main conclusions of this book that employees' relocation decisions are likely to be dominated by work-related factors. Therefore, it is probably within the powers of the employer considering relocation to assess his own chances of transferring his labour force. This is an important practical point. The employer can analyse its skill composition, measure wage-rates against alternative local ones, and even make some estimate from labour turnover and stability, absenteeism, and strikes, as to his reputation as a 'good' or a 'bad' employer in the senses I have specified above. If he concludes that his reputation is good, he can then attempt to transfer his employees with the possibility of success.

However, this is no easy matter. Very few employees would move unless

[28] Nearly all those saying they would move to any of these places were drawn from the actual movers. In response to Survey 1, question 19.
[29] Such as the proposed developments of Telford, Milton Keynes, Peterborough, and South Hampshire.
[30] E. Hammond, *London to Durham*, p. 23.
[31] *Ibid.* pp. 36–7.

they were positively persuaded to, and their inducement must include the covering of the costs of the actual relocation as well as the offer of an attractive job after the relocation. This involves two main relocation policies, one to cover the housing problems of employees, the other to cover their financial costs (though the two are obviously interconnected), and must be the corner-stone of any attempt to relocate any group of employees, no matter how satisfied with their employment they migh be. This is for two reasons. If employees had to pay their own costs they would then have to add them to their cost–benefit analysis of the moving decision itself, and, as the analysis of the Birds employees was dominated by economic considerations, this would probably make moving less attractive.

But the second reason is the more important one: most employees would feel that their employer had an obligation to pay these costs, and if this was not fulfilled then they would be much less willing to place their future in his hands by relocating. In Chapter 4 we found that, though industrial relations were by then good, employees reacted to the first news of the relocation with hostility and a strong sense of betrayal. Throughout the relocation negotiations, according to a union representative, 'there was this terrible suspicion behind everything'. We can only understand this suspicion by referring to the concept of job property rights which Turner and his collaborators have identified as one of the two bases of post-war industrial relations. They state:

> The concept of 'job property rights' is . . . an idea with far-reaching implications. In manual workers' terms, it extends not merely to the sense that operatives should not be turned off *en masse* when it is no longer profitable to employ them, or that the individual worker should not be deprived of his property rights established by service without appeal from the decision of a management which now finds his presence undesirable: it also includes the idea of rights to a particular job at a particular place, and may extend to the right to consultation in anything which may affect the future value of his 'property.[32]

Nearly all the Birds workers considered that they had a right to their jobs in this way. The relocation seemed to them to threaten this right and it could only be tolerated if it interfered minimally with their economic security and their work-life. From their point of view, the relocation policy had to contain assurances of future employment with the company, had to cover the costs of moving, had to guarantee alternative employment in Birmingham. The company's relocation policy went extremely

---

[32] Turner *et al., Labour Relations in the Motor Industry,* p. 337.

close to providing these three items in their entirety and so was generally regarded as being 'fair' by employees. It was not considered an unexpected act of generosity, but rather the fulfilling of an obligation.[33]

It was the achievement of Alfred Bird and Sons Ltd that its management sensed this mood, and took trouble throughout the relocation to be seen to act 'fairly' – to look after the interests of the non-movers as well as the movers, to admit financial responsibility for the inconvenience, and to move closer than it had in the past toward guaranteeing employment, through the institution of 'Personal Grades'.[34] Most employees relocated because they trusted the company to provide them a secure future – reinforcement for this trust came from the company's relocation policy. It could easily have turned out otherwise; many of the cases of relocation failures referred to in Chapter 2 probably foundered on this lack of trust. Indeed, it took Birds a formidable amount of effort to put across to employees its relocation policy and the image of fairness it contained. Its policy was not, of course, invented by the company but was derived in part from the parent company's American experience. It is to be hoped that other companies will learn from Bird's experience.

Indeed, other companies can be warned of the difficulties that are probably inevitable as well as those that can be skirted. Though I have emphasised the successful nature of this relocation, I have also chronicled the crises and failures. Any company which, like Birds, attempts to run two factories simultaneously in the transition phase of a relocation will inevitably encounter the problems of co-ordination and of an influx of temporary workers and supervisors. And only the most accurate of planning could ensure that homes and jobs were transferred simultaneously and that commuting problems would not occur. Naturally if the relocation was over a much greater distance than the 42 miles involved here, commuting would be impossible and a different range of problems would present themselves. It is as well to think ahead of contingencies to be met if planning does prove inaccurate.

Two other developments encountered by Birds may well be experienced in other relocations. One is increasing unionisation and the other is intra-management rivalry. These are obviously linked problems, arising from the tendency of a relocation to increase the work dependence of transferred employees,[35] particularly if the move is to a small town with little alternative employment for the men.

---

[33] Indeed, many employees still took the precaution of joining a trade union for the first time. See Chapter 4.
[34] See Chapter 7.
[35] Wilensky has also noted that geographical mobility within one firm strengthens the employee's commitment to it; 'Work, Careers, and Social Integration', p. 556.

Conclusions

But the intensity of the managerial struggles between the 'thrusters' and the 'dependables' or 'sleepers' derives from another source. Relocating companies are modernising companies, and thus are changing in many ways at the time of the relocation. New types of manager are needed for the new functions and skills but these men co-exist with the older, less educated, more settled staff. As at Birds, management may polarise, with each extreme finding a group consciousness concerned to defeat the strategies of the other. At Birds, the relocation came at a critical stage of the rivalry, with neither group having achieved dominance. The crucial decision of whether to discharge managers thought to be inefficient was thus ducked and postponed until after the move, thereby creating a much worse situation. The top managements of modernising companies often seem to feel the need for periodic purges; relocation will certainly crystallise dilemmas about this. This, too, is a problem to be faced by those who propose to relocate.

THE DESIRABILITY OF THIS INDUSTRIAL RELOCATION

There is one final aspect of this case-study of industrial relocation to be considered, and that is its overall desirability. I cannot claim to give a final answer on this point because I have not considered the effects of other policy alternatives to the problem of relieving urban and industrial congestion. Nor have I investigated all the effects of this particular policy. But one or two of the effects of this relocation can contribute to an overall analysis of the problem. First let us consider the beneficial effects.

The most important apparent desirable consequence of the Birds relocation was that nearly 650 households and 2,000 people were moved out of the Birmingham area, releasing their housing for other users.[36] Moreover, their jobs, nearly 700 of them, were moved out too, and the company's considerable expansion programme has begun to take place well away from the congested conurbation of Birmingham. However, because of a loophole in planning controls, neither fact contributed anything to the alleviation of Birmingham's overcrowding problems. Birmingham Corporation did not have the power to stop another company from buying and using the Birds factory. This loophole will be

[36] Only 11 per cent of movers did not vacate their accommodation completely. This is in marked contrast to the 46 per cent of London overspill tenants whom Cullingworth found did this. 'Household splitting' would seem, then, to occur only when the migrants were living before their move in grossly overcrowded accommodation and is not therefore undesirable from a town planning point of view. See Cullingworth, *Memorandum to the Milner Holland Committee*, and Chapter 1 above.

discussed later on. Obviously if industrial relocation is to be used as a method of solving conurbation problems, it must be filled. If this had been done, a not inconsiderable step toward easing the burden of housing, industrial, and other overcrowding in Birmingham would have been taken by the Birds relocation alone. It would not take a large number of such relocations to remove that burden.

The second beneficial effect was on the town of Banbury. Whether the general effect of Birds on Banbury was desirable is a complex question which is not investigated here. But in one respect the Birmingham overspill that Banbury received had one great advantage over that received in all other known overspill schemes: it contained a fairly balanced age-structure. The balance was obviously a consequence of the success the company had in persuading most of its employees to move. I have argued that the younger men moved because the company seemed to offer career advancement[37] (within the company for manual workers, and partly outside of it for office workers), and the older men because security was offered. As I have also argued, there will be many other companies able to do the same, and so there should be more age-balanced overspill groups in the future.

The third, and last, major beneficial effect was felt by the group of movers who said they were 'pleased' that Birds had relocated – about half of the movers in fact. Many of them desired to get away from Birmingham, and while Birmingham remains congested and while there remains 'class conflict' within its housing market, it is to be expected that there will be many more of its present residents who would also like to move away. I produced evidence to suggest that there may be a general desire among modern English people for low-density living. This can be reconciled with their shopping and social needs by high-speed communication and transport facilities. Certainly, if these desires were general in the population and were catered for, then the whole of the area between London and Birmingham, for example, would consist of 'urban sprawl' – but then if this is what is wanted, should it not be planned for?

The disadvantages of the relocation were felt most severely by the non-movers. Only 5 per cent of them – and for very idiosyncratic reasons – said they were pleased at the move. The rest had suffered a disruption of some sort. Yet we saw in Chapter 8 that only a few of them had suffered severely as a result of leaving the company.

We also saw that the other half of the movers were not 'pleased' with the move, and their lives too had undergone disruption. But as time passed

---

[37] A few of them actually moved for housing advancement, but this has been so of a much larger proportion in other overspill schemes. See Chapter 2.

in their new locality, all but a few seemed to accept, and even enjoy, the consequences of their move.

It is true that the majority of the sample were not pleased with the move, and that if we considered only their short-term interests we would have to decide against industrial relocation as a means of solving congestion problems. But in the long-run it might be found that all the movers – who, after all constituted three-quarters of the labour force – benefit from a move which might ensure the continued prosperity of their employer as well as probably their own. Above all, we must remember that advantages have accrued, as a result of the Birds relocation, to many people outside the company. The fact that they too benefit seems to have made this particular relocation desirable as well as successful. I have already argued that its success can be repeated by other companies – is it desirable that public policy should encourage other relocations? Finally, then, I will consider the implications of this case-study for the public policy issues discussed in Chapter 1.

INDUSTRIAL RELOCATION AND PUBLIC POLICY

Little support can be given to the policy of rebuilding the conurbations at high-densities. As I have already remarked, there existed in this sample an almost uniform desire for low-density living, for a semi-detached or detached house with a garden in a residential area of similar houses. Furthermore, few of the sample felt any great tie to local conurbation 'communities'. Half the movers were in any case glad to get out of the Birmingham conurbation, while very few mentioned the break with family, friends or Birmingham community as being a disadvantage of the move. Nor were many of the non-movers motivated by a strong desire to retain community ties. Nearly all were employees without much dependence upon the company, while council house tenants (i.e. those who had already attained their desired housing advancement) were over-represented among them. In particular, we saw that a majority of those in the sample who lived in the traditional working-class areas of Birmingham did not even like their supposed 'communities'. An improvement in housing conditions in those areas, through rebuilding at relatively high densities, would reduce this dislike but not remove it, for it was based partly on a dislike of the other inhabitants. This in turn proved to be partly but not wholly based on racialism. In these attitudes the sample is probably not untypical of conurbation populations in general. The attractions for professional and managerial groups of living in west central London should not blind us to the fact that probably this does not extend to other groups, nor other

235

conurbations – elsewhere the attractiveness of a residential area is probably positively correlated to its distance from the conurbation centre. Thus there are probably no compelling social reasons why public policy should centre on rebuilding the conurbations at high densities.

My results also support the notion widespread among planners that fringe overspill is a 'second-best' policy. While my sample wanted 'suburban' living they did not appear to demand that this be as close as possible to their former residence. The distance of about 40 miles between Banbury and their former residence was not too great for the vast majority of movers to maintain the relations they desired with family and friends. The development of the 'modified extended family' and the spread in car and telephone ownership have probably eliminated the social benefits of short-distance overspill. If, in the absence of social benefits, economic costs of transport and employment congestion are incurred through fringe overspill, this surely renders it an unattractive policy, justifiable only if industry can prove the necessity for a central conurbation location. If locational analysis did conclude that most factories and offices in the conurbations should remain there, both high-density rebuilding and fringe housing overspill would remain practicable alternative policies.

At the moment, however, the case for industrial immobility is not proved. Even if it were, we would still have a situation where, while much of the population was prepared to move out of the conurbation to solve their own congestion problems, they were either prevented from doing so or were forced to commute back to the central areas after they moved by industry's attitude. There is thus a very strong case for making industry pay for the congestion it causes in the form of a differential location tax. If one of the objects of such a tax were to force industry to comply with the wishes of its employees to move out, the tax might well be assessed on numbers employed rather than floor-space occupied. The economics of industrial location would certainly be changed by such a tax. Moreover, some writers have suggested that a sleepy conservatism, unrelated to economic considerations, is at the root of industry's attitude – a light tax might then be the kind of sharp, but not too painful, jab needed to wake up a sleeping giant. It seems worth exploring.

If overspill to new and expanded towns is the policy most in accord with people's preferences, what form should it take? Industrial relocation seems to have two advantages over housing relocation. First, if it is successful, i.e. if most of the labour force accepts transfer, a balanced age-structure results. I have tried to show in what circumstances this success can be achieved, concluding that many of the organisations likely to consider relocation will also be likely to achieve success. Secondly, it is a rather easier policy to administer. It is far easier to plan for the reception

236

of migrants in large batches through industrial relocation schemes than in a stream of individual rehoused families; much of the organisation of the relocation becomes an internal matter for the firm concerned; and the vagaries of the Industrial Selection Scheme became less critical hurdles to surmount than they are in housing overspill.[38] Yet there appear at first sight to be two disadvantages to offset these: the fact that in industrial relocation those overspilled are not those in the greatest housing need, and many of them are likely to be less pleased about the move than housing overspillees.

The first point applies more to working-class than middle-class migrants, for few of the latter will be in dire housing need whatever the form of the overspill. But whereas most of the manual workers recruited through Industrial Selection Schemes will be council house applicants in overcrowded under-equipped dwellings in the conurbation, the housing conditions of workers transferred with their employer will more resemble a cross-section of working-class housing, with only a minority in serious housing need. Industrial relocation does not necessarily solve the housing problem though it obviously relieves congestion. The crux of the matter is surely whether 'household splitting' occurs. If it does, then little contribution is made to serious housing problems – while the average occupancy rate of dwellings in good condition is pushed down still further. If it does not – if the worker's former dwelling is left empty – then provided other policies prevent further immigration to the conurbations we can assume that a chain of housing moves will be set in motion culminating in a reduction of overcrowding. 'Household splitting' can occur anywhere along this chain, but in this case it occurred in only a small minority of the relocating households themselves. This is some evidence towards dismissing the first objection to industrial relocations. Housing problems may be alleviated without initially rehousing those in greatest housing need.

The second objection, that transferred workers are less likely to welcome a move than rehoused migrants, has more validity. In rehousing schemes the migrant is offered an incentive to move but he is only prevented from continuing his present existence if his dwelling is to be forcibly demolished. Thus his move is more voluntary than that of the transferred worker who is offered a disincentive to stay behind, namely to lose his job, but no positive incentive to move – by moving he maintains his present circumstances but does not improve them. This is an oversimplification, for we have seen that about half the movers in this case-study thought that they had improved their circumstances, mostly by achieving

[38] In this case the Scheme was felt to be inefficient by the recruitment managers of the company who estimated that it took up to six months of elaborate negotiating to recruit one man.

housing advancement. Nevertheless, the other half did not, which suggests less positive satisfaction with overspill than is usually found in schemes centring on rehousing.[39] It is only a partial answer to say that very few of the movers felt positive dissatisfaction about the move, for nearly all the non-movers were dissatisfied (understandably so in view of their difficulties in finding comparable employment). There is, in fact, no way of avoiding this disadvantage of industrial relocation which must be weighed against the advantages already mentioned in any final decision between the two overspill policies.

It may be that the issue will be decided by the exigencies imposed by the need to persuade industry to relocate. A differential location tax might be the 'stick' to wield at industrialists, but perhaps 'carrots' might alone overcome their reluctance. A propaganda exercise similar to that conducted in London by the Location of Offices Bureau might persuade industry of the advantages of a new, decongested environment without any need of sanctions. And an effective part of such an exercise would undoubtedly be the assurance that trained employees would be likely to accept transfer, many of them gladly. Industry would probably want to transfer its labour force, and this might well be the deciding factor in favour of a policy of centring overspill on the relocation of employers of labour. Planners are now calling for the co-ordination of overspill programmes, that is for closer links between the relocation of jobs, houses and social amenities.[40] Effective co-ordination may result through basing overspill on industrial relocation.

However, two specific problems emanating from industrial relocation must be dealt with by public policy. Both involve the allocation of public funds to overspill. The first arises from the fact that when a company relocates from a conurbation its vacant premises can be used for similar industrial or commercial purposes by another company. The only way of stopping this occurring is for the local authority to buy the premises in the open market, and at the moment it rarely has the funds available for this purpose. Thus, the Birds relocation has probably contributed little to the alleviation of Birmingham's congestion because the Birds factory and offices have been bought and used by other companies. Whether I.D.C. and O.D.P. policy can be amended to prevent this, and whether money for site purchase is to come from the funds of local or central government, clearly something has to be done to prevent this generally happening.[41]

The second financial problem derives from the costs incurred by the

[39] E.g. the satisfaction reported in the study by Sykes *et al.*, *Cumbernauld '67*.
[40] See, for example, *East Anglia: A study*, p. 10.
[41] This problem is discussed in West Midlands Economic Planning Council, *The West Midlands: Patterns of Growth*, pp. 25–29, and in South East Economic Planning Council, *A Strategy for the South East*, p. 51.

relocating company itself. In this case-study, the company justified the expense of the move itself in terms of the expansion and higher productivity obtained at the new location. Yet the costs of the move itself and the special costs incurred in inducing employees to transfer were considerable.[42] The small firm might find itself unable to afford such expenditure, particularly as regards the cost of obtaining expertise on various aspects of the move.[43] There is thus a strong case for some public provision of advice and expertise to firms similar to that provided in London by the Location of Offices Bureau.

In these two instances, industrial relocation policy will cost more than the public exchequer seems to have realised. All public policies have unintended consequences – these are relatively minor ones. Rather more severe, though only in the long-term, are the trends toward increasing the concentration in the conurbations of 'problem' sections of the population.

Whether we concentrate on relocating jobs or housing, three main social groups are under-represented in the reception areas, and could eventually be over-represented in the conurbations. These are the older unskilled worker (i.e. over 40), the coloured worker, and those of retirement age. All three form a much lower proportion of migrants to all the New and Expanded Towns than of the population of the country as a whole. Even when jobs as well as dwellings are relocated these trends remain, though weakened. Just as those of retirement age are not generally on local authority housing lists, they are only rarely in employment. However, more will relocate indirectly through factory relocation, as we saw in this case, for where middle-aged workers are transferred their households will contain more grandparent pensioners than will those of younger workers. Moreover, even among the middle-aged unskilled workers a higher proportion will probably accept job transfer than is normally found in housing overspill schemes. It was only those in this sample who already possessed adequate council housing in Birmingham who were unlikely to relocate, and this made little impact on the relocating propensity of the whole middle-aged group.

However, the coloured worker represents a different kind of problem. Very few coloured families have yet acquired the necessary residence qualifications for acceptance on a council house waiting-list, and thus very few have moved to the New and Expanded Towns.[44] This barrier to

---

[42] Birds paid out on average about £500 on personnel policies to relocate one employee.
[43] And the 1967–8 Annual Report of the *Location of Offices Bureau*, found that smaller firms were more likely to abandon the idea of decentralisation once they had considered it (pp. 38–9).
[44] See Sample Census 1966, Great Britain, *Commonwealth Immigrants Tables* (H.M.S.O., 1969) Table 1.

their movement is absent in the case of industrial relocation, but in this case very few of the coloured workers did accept the opportunity to move to Banbury. Indeed, the coloured workers were almost unique in their relative attachment to their local Birmingham communities, and this is what prevented their relocation. But, of course, we cannot say that they are 'immobile' – most have already moved thousands of miles to advance their standard of living, severing original community ties in the process. The reason for rejecting the relocation offer given by the few coloured workers in this sample was not that they were opposed to any kind of movement away from their Birmingham community, but that Banbury was not a congenial destination because it did not already contain a coloured community. An all-white English small town appeared to offer them a harsh alien environment: as one of them said 'I don't want to be stared at all my life.' This attitude perpetuates a vicious circle, of course: if coloured workers will not move to New and Expanded Towns because coloured people do not already live there, how can any coloured people ever live there?[45]

This represents an increasing social problem confronting regional planners. Many are already aware of the special problems posed by inner London whose population is increasingly composed of the highest and the lowest social strata. In the other conurbations, the highest stratum is tending to move out in similar proportions to the rest of the middle class. Now we have seen that many young and many skilled and semi-skilled manual workers are likely to join the emigration. Among those who are left the elderly, the confirmed unskilled (i.e. those in unskilled jobs in middle age or beyond) and the coloured are tending to be over-represented.[46] Thus, whether long-distance overspill is centred on housing or on jobs it may lead to a concentration of 'social problems' in the conurbations. Perhaps we should look to the experience of the American cities as a warning not against traffic congestion but against poverty and race war.

In this book I have shown that the New and Expanded Towns policy can be justified on the grounds of popular preferences, and I have also argued the case for basing overspill on genuine industrial relocation. My evidence thus gives support to those planners who wish to fulfil the overspill schemes at present projected and to exert more pressure on industrialists to relocate. If their plans are adopted, however, all the possible

---

[45] We may note that in an American case-study of factory relocation between towns which both possessed large Negro populations, the Negro workers were *more* likely to relocate than the whites (because of their greater fear of unemployment). See Gordon and McCorry 'Plant Relocation and Job Security . . .'.

[46] This worrying trend is briefly noted in *A Developing Strategy for the West Midlands*, p. 33.

consequences must be considered and, if necessary, policy must be amended. It seems that one serious consequence of the overspill programme may be the strengthening of 'ghetto' situations in the conurbations. If this is considered undesirable, and the overspill programme is to be continued, amendments will have to be introduced to the programme. The most obvious amendment would be the adoption of a 'quota' system for overspill, whereby a certain proportion of houses or jobs were offered to coloured people. An alternative would be to offer greater inducements to relocate to firms employing a large proportion of coloured workers. Quota systems, formal or informal, are of course political dynamite (though no-one objects to the fact that for years New Town planners have discussed and implemented quota housing schemes to boost the number of pensioners resident there). Furthermore, such a policy would have an effect on existing policy. For example, we have seen that some of the workers in this study accepted transfer to get away from coloured people. What would be their reaction if coloured people were also to be transferred?

All this serves to emphasise that social planning problems are unfailingly complex and never-ending. Each policy adopted causes chain reactions in other areas, and modifies the existing 'market' in which the population makes its choices about housing, community, job etc. Thus continual research into financial costs, and popular and interest-group preferences must be undertaken by those who seek to plan for people. The planners have been doing this for some time now, but to date their sociological expertise seems to have been limited to the use of sample social surveys. Yet we have seen throughout this study that the results of sample surveys can be utilised more if we can fit them into an overall framework of sociological theory. I hope, then, to have shown that applied sociology – sociology which can be of use to the population in general – must be theoretical as well as empirical.

Appendix

The two main interview surveys took place in December 1964–January 1965 and February–March 1967, before and after the company's main relocation. The first survey was preceded by a pilot survey which was relatively flexible in form as the interview schedule changed somewhat between first and last interviews. The pilot sample of 40 and the full sample of 300 were drawn by the same method. At that time the company's personnel cards were grouped by department. Within each department the arrangement of cards was alphabetical. The sampling method was to make use of the departmental grouping to ensure representativeness of the jobholders selected in the sample, but to select randomly within departments. The pilot sample consisted of every thirtieth employee card, and the full-scale sample of every fourth one.

In the full-scale survey interviews were requested of these 300 people. The first questionnaire, although taking at least half an hour to complete, was fully answered by 274, and partial answers were obtained from another 6. Moreover, some details on all 300 were obtainable from company records. Thus the response rate never fell below 90 per cent and on some issues was 100 per cent.

Though Survey 1 was intended as a pre-move survey, the sample in fact included a few employees who had already moved into the Banbury area.[1] This was impossible to avoid, for the research started only in the summer of 1964, at which point some employees had already moved. Thus the questionnaire took two basic forms according to whether the respondent had already moved. If he or she had done so than every attempt was made through the questions to reconstruct the person's situation before the move as well as to probe reactions to the new environment.

The questionnaire was administered by an interviewer who recorded the answer without additional prompting. Half the hourly rated (manual) respondents were seen in works premises during their working hours, and half at home. All the salaried respondents except two were seen at home (these two specially requested to be seen in their offices as their homes were in turmoil just before the move). It was anticipated that dif-

[1] See Chapter 5 for an explanation of this.

242

ferences between the manual worker groups seen at home and work would emerge, but this did not happen.[2] No notice has therefore been taken of the place of interview in the analysis. A third of the interviews were conducted by myself. The remainder were divided among seven students who counted the work as part of the practical work necessary to secure the Oxford University Diploma in Social and Administrative Studies. There was no significant interviewer bias.

The same sample was used for the post-move survey. Much less information than in the first survey was needed, and this made possible a questionnaire short enough to be sent through the post. Two variations on the questionnaire form are included later in this Appendix; one for movers still with the company (slightly varied for those who had moved and then left), and a second for non-movers. The response after two reminding letters was 70 per cent and I then visited the address of all non-respondents, bringing the total response to 93 per cent. There were only 2 actual refusals, the remaining non-respondents being people who had moved to an unknown address. It is significant that 11 of the 20 actual refusers in Survey 1 consented to fill in the second questionnaire – familiarity seemed to lead to helpfulness on their part (though one person who had co-operated in the first survey refused in the second). Thus 88 per cent of the sample completed in full both questionnaires.

The company had agreed during relocation negotiations to accept new employees recruited through Banbury's Industrial Selection overspill arrangement with the (then) London County Council.[3] A small-scale postal survey was made of these employees, and some of the results are included in Chapter 7. One in four of all London overspill employees at 1 December 1966 were randomly selected, yielding 38 persons, all men. Thirty of them filled in the questionnaire. Five of the non-respondents had moved back to London, and thus this sample may be slightly biassed.

The number of men who stayed in Birmingham was small, and additional unstructured interviews were made with non-movers not in the sample. But this information cannot be added to the survey results for statistical purposes, and is used only illustratively, like the material deriving from the tape-recorded interviews with a small number of the movers in their new homes.

---

[2] Tests were conducted on their attitudes to the company (question 85, Survey 1), their intending moving decisions (question 1, Survey 1), and their attitude to the area they were living in (question 88, Survey 1). No differences were observed in the replies of the two groups.

[3] Thus these men were accepted for employment by the company before they were allocated council housing by the Banbury authorities. See Chapter 5.

The results of the two interview surveys form the main bulk of the evidence from the case-study. Thus the adequacy and representativeness of the sample must be convincingly demonstrated.

It is ironic that the major defect of the sample stems from its very representativeness. Drawn from all sections of the firm, it includes the major sub-groups in exactly their proportions in the total labour force of the company – 36 per cent women, 21 per cent salaried male staff and 43 per cent male manual workers. But more careful preparation (and the timetabling above shows that the first survey was very rushed) would have made clear the fact that the moving decisions of women employees were relatively uninteresting, being almost entirely predictable (see the beginning of Chapter 7). In fact, women are barely considered at all in this thesis, which is rather a waste of 36 per cent of my sample. Rather small numbers in the interesting sub-groups (the hallmark of the graduate student's thesis) are the result. Thus the numbers are often inadequate for cross-tabulating three or four variables at once. Moreover, small numbers also make it rather difficult to obtain acceptable levels of significance for *chi*-squared tests, which are, of course, very susceptible to sample size. But many of the interesting findings of the study are actually absences of relationships, where from previous studies, we might expect very strong ones to emerge, and thus the comparative smallness of the sample is not such a great disadvantage.

Turning from the question of adequacy to representativeness, we must ask two questions, was the sample, and were the respondents in the sample, typical of the labour force? We will answer these questions by looking for sample bias on the most important variable, the actual relocation decision of the employees. We want to know whether the sample and the respondents contained the same proportion of movers and non-movers as the whole labour force. This is actually a very complicated matter, raising an important methodological issue not only for this study but for all other relocation studies.

It can easily be said that a certain number of the male employees moved with the company. But it is very difficult to estimate what proportion of the labour force this represents. If the warning of the move and the entire relocation itself had occurred on the same day, there would be no problem and only two categories, 'movers' and 'non-movers' (apart, that is, from the few employees commuting to Banbury from their old address). But, as in the other relocations described in Chapter 2, the length of the planning period of a relocation introduces further groups. In this case three and a half years elapsed from the first warning to the last job relocation.

244

During this period many employees left and were replaced. In the case of non-manual employees the replacements were also entitled to move. So now a third category emerges, and if we simply take the number moving as a percentage of the total labour force (assuming that to be constant) to represent our final proportion of movers to non-movers, we take no account of the doubtless biassed selection process at work during these years. Moreover, can we even be sure that all those who left the company in this period did so as a consequence of the move? Some could be part of 'normal' labour turnover, and we should therefore allow for the effects of this fourth group.

The problem is slightly different for manual and non-manual workers. The company was finally committed to relocating at the beginning of 1963, and no manual worker who joined the company after about the beginning of 1964 was at first eligible to move. Between these dates, practically no workers were recruited on a permanent job basis. So the proportion of movers among manual workers with the company at the end of 1962 is not biassed by the selection of replacements. This is not the case with non-manual workers.

With these reservations in mind we can turn to the figures. Table 1 includes three separate populations in its rows. The first two rows contain male labour force totals at 1.12.1962 and 1.12.64 respectively. The second of these acts simply as a check on the third population which is a random sample of employees at 1.12.1964. Let us first study the figures for manual workers alone.

Rows 2 and 3 show fairly similar percentages, indicating that the sample

Table 1: *Moving decisions of male sample and whole labour force[a] (percentages)*

	Hourly-rated men			Salaried men		
	Movers	Non-movers	N	Movers	Non-movers	N
	%	%		%	%	
Row 1						
Whole labour force at 1.12.62	60	40	456	61	39	188[b]
Row 2						
Whole labour force at 1.12.64	63	37	431	88	12	223[b]
Row 3						
Sample selected at 1.12.64	70	30	128	84	16	62

[a] In this respect, there are no biassing problems regarding women. See Chapter 7.
[b] Plus four persons excluded from this analysis who were still commuting between Birmingham and Banbury at 31.12.68.

was only very slightly biassed on the moving/ not moving criterion when it was drawn. But it can also be seen that Population 1 shows a lower proportion of movers than Population 2. The difference is due to the fact that between the two dates 25 men who were eligible to move left the company. The problem comes in deciding how many of these represent normal turnover and how many were leaving because of the move. It proved impossible to locate many of these for interview; at least 12 had left the district by the summer of 1965, most of them being of foreign or Irish extraction. This shows that though they might have objected to Banbury they were not opposed to moving *per se*. Of the rest, nine (i.e. all who could be contacted) were interviewed informally in their own homes. It proved difficult to sort out their reasons for leaving. Even when asked 'Was the move to Banbury the main reason, or one of the reasons for your leaving?', they tended to equivocate. Only four answered definitely 'yes' even to this leading question, while only two had mentioned the move spontaneously as a reason. Most of them were dissatisfied with the particular job they were doing, and had been unable to secure transfer to a better job. The majority were night-shift packers who were finding transfer difficult for the reasons mentioned in Chapter 4. They were also short-service employees, and mostly in their early twenties. In short, they seemed the 'normal turnover type'. It seems safe to say, therefore, that the biassing effects of selective turnover upon the sample of manual workers was minimal. However, it is worth noting that the labour turnover rate for these two years was well down on the normal annual average in the company.[4] So management not only had the satisfaction of moving 60–70 per cent of male manual workers, but also of a lower turnover for two years as a result of the move.

The bias among non-manual males is more serious. Newly joined employees in this group were allowed to move no matter how short their service to the company. Moreover, there was a large turnover among them in the years 1962–5, higher than the previous annual average. This results in a considerable discrepancy between row 1 and rows 2 and 3 (though, again, the similarity of 2 and 3 shows the sample to be fairly representative at the time it was drawn), 61 per cent moving in row 1 and 84 per cent and 88 per cent in 2 and 3. The sample is considerably biassed by the effects of selective turnover among salaried men, and there will be much less discussion of their situation than that of the manual workers.

It is worth adding that these elaborate calculations are of no interest to the company's management: for them it is sufficient to know that at the

---

[4] Because of the extra termination allowance offered to non-movers who continued working with the company until the factory actually shut down.

time of the relocation itself almost all the male staff made the move. Perhaps the efficiency of company in Banbury has suffered from having so many short-service employees in positions of responsibility, but we saw in Chapter 7 that some top management argue the opposite.

Now we must consider the question of a biassed response-rate. Table 2 shows that movers were, in fact, slightly more likely to be interviewed than non-movers. However, this slight bias is rendered less important by the fact that the most important characteristics of the sample which I discuss above are generally those on which I have been able to collect information on the whole sample from company records. Furthermore, we must note that the total response-rate (91 per cent among the men in survey 1, and 88 per cent in both surveys) is extremely high.

Only two persons in the sample told me relocation decisions in Survey 1 which subsequently proved unreliable: one man said that he would move, but did not in fact do so, and one woman moved after having said she would not. In addition, 27 employees said they were still undecided about the relocation in the survey, and these later split into 17 movers and 10 non-movers – almost exactly the same proportion as in the rest of the sample.

Table 2: *Response rate in Survey 1 by actual moving decision – men only[a]*

| | Movers | | Non-movers | | All | |
	N	%	N	%	N	%
Respondents	132	93.6	42	84	174	91.1
Non-respondents	9	6.4	8	16	17	8.9
Total	141	100	50	100	191	100

[a] Bias among the women was negligible: 93.3 per cent of the movers were interviewed successfully, compared with 91.1 per cent of the non-movers (N = 109).

ADDITIONAL TABLES: VIEWS ON THE RELOCATION POLICY

Table 3: *Sample: moving decision by suggestions made for further help to movers. Survey 1, question 72* [a]

	Number of suggestions made concerning							
	More help with housing	More help with travelling	More information	More money	Allowance scales unfair	Other	Total suggestions	Number of persons
Movers	16	14	11	12	9	21	83	157
Non-movers	3	2	4	1	2	6	18	117
Total	19	16	15	13	11	27	101	274

[a] Men and women have been treated together in these tables – there was no significant difference between them, though women were far less likely to move.

Table 4: *Sample: moving decision by suggestions made for further help to non-movers. Survey 1, question 73*

	Number of suggestions concerning				
	More help in finding other job	Bigger termination allowances	Other	Total suggestions	Number of persons
Movers	13	7	17	37	157
Non-movers	18	9	9	36	117
Total	31	16	26	73	274

Table 5: *Sample: moving decision by opinion of fairness of relocation policy. Survey 1, question 74*

	Company unfair regarding					
	Relocation allowance scale	Travelling allowance scale	Single people	Other	Total mentions	Number of persons
Movers	23	14	2	15	54	157
Non-movers	9	4	6	9	28	117
Total	32	18	8	24	82	274

248

Table 6: *Sample: moving decision by desire for further information on the move.*
Survey 1, question 75

	More information on						Total mentions	Number of persons
	Banbury	Moving dates	Nature of own job	Hours or shifts	Future of company	Other		
Movers	14	8	9	9	8	10	58	157
Non-movers	2	7	5	2	0	4	20	117
Total	16	15	14	11	8	14	78	274

Questionnaires used

This Appendix contains the substance of the main survey questionnaires. For the sake of space, they have been compressed – questions have been occasionally abridged, and many coding categories removed. Only the main pre-move questionnaire and the main post-move questionnaires for movers and non-movers have been reproduced here. This omits the pre-move variant for those already living in Banbury, the variant for the movers who left Birds after they relocated, and the London overspill questionnaire.

The full texts of all the questionnaires can be consulted in the thesis on which this book is based.[1]

Survey 1

1–4 Do you intend to work for Bird's in Banbury? I mean for longer than the starting-up period. Why (not)?

5. *If yes or undecided.* If you do work in Banbury, will you move house or will you stay here?

6. *Movers only.* When will you move?

7. Where are you moving to? Why have you chosen this particular place?

8. Do you like the area where you are living now? Why do you think this?

9. What are the main advantages and disadvantages of Banbury itself as a place to live?

10. Do you know whether the employees already living in the Banbury area like it there? do they like it there? Why?

11. Did you know anything about Banbury before the move was announced? What did you know?

12. Have you visited Banbury since the move was announced? How many times have you visited it?

13. Would a move to the Banbury area mean an overall financial gain or loss for you or wouldn't it make any difference financially? How much difference would it make? Why do you think this?

14. If most of your neighbours were Bird's employees, would you consider this an advantage, a disadvantage, or neither an advantage or a disadvantage?

15. Is your job being transferred to Banbury?

16. When is your job or area being transferred to Banbury?

17. When was the first date that the company asked you to be in Banbury by?

18. *Non-movers only.* How long will you continue working for Bird's? Will you get another job when you do leave? *If no.* Why not?

19. Suppose that the company had not decided to go to Banbury but had gone to any of the following places. Would you have gone with them if they had offered the same assistance? Why (not)? Liverpool, Cardiff, Gloucester.

20. How many employers have you worked for in the last five years?

21. Have you been unemployed in the last ten years? I mean for a month or longer.

22. Have you looked round for another job since first hearing about the move in case you didn't move? *If yes.* Have you actually applied for another job? Where was this job?

23. If you left Bird's now would you have any difficulty finding another job at a similar level of pay in Birmingham?

24. If you left Bird's now would you have any difficulty finding another job at a similar level of pay in Banbury?

25. Can you tell me the names of two companies with factories in Banbury? What are they?

26. Are you, married, single, widowed, divorced/separated?

27. Does your wife (husband) go out to

[1] M. Mann, *Sociological Aspects of Factory Relocation: a Case Study* (University of Oxford, D. Phil. thesis, 1970).

work? Does she (he) work full or part time? Does she (he) work at Bird's? How much does she (he) earn per week? £5, £6.10, £11.20, £20+?
Have you attempted to get her (him) a job at Bird's so that you would be able to move more easily?
If yes. What happened? *If no.* Why not?

28 Have you any children who live here with you? How many? Are they at school, are they working, or are they looking for work? Where? How much do they earn?

29 Have you any children who don't live here? How many? *If yes.* Where do they live? How far is that from here? How regularly, if ever, do you (or your wife/husband) visit any of them, or do any of them visit you (or your wife/husband)? More than once a week, once a week, once a month, less, never.
When was the last time? Last week, last month, longer.

30 What do you think would be the effects of a move nearer Banbury on your children? (*Except Banbury sample*)

31 *Banbury sample only.* What do you think has been the effect on your children of this move?

32 Is there anyone else living with you in this household? Anyone at all, including relations, friends, or lodgers.
If yes. Who? Are any of them working full or part time? If so, how much do they earn per week?

33 Have you tried to get any of these or anyone else (apart from your wife/husband) a job at Bird's so that you would be able to move more easily?
If yes. Who did you try to get a job, and what happened?

34 *Movers only.* Is there anyone at present living in your household who isn't moving with you?
If yes. Who, and where will they live?

35 Where do your parents live? (Including your wife's/husband's parents)

36 How regularly, if ever, do you (or your husband/wife) visit any of them, or do any of them visit you (or your wife/husband)? (I mean those that don't live here.) More than once a week, once a week, once a month, less, never.

37 Where do your three best friends live? How far away is this?

38 When was the last time that you (or your wife/husband) visited one of them or when one of them visited you (or your wife/husband)? Last week, last month, longer.

39 Are any of these three Bird's employees? How many?

40 Have you any other relations working for Bird's? How many?

41 Do you go to church or to the meetings of any other religious organisation?
If yes. Which, and when did you last attend a service? C of E, other prot., R.C., other (specify). Last week, last month, last year, longer.

42 Have you been to a meeting of club or association in this area in the last year? I mean any sports, social, or political club, apart from a trade union.
If yes. Which club(s) and when did you last attend a meeting (of each)?

43 Do you ever go out for your entertainment or do you always stay at home?
If out. When you do go out for entertainment, where do you go out to? For each item, tell me when was the last time you did it (and whether you would be able to do it in Banbury). Item, last week, last month, longer, in Banbury.

44 How long does it take you to get from your home to work? – 15 min, 16–30 min, 31–60 min, 60+ mins.

45 Where were you born? How far away from here is that? – 1 mile, 1–5 miles, 6–10 miles, 11–30 miles, 30+ miles.

46 How long have you lived in this house/flat? Whole life, 10 + years, 5–10 years, 1–5 years, – 1 year.

47 Where did you move from when you came here? How far away from here is that? – 1 mile, 1–5 miles, 6–10 miles, 11–30 miles, 30 + miles.

48 Why did you move here?

49 How many moves have you made in the last 5 years?

50 Has this house/flat got an indoor toilet? a bathroom with h and c running water? an unshared garden?

51 How many bedrooms has it got?

52 Can you give me details of what your present accommodation costs you? Are you Buying, renting from the council, renting privately, living rent free, paying board and lodging.

53 What do you have to pay in: Rent, rates, water rates, ground rent, mortgage, other (specify), total?

54 *If renting privately* is it furnished or unfurnished? Is it controlled or decontrolled? I mean can the landlord put up the rent when he wants to? Are you responsible for interior decorating? Are you on a council house waiting list, and when, if ever, do you think you will be successful?

55 *If buying.* When did you come into the ownership of this house/flat?

56 How much was it worth when you came into the ownership?

57 How much do you think it is worth now?
58 Is it freehold or leasehold?
If lease. When does the lease run out?
59 Could you get a similar house in the Banbury area for about the same price as this would fetch?
60 *If no.* Would it cost more or less, or wouldn't you be able to get a similar house at all there? How much more or less?
61 Do you mind if I get details of your income from Bird's?
62 Have you any income from other sources? How much from: spare time earnings, income from lodgers, pensions, interest or dividends, rent from property, family allowance, other (specify), total?
63 Have you any savings put by in cash, in a bank, in savings certificates or premium bonds, with a building society, or in stocks and shares? If you have, could you tell me the approximate amount that you (and your wife/husband) have altogether? Is it: Less than £50, £51–100, £101–500, £500 + ?
64 (a) Do you own or rent any of these things? Car, T.V., washing machine, refrigerator.
  (b) *Banbury sample only.* Did you also own or rent these where you lived before?
65 Have you any hire purchase commitments?
If yes. How much are you paying out altogether? Is it: − £1 per week, £1–3 £4–6, £6 + ?

Movers only

66 Do you intend to buy a house, will you rent from the council, rent privately, or live in your family home?
67 *If buying.* What is the price range for a house that you are looking for?
  − £2500, £2501–3000, £3001–4000, £4001–5000, £5000 + .
68 Have you already bought a plot of land or a house?
If yes. How much have you paid, for the land? for the house?
If no. Are you at present engaged in negotiations for a house or plot of land?
70 *If renting.* How much do you intend to pay in rent per week? − £2.10s, £2.10s.–£3, £3–£4, £4 + .
71 What are you doing with your present accommodation when you move? *If buying,* Are you selling it? *If renting.* Is your family vacating it completely?

72 Is there any other assistance you would like the company to give to those who are moving? What other assistance would you like them to give?
73 Is there any other assistance you would like the company to give those who aren't moving? What other assistance would you like them to give?
74 Do you think that the company is being fair to everyone in its relocation policies? Why do you think this?
75 Is there anything you want to know about Banbury or about the move which the company hasn't told you? What is this?
76 What happens to your pension rights if you don't move?
77 The company gives everyone who moves a relocation allowance, a lump sum to cover all expenses of moving which are not readily identified. How much relocation allowance would you receive if you were to move? (How much have you received?)
78 Are you an hourly rated, a weekly salaried, or a monthly salaried employee?
79 What is your present job at Bird's?
80 What are your hours of work?
82 Are there any hours or shifts you wouldn't like to work, or don't like working? Which are these? Why?
83 Is your present job your normal job, have you been moved on to it from your normal job, or have you been moved about between several jobs recently (in the last two weeks)?
If several moves. Have you a normal grade? What is it?
If moved from normal job. When, if ever, do you expect to be moved back to your normal job? What is your normal job? Is there any difference in pay between this job and your normal job? How much?
84 *If has already left Bird's.* Why did you leave? What is your present job? What was your last job at Bird's? Are you getting paid more, less, or the same as at Bird's? How much more (or less)?
85 What do you think of Bird's as a company to work in?
86 Has your attitude to Bird's become more or less favourable, or has it remained the same, since you started working here?
If more or less. In what way has it?
87 Has your attitude to Bird's become more or less favourable, or has it remained the same, as a result of the way it has handled this move?
If more or less. In what way has it?
88 How do you feel about the job you do

at Bird's? Are you satisfied, dissatisfied, or don't you feel strongly either way about it? Why?

89 How do you feel about the work your department is doing? Are you satisfied? Dissatisfied? Or don't you feel strongly either way about it?

90 Is your pay good, average, or bad?

91 Is the security of your job good, average, or bad?

92 Do your supervisors do a good job, an average job, or a bad job?

93 Do promotion prospects matter to you? Are they good, average, or bad?

94 Do you feel that there is too much pressure on you at Bird's to get the work out?

95 Should trade unions have a place at Bird's? Why do you think this?

96 Do you think that the company wants the unions to have a place at Bird's? Why do you think this?

97 Would you mind telling me if you are a member of a trade union? Which one?

98 Taking everything into consideration, are you pleased that Bird's decided to move, or would you have preferred to remain working for them in Birmingham? Why?

99 Is there anything else you'd like to say about the move?

Survey 2: Movers (postal questionnaire)

1 Are you pleased you moved with Bird's? Yes, no, not sure.

2 Do you want to go back to the Birmingham area? Yes, no, not sure.

3 What are the most important advantages and disadvantages of having moved? Please indicate which advantage and which disadvantage is the most important.

4 Do you like the area where you live? Yes, no, not sure.

5 How often, if ever, do you visit the Birmingham area? Never, every week, every month, less.

6 How often, if ever, do you meet socially with the following types of people? Never, every week, every month, less. Relations? Bird's employees (not relations or London overspill)? Friends in the Birmingham area? Friends in this area who were born here or have lived most of their lives here? Friends who have moved more recently into this area (and not with Bird's)? London overspill tenants?

7 Do you own or rent any of these things? A car, a television, a refrigerator, a washing machine.

8 When was the last time, if ever, you took part in these local activities? Never, last week, last month, longer ago. Cinema or theatre, dancing, local clubs, sporting activities, pubs, church, exchanging visits with friends, any other activities (please name them).

9 Were you buying a house in the Birmingham area before the move? If you were, what was its selling price?

10 (a) What is the position with your present house? Buying it, renting from Council, renting privately, other (e.g. paying board and lodging),
(b) *If you are buying it*: What was its cost price (including the price of the land if it is freehold)?

11 How much per week are you paying in rent or mortgage and interest payments and in rates and ground rent if any? Add all the payments together.

12 Could you give some details of all the people living here besides yourself? Relationship to yourself (e.g. wife, brother-in-law, etc.) Is he or she working? What are his or her average weekly earnings? If at school give type of school (e.g. primary, secondary modern, etc.).

13 For adults (aged 15 or above) listed above, could you say whether they think they are better off, worse off, or about the same, as a result of the move. For children say whether their parents think the children are.

14 As a result of moving with Birds have you had to; use any savings you had before the move? Sell any of yours, or the family's property? Move house again in the Banbury area? Economise on yours, or on the family's expenses or postpone intended expenditure? Enter into more hire purchase agreements or into loans other than house loans?

15 What is your best estimate of the actual cost to you and your family of your moving, including all expenses directly or indirectly involved, over and above what the company gave you? Nothing, less than £50, £50–100, £100–200, £200–500, more than £500.

16 What do you think of Bird's as a company to work in? Please feel free to reply at length if you want to.

17 Has your attitude to Birds become more or less favourable, or has it stayed the same, as a result of the move?

18 What is the title of your present job? Which department is this in?

19 Are the following aspects of your job good, average or bad? Pay, security, promotion prospects, supervision.

20 Are you now trying to find another job

outside Bird's. Yes, actively; Yes, inactively; no; other comments. Please write here any other comments you would like to make about the move.

Survey 2 – non-movers (postal)

1 Do you wish that you had moved with Bird's after all?
2 Have you now got a job? Full-time or part-time?
3 If you have not got a job, why haven't you?
4 (a) If you have got a job, is it better, worse, or the same as your normal job at Birds in the following details. Pay, security, promotion prospects, General attitude of the company to you.
  (b) All in all, do you prefer your present employment, or that at Bird's? Present, Bird's, undecided.
5 As a result of leaving Bird's, have you had to: Use any savings you had when you left? Sell any of yours, or the

family's property? Move house? Economise on your's or on the family's expenses or postpone intended purchases?

(The remaining questions asked for details of *all* jobs held since leaving Birds.)
6 How long, if at all, were you unemployed before starting this job?
7 How did you get this job (e.g. through Bird's, the Labour Exchange, a friend, etc.)?
8 What was (is) the job title?
9 What town, or district of Birmingham, was (is) the work in?
10 What was (is) the average take-home pay per week.
11 If you were (are) working overtime or shifts, please give details.
12 Why did you leave this job?
13 How long were you employed in it?

Please write here any other comments you would like to make about the move.

Bibliography

Aucott, J. V., 'Dispersal of offices from London', *Town Planning Review*, 31 (1960).

Baldamus, W., *Efficiency and Effort* (Tavistock Publications, 1961).

Bell, C., *Middle Class Families* (Routledge and Kegan Paul, 1969).

Bell, C., Batstone, E. and Murcott, A., 'Voluntary associations in Banbury', unpublished paper, Banbury Social Survey (1968).

Berger, B. M., *Working-class suburb: a study of auto workers in suburbia* (University of California Press, 1960).

Blauner, R., *Alienation and freedom: the factory worker and his industry* (University of Chicago Press, 1964).
  'Work satisfaction and industrial trends in modern society' in W. Galenson and S. M. Lipset (eds.) *Labor and Trade Unionism* (John Wiley, 1960).

Brennan, T., 'Gorbals – A study in redevelopment', *Scottish Journal of Political Economy*, 4 (1957).

Bright, J., *Automation and Management* (Harvard University Press, 1958).

Brown, C. M., 'The Industry of the New Towns of the London Region' in J. E. Martin (ed.) *Greater London: an Industrial Geography* (G. Bell, 1966) pp. 238–52.

Bull, D. A., 'New Town and Town Expansion Schemes: Part I', *Town Planning Review*, 38 (1967).

Cannon, I. C., *The Social Situation of the Skilled Worker* (unpublished Ph.D. thesis, University of London, 1961).

Census, 1961, England and Wales, *Migration Tables* (H.M.S.O., 1966).

Census, 1961 *Oxfordshire County Report* (H.M.S.O. 1964).

City of Birmingham Abstract of Statistics (City of Birmingham Central Statistical Office) (1964) No. 9.

City of Birmingham Development Plan, Approved Statement (1960).

Clark, S. D., *The Suburban Community* (University of Toronto Press, 1966).

Clarke, D. G., *The Industrial Manager – His Background and Career Pattern* (Business Publications, 1966).

Cotgrove, S., 'Alienation and Automation', unpublished paper, University of Bath.

Crossman, E.R.F.W., ''Automation and Skill', D.S.I.R. *Problems of Research in Industry*, No. 9 (1960).

Cullingworth, J. B., *English Housing Trends: a Report on the Rowntree Trust Housing Study* (G. Bell, 1965).
  Housing and Labour Mobility (O.E.C.D., 1969).
  Housing Needs and Planning Policy (Routledge and Kegan Paul, 1960).
  'Memorandum to the Milner Holland Committee', *Housing Review*, 14 (Jan.– Feb. 1965).
  'Overspill in South East Lancashire: The Salford–Worsley Scheme', *Town Planning Review*, 30 (1959).
  'The Swindon Social Survey: Second Report on the Social Implications of

Overspill, *Sociological Review*, 9 (1961).

A Profile of Glasgow Housing (Oliver and Boyd, 1968).

Cutriss, C. H., the *Relocation of industry with reference to both the human and the economic factors*. Report of the proceedings of the Town and Country Planning Summer School (published under auspices of the Town Planning Institute London) (Cambridge, 1955).

Dalton, M., 'Worker response and social background', *Journal of Political Economy*, 55 (1947).

Daniel, W. W., 'Automation and the quality of work', *New Society* (29.5.1969).
Strategies for Displaced Employees (Political and Economic Planning, 1970).

Dennis, N., *People and Planning* (Faber and Faber, 1970).

Department of Employment and Productivity, *Labour Costs in Great Britain* (H.M.S.O. 1968).

Department of Scientific and Industrial Research, *Automation* (H.M.S.O., 1956).

Dobriner, W. M., *Class in Suburbia* (Prentice-Hall, 1964).

Doeringer, P. B., 'Determinants of the structure of industrial type internal labor markets', *Industrial and Labor Relations Review*, 20 (1967).

Dubin, R. 'Industrial Workers' Worlds: a study of the "central life interests" of industrial workers', *Social Problems*, 3 (1956).

Dunning, J. H., *Economic planning and town expansion: a case study of Basingstoke* (W.E.A., 1963).
'Manufacturing industries in the new towns', *Manchester School of Economics and Social Studies*, 28 (1960).

East Anglia Economic Planning Council, *East Anglia: A Study* (H.M.S.O., 1968).

Economist Intelligence Unit. *A Survey of Factors Governing the Location of Offices in the London Area* (Location of Offices Bureau, 1964).

Elias, N. and Scotson, J. L., *The Established and the Outsiders* (Frank Cass, 1965).

Etzioni, A., *A Comparative Analysis of Complex Organisations* (The Free Press, 1961).

Everitt, G. F., 'The First report of the East Anglia Economic Planning Council seen in relation to the London Town Development Programme', *Town and Country Planning Association*, Conference on 'East Anglia – a Study', Bury St. Edmunds, February 1969.

Eversley, D.E.C., 'Social and Psychological Factors in the Determination of Industrial Location' in T. Wilson (ed.) *Papers on Regional Development* (Blackwell, 1965).

Field, D., 'New Town Expansion Scheme: Part II', *Town Planning Review*, (1968).

Firth, R., Hubert, J., and Forge, A., *Families and their Relatives* (Routledge and Kegan Paul, 1969).

Food Manufacturing Economic Development Council, *A Study of Labour Turnover* (National Economic Development Council, 1968).

Fox, A., *The Milton plan* (Institute of Personnel Management, 1965).

Fullan, M., 'Industrial technology and worker integration in the organisation', *American Sociological Review*, 35 (1970).

Gans, H. J., *The Levittowners* (Allen Lane, 1967).

Gavron, H., *The Captive Wife* (Penguin Books, 1966).

Goldthorpe, J. H., Lockwood, D., Bechhofer, F., and Platt, S., *The Affluent Worker: Industrial Attitudes and Behaviour* (Cambridge University Press, 1968).

The Affluent Worker in the Class Structure (Cambridge University Press, 1969).

Gordon, M. S. and McCorry, A. H., 'Plant relocation and job security: a case study', *Industrial and Labor Relations Review*, 11, (1957).

Government Social Survey, *Labour Mobility in Great Britain 1953–1963* (H.M.S.O., March 1966).

Greater London Development Plan, *Report of Studies* (Greater London Council, n.d. – 1968?).

The Guardian, *Moving Out of London* (Manchester Guardian and Evening News Ltd, 1964).

Hall, P., *London 2000* (Faber and Faber, 1963).

'Moving house in the aetiology of psychiatric symptoms', *Proceedings of Royal Society of Medicine* (February, 1964).

Hammond, E., *London to Durham* (University of Durham, Rowntree Research Unit, 1968).

Harvard Business School, Case studies, Labor, Nos. 519 and 520 (1966).

Heraud, B. J., 'Social Class and the New Towns', *Urban Studies*, 5 (1968).

Hole, V., 'The social effects of planned rehousing', *Town Planning Review*, 30 (1959).

Hollowell, P., *The Lorry Driver* (Routledge and Kegan Paul, 1968).

Hubert, J., 'Kinship and geographical mobility in a sample from a London middle-class area', *International Journal of Comparative Sociology*, 6 (1965).

The Hunt Committee, *The Intermediate Areas* (H.M.S.O., 1969) CMND 3998.

Hunter, L. C. and Reid, G. L., *Urban Worker Mobility* (O.E.C.D. 1968).

Ingham, G. K., *Size of Industrial Organisation and Worker Behaviour* (Cambridge University Press, 1970).

Jackson, J. N., 'Dispersal – success or failure', *Journal of the Town Planning Institute*, 45 (1959).

Jansen, C., *Social Aspects of Internal Migration* (Bath University Press, 1968).

Jefferys, M., *Mobility in the Labour Market* (Routledge and Kegan Paul, 1964).

Jephcott, P., *Homes in High Flats* (Oliver and Boyd, 1971).

Kahn, H. R., *Repercussions of Redundancy* (Allen and Unwin, 1964).

Karpik, L., 'Urbanisation et Satisfaction au Travail', *Sociologie du Travail*, No. 2. (1966).

Klein, J., *Samples from English Cultures* (Routledge and Kegan Paul, 1965) Vol. 1.

Kornhauser, A., *The Mental Health of the Industrial Worker* (Wiley, 1965).

Lerner, S. W. and Marquand, J. 'Regional variations in earnings, demand for labour and shop stewards' combine committees in the British engineering industry', *The Manchester School of Economic and Social Studies*, 31, (1963).

Lipset, S. M. *et al*, *Union Democracy* (Free Press, 1956).

Litwak, E., Geographic mobility and extended family cohesion', *American Sociological Review*, 25, No. 3 (1960).

Loasby, B., 'The Experience of West Midlands Industrial Dispersal Projects', *Town and Country Planning* 29 (1961).

Location of Offices Bureau, *Annual Reports* 1965–6, 1966–7, and 1967–8 (L.O.B.).

Offices in a Regional Centre: Follow-up Studies on Infrastructure and Linkages (Location of Offices Bureau, October 1969).

Relocation of Office Staff: a study of the reactions of office staff decentralized to Ashford (L.O.B., March 1969).

White Collar Commuters – A Second Survey (L.O.B., June 1967).

Luttrell, W. F., *Factory Location and Industrial Movement* (National Institute of Economic and Social Research 1962, 2 vols).

McCarthy, W. E. J., 'The role of shop stewards in British industrial relations', *Royal Commission on Trade Unions and Employers' Associations Research Report*, No. 1 (H.M.S.O., 1967).

The Closed Shop in Britain (Basil Blackwell, 1964).

Mallet, S., *La Nouvelle Classe Ouvrière* (Editions du Seuil, 1963).

Mann, F. C. and Hoffman, L. R., *Automation and the Worker* (Henry Holt, 1960).

Mann, M., *Sociological Aspects of Factory Relocation: a Case Study* (University of Oxford, D. Phil thesis, 1970).

Consciousness and Action in the Western Working Class (Macmillan, 1972).

Mercer, D. E. and Weir, D. T. H., 'Orientations to Work among White-Collar Workers' in Social Science Research Council (eds.) *Social Stratification and Industrial Relations* (S.S.R.C. 1969).

Ministry of Labour Gazette (February 1963) 'Redundancy in Great Britain'.

Mogey, J. M., *Family and Neighbourhood* (Oxford University Press, 1956).

Morris, R. N. and Mogey, J., *The Sociology of Housing: Studies at Berinsfield* (Routledge and Kegan Paul, 1965).

Moss, J. A., 'New and Expanded Towns: a survey of the demographic characteristics of the movers', *Town Planning Review*, 39 (1968–9).

Mott, P. E. *et al.*, *Shift Work* (University of Michigan Press, 1965).

Naville, P., 'The Structure of Employment and Automation', *International Social Science Bulletin*, 10 (1958).

Naville, P., *L'automation et le travail humain* (C.N.R.S., 1961)
Vers l'automatisme social? (Gallimard, 1963)

Nicholson, J. H., *New Communities in Britain* (National Council of Social Service, 1961)

Organization for Economic Co-operation and Development, *International Joint Seminar on Geographical and Occupational Mobility at Castelfusant, Italy, 1963*, 2 vols (O.E.C.D., 1964).

Wages and Labour Mobility (O.E.C.D., 1965).

Orzack, L. H., 'Work as a "central life interest' of professionals', *Social Problems*, 7 (1959).

Osborn, Sir F. and Whittick, A., *The New Towns – the answer to Megalopolis* (Leonard Hill, 1963).

Pahl, R., 'Urbs in Rure: the metropolitan fringe in Hertfordshire', *L.S.E. Geographical Papers* No. 2 (1965).

Palmer, G. L. *et al.*, *The Reluctant Job-Changer* (University of Pennsylvania Press, 1962).

Park, R. E. *et al*, *The City* (University of Chicago Press, 1923).

Plowman, D. E. G. *et al.*, 'Local social status in England and Wales', *Sociological Review*, 10 (1962).

Political and Economic Planning, *Thrusters and Sleepers: A P.E.P. Report* (Allen and Unwin, 1965).

Purcell, T. V., *Blue-Collar Man: Patterns of Dual Allegiance in Industry* (Harvard University Press, 1960).

Raimon, R. L., 'The indeterminateness of wages of semi-skilled workers', *Industrial and Labor Relations Review*, 6 (1953).

Rankin, N. H., 'Social Adjustments in a North-West New Town', *Sociological Review*, 11 (1963).

Rees, A. and Schultz, G. P., *Workers and Wages in an Urban Labor Market* (Chicago University Press 1970).

Rex, J. and Moore, R., *Race, Community and Conflict* (Oxford University Press, 1967).

Reynolds, L. G., *The Structure of Labor Markets* (Harper and Row, 1951).

Robinson, D. (ed), *Local Labor Markets and Wage Structures* (Gower Press, 1970).

Rosser, C. and Harris, C., *The Family and Social Change*, (Routledge and Kegan Paul, 1965).

Rossi, P. H., *Why families move: a study in the social psychology of urban residential mobility* (Free Press, Glencoe, 1956).

Royal Commission on Local Government in England, *Research Studies*, No. 9, 'Community Attitudes Survey: England' (H.M.S.O., 1969).

Royal Commission on Trade Unions and Employers' Associations 1965–8, *Report* (H.M.S.O., 1968).

Sample Census 1966, England and Wales, *County Reports: Warwickshire* (H.M.S.O., 1967).

England and Wales, *Housing Tables, Part I* (H.M.S.O., 1968).

England and Wales. *Migration Summary Tables*, 2 vols. (H.M.S.O., 1968 and 1969).

Great Britain, *Commonwealth Immigrants Tables* (H.M.S.O., 1969).

Scargill, D. I., 'Town Expansion at Aylesbury', *Town and Country Planning*, 33 (1965).

Scott, W. H. *et al.*, *Technical Change and Industrial Relations* (Liverpool University Press, 1966).

Self, P. *Cities in Flood* (Faber and Faber, 2nd edition, 1961).

Shankland, Cox and Associates *Ipswich Draft Basic Plan: consultants' proposals for the expanded town* (H.M.S.O., 1968).

Smith, B. M. D., 'Industrial overspill in theory and practice: the case of the West Midlands', *Urban Studies*, 7 (1970).

Smith, C. S., *The Planned Transfer of Labour with Special Reference to the Coal Industry* (University of London, PH.D. thesis, 1961).

Smith, L. M. and Fowler, I. A., 'Plant Relocation and Worker Migration' in A. B. Shostak and W. Gomberg, *Blue-Collar World* (Prentice-Hall, 1964).

Sofer, C., *Men in Mid-Career* (Cambridge University Press, 1970).

South-East Joint Planning Team, *Strategic Plan for the South East* (H.M.S.O., 1970).

Stacey, M., *Tradition and Change: a study of Banbury* (Oxford University Press, 1960).

Swindon: A Study for Further Expansion, a study undertaken by joint teams of officers of Swindon Borough Council, Wiltshire County Council, and Greater London Council, October 1968.

Sykes, A. J. M. *et al.*, *Cumbernauld '67: a Household Survey and Report* (University of Strathclyde, Dept of Sociology, n.d.).

Taylor, G. B., 'Social Problems of New Towns' in P. Kuenstler (ed.) *Community Organization in Great Britain* (Faber and Faber, 1961).

Taylor, Lord and Chave, N. S., *Mental Health and Environment* (Longman Green and Co., 1964).

Taylor, R. C., *The Implications of Migration from the Durham Coalfield: an Anthropological Study* (University of Durham, Ph.D. thesis, 1966). Summarised in his 'Migration and Motivation: a study of determinants and types' in J. A. Jackson (ed.) *Migration* (Cambridge University Press, 1969).

Thomas, R., *Aycliffe to Cumbernauld: a study of seven new towns in their regions* (Political and Economic Planning, 1969).

London's New Towns: a study of self-contained and balanced communities (Political and Economic Planning, 1969).

Touraine, A., *L'évolution du travail ouvrier aux usines Renault* (C.N.R.S., 1955).

La Conscience Ouvrière (Editions du Seuil, 1966).

Touraine, A. and Ragazzi O., *Ouvriers d'Origine Agricole* (Editions du Seuil, 1961).

Town and Country Planning Association, *The Paper Metropolis* (authors, 1962).

London Under Stress (author, 1970).

Townsend, P., *The Family Life of Old People* (Routledge and Kegan Paul, 1957).

Trotman-Dickens, D. I., 'The Scottish Industrial Estates' *Scottish Journal of Political Economy*, 8 (1961).

Turner, A. N. and Lawrence, P. R., *Industrial Jobs and the Worker* (Harvard University Press, 1965).

Turner, H. A. L., Clack, G. and Roberts, G., *Labour Relations in the Motor Industry* (Allen and Unwin, 1967).

University of Liverpool, Department of Social Science, *Urban redevelopment and social change* (Liverpool University Press, 1961).

Walker, C. R. and Guest, R. H., *The Man on the Assembly Line* (Harvard University Press, 1952).

Watson, W., 'Social mobility and social class in industrial communities' in M. Gluckman (ed.) *Closed Systems and Open Minds* (Oliver and Boyd, 1964).

Weber, A. R., 'The interplant transfer of displaced employees' in G. Somers *et al.* (eds.) *Adjusting to technological change* (Harper, 1963).

Wedderburn, D., 'The Conditions of Employment of Manual and Non-Manual Workers' in Social Science Research Council (eds) *Social Stratification and Industrial Relations* (author, 1969).

'Redundancy' in D. Pym (ed) *Industrial Society: Social Sciences in Management* (Penguin Books, 1968).

Redundancy and the Railwaymen (Cambridge University Press, 1965).

White-Collar Redundancy: A Case Study (Cambridge University Press, 1964).

Wedderburn, D. and Crompton R., *Workers Attitudes and Technology* (Cambridge University Press, 1972).

Welford, A. T., 'Ergonomics of Automation', D.S.I.R., *Problems of Research in Industry*, No. 8 (1960).

Westergaard, J. H., 'The Structure of Greater London' in Centre for Urban Studies (eds.) *London: Aspects of Change* (MacGibbon and Kee, 1964).

West Midlands Economic Planning Council, *The West Midlands: Patterns of Growth* (H.M.S.O., 1967).

The West Midlands: an Economic Appraisal (H.M.S.O., 1971).

West Midlands Planning Authorities, *A Developing Strategy for the West Midlands* (West Midlands Regional Study, 1971).

Whitman, E. S. and Schmidt, W. J., *Plant Relocation: a Case History of a Move* (American Management Association, 1966).

Whyte, W. F. *et al. Money and Motivation* (Harper and Row, 1955).

Whyte, W. H., *The Organisation Man* (Penguin Books, 1960).

Wilensky, H. L., 'Orderly careers and social participation: the impact of work history on social integration in the middle mass', *American Sociological Review*, 26 (1961).

'The moonlighter: a product of relative deprivation', *Industrial Relations*, 3 (1963).

'Work, careers and social integration', *International Social Science Journal*, 12 (1960).

Williams, G., *Recruitment to Skilled Trades* (Routledge and Kegan Paul, 1957).

Willmott, P., *The Evolution of a Community: a Study of Dagenham after Forty Years* (Routledge and Kegan Paul, 1963).

'East Kilbride and Stevenage: some social characteristics of a Scottish and an English New Town', *Town Planning Review*, 34 (1964).

Willmott, P. and Young, M., *Family and Class in a London Suburb* (Routledge and Kegan Paul, 1960).

Woodward, J., *Industrial organisation: theory and practice* (Oxford University Press, 1965).

Wragg, M., 'Starting Life in a New Town', *Town and Country Planning*, 19 (1951).

Young, M. and Willmott, P., *Family and Kinship in East London* (Routledge and Kegan Paul, 1957).

Index

age-structure, 9, 13–15, 26–32, 64, 212, 234, 236, 239; of Birds employees, 113, 114, 134–5, 141–3, 154–5, 164, 186–7, 196–8, 234.

Alfred Bird and Sons Ltd (General Foods, Ltd), vii, ix, 68–128, 193–4, 213, 232; *see also* General Foods Corporation, U.S.A.

Ashford, 2, 170
Aucott, J. V., 6
Aylesbury, 28

Baldamus, W., 51, 127
Banbury, vii, 28, 105, 115, 121, 130, 144, 165, 196–201, 234; Borough Council, 105–6, 109–10, 116–17, 144–5; attitudes of Birds employees to, 150, 154–6, 166–7, 173–83, 229–30
Basildon, 198
Bell, C., 10–13, 165, 183
Berger, B. M., 22
Bethnal Green, 13, 19–23, 160–1, 223
Birmingham, vii, 1–7, 45, 66, 68, 85–7, 100, 105, 109, 161, 226–7, 230, 233; City Corporation; 109, 145, 150–2, 233, 255; attitudes of Birds employees to, 150–5, 234–5
Blackburn, R. M., 43
Blauner, R., 53–60, 91, 98–9, 217–19, 223
Board of Trade, 5–7, 105
Brennan, T., 19,
Bright, J., 53, 61, 216
British Aluminium Company, 34–5, 37, 116–17, 212
British Motor Corporation, Ltd, 87, 199, 208, 210–11
Brown, C. M., 28, 30, 37
Bull, D. A., 3

calculative involvement, *see* instrumentalism
Cannon, I. C., 57
Cardiff, 229–30, 250
careers, 10–15, 25, 38, 48–9, 61–3, 65–6, 215–19; at Birds, 134–5, 209, 213, 215, 217, 234
Census, 1961, 9. 145, 161, 197; 1966 sample, 16–17, 145, 239
Chorley-Leyland (new town), 2
Clark, S. D., 22–3
Clarke, D. G., 12
coffee, production, 68–9, 74–5, 79, 117, 122–3, 222; process workers, 74–7, 79–82, 91–100, 103–4, 123–4, 126,

136–9, 157–60, 180, 217–21
community attachment, viii, 13–14, 19, 36–7, 45, 63, 65–6, 223–8; among Birds employees, 151–4, 159–61, 163–4, 175–87, 198–201, 235
commuting, 21, 232; between Birmingham and Banbury, 118–19, 128, 130, 244, 245
conurbations, vii, ix, 1–8 17, 20, 39, 152, 227, 235; *see also* Birmingham, Glasgow, Liverpool and London
Cotgrove, S., 60, 98
Crawley, 30
Crossman, E. R. F. W., 53, 75, 216
Cullingwoth, J. B., 9, 10, 18, 20–5, 31–2, 145, 172, 182–6, 229, 233
Cumbernauld, 22, 31
Cutriss, C. H., 30, 144

Dalton, M., 47
Daniel, W. W., 37, 61, 63, 125
Dennis, N., 25, 224
Department of Employment and Productivity, 70, 85, 88–90, 113, 211
Department of Scientific and Industrial Research, 53
dependence upon employment, ix, 14, 38–9, 40–53, 57–67, 228; at Birds, 91, 94–5, 102–4, 124–5, 134–43, 150, 163–4, 194, 215–21; dependence upon work, 14, 40, 42, 50–2.
development districts, 2–6, 105, 111, 228
Dobriner, W. N., 22, 175
Doeringer, P. B., 49, 61, 217
Dubin, R., 40–1
Dunning, J. H., 28, 30, 33, 228
Durham, 23, 230

East Anglia Economic Planning Council, 8, 238
Economist Intelligence Unit, 5, 6, 7, 35
Elias, N. (and Scotson, J. L.), 198–9
Etzioni, A., 41, 101, 215
Everitt, G. F., 228
Eversley, D. E. C., 5, 6

family, life-cycle, 9–10, 18, 25, 27, 30, 38, 46–7, 59, 186; structure (extended, nuclear), 19–25, 63, 65–6, 223–6, 236; structure of Birds employees, 155–62, 167, 176, 181–7, 225
Field, D., 3
Firth, R. *et al.* 24
foremen at Birds, 127, 135, 190–3

Fox, A., 34, 37–8, 116–17, 212
fringe benefits, 50, 52–3, 62, 216, 222;
  at Birds, 70, 87–90, 113, 125, 189
Fullan, M., 55

Gans, H. J., 22–3
Gavron, H., 184, 224
General Foods Corporation, U.S.A., 108,
  111, 113, 228
Glasgow, 18, 19
Gloucester, 229–30, 250
Goldthorpe, J. H. *et al*, 41, 44–6, 56, 63,
  90, 100–1, 141, 214–15, 224
Gordon, M. S. and McCorry, A. H., 27,
  36, 240
Government Social Survey, 12, 15
Guardian, The 34

Hall, P., 1, 4, 5, 22, 183
Hammond, E., 169, 185, 230
Harvard Business School, 108, 111
Haverhill, 28
Hemel Hempstead, 28
Heraud, B. J., 32
Hole, V., 33
Hollowell, P., 43
'household splitting', 32, 233, 237
housing, condition and tenure, 10–11,
  15–22, 30–1, 38–9, 65, 145, 226–8; of
  Birds employees, 108–10, 113–14, 116,
  117–18, 131–2, 138, 143–50, 163,
  168–71, 226–9
Hubert, J., 24
Hunt Committee, 6
Hunter, L. C. and Reid, G. L., 44

Industrial Selection Scheme, 3, 27, 29,
  31–2, 106, 110, 237, 243
Ingham, G. K., 44, 46
instrumentalism, 40–2, 44–7, 151, 59, 60,
  63–5, 214–15

Jackson, J. N., 21
Jansen, C., 9, 41, 145, 155, 159
Jefferys, M., 26–7, 211
Jephcott, P., 20
job satisfaction, 40, 42, 50, 53–7, 60–2,
  70–1, 216, 219; at Birds, 90–1, 96–102,
  187–94, 214, 217; and relocation
  decisions at Birds, 131–3, 215

Kahn, H. R., 44–5, 210–11
Karpik, L., 45
Klein, J., 157–8

labour market, internal, ix, 48–53, 58–62,
  66–7, 76–7, 82–3, 92–4, 215, 217–21;
  external, 42–53, 57–62, 66–7, 220
Lerner, S. W. and Marquand, J., 85
Lipset, S. M. *et al*, 57
Litwak, E., 24, 160, 186, 225
Liverpool, 14, 19, 22, 229, 250; University
  of, 19, 260

Loasby, B., 7, 37
Location of Offices Bureau, 5, 6, 7, 14,
  15, 35, 170, 185, 238–9
London, 1, 5–6, 12, 14, 17, 18, 21, 24, 27,
  29, 30, 37, 230, 235; overspill to
  Banbury, 106, 109–10, 121, 178–83,
  187–8, 196–201, 243; Greater London
  Development Plan, 6, 17–18
Luton, 41, 46, 63, 206
Luttrell, W. F., 34

McCarthy, W. E. J., 58, 80, 84
maintenance workers, *see* skilled workers
Mallet, S., 220
Mann, F. C. and Hoffman, L. R., 63
Mann, M., 40, 43, 220, 250
Mercer, D. E. and Weir, D. T. H., 46
Milton Keynes, 2, 230
Ministry of Housing and Local
  Government, 5
Ministry of Labour, *see* Department of
  Employment
mobility, geographical, 8–18, 45–6, 63–4,
  157, 160–1, 223, 228; social, 45–6, 63–4,
  92–4, 136–7
Mogey, J. M. 185
Morris, R. N. and Mogey, J., 199
Moss, J. A., 198
Mott, P. E. *et al*, 44, 47, 63

Naville, P., 53, 60, 216–17
new and expanded towns, vii, 2–8, 26–34,
  109–10, 176, 198, 228–30, 239–41
Nicholson, J. H., 29, 182
non-manual workers, 10–17, 25, 32, 62–3,
  213, 215, 223–6, 230; at Birds, 70–4,
  102–3, 107, 115, 119, 134–5, 149, 157–60,
  180, 190, 209, 222, 225, 245–7; groups,
  rivalries among, 71–4, 102, 119–20,
  191–4, 232–3
Northampton, 2

Organisation for Economic Co-operation
  and Development, 37, 46, 72
orientation to work, 43–7, 56, 67, 223
Orzack, L. H., 40–1
overspill policies, vii–ix, 1–8, 14, 18–25,
  187, 235–41

Pahl, R., 175
Palmer, G. *et al*, 50–2, 65, 141
Park, R. E. *et al*, 226
Peterborough, 2, 43, 230
Plowman, D. E. G. *et al*, 226
Political and Economical Planning,
  72–3, 102
promotion, *see* labour market, internal
Purcell, T. V., 126

race, 36, 144, 153–4, 163–4, 224, 226–7,
  239–41
Raimon, R. L., 59
Rankin, N. H., 22

Rees, A. and Schultz, G. P., 49
relocation, of factories and offices, vii,
    ix, 1–8, 34–7, 233–41; decisions of
    employees, vii, 3, 7–8, 14, 26–38, 52,
    62–6, 116–17, 229–32; of Birds, vii, 39,
    105–28; decisions of Birds employees,
    66–7, 74, 107, 115, 129–64, 209, 213,
    215, 229, 234, 244–7; economic
    hardship of, 169–72, 205–6
Reynolds, L. G., 44, 49, 51
Rex, J. and Moore, R., 153, 226
Robinson, D., 52, 57
Rosser, C., and Harris, C., 19, 24–5, 185–6,
    223, 225
Rossi, P. H., 9
Royal Commission, on Local Government,
    152, 159, 161, 225; on Trade Unions,
    57

Scargill, D. I., 28
Scott, W. H. *et al.*, 80
security of Employment, 50–3, 60–1,
    216–19; at Birds, 87, 100, 122, 140–1,
    189–92, 208, 218, 234
Self, P., 1
Shankland, Cox and Associates, 31
shiftwork, 43, 47, 61, 63–4, 75, 85–6, 95,
    171, 189, 216
skilled workers, 16–18, 32, 51, 52, 54–5,
    57–8, 64; at Birds, 75, 78–9, 85–6,
    92–9, 106, 114, 119, 123, 136–9, 157–60,
    180, 221
Smith, B. M. D., 4, 7
Smith, C. S., 163
Smith, L. M. and Fowler, I. A., 36
Smith, W. H., Ltd., 31
Sofer, C., 12
South-East Joint Planning Team, 35
South Hampshire, 2, 230
Stacey, M., 165, 200
Stevenage, 31, 198, 206
Sunderland, 25, 224
Swansea, 12–13, 17, 19, 24–5
Swindon, 2, 3, 21–5, 28–9, 31, 105
Sykes, A. J. M. *et al.*, 22, 31, 238

Taylor, G. B., 28–9, 182, 198
Taylor, Lord and Chave, S., 22
Taylor, R. C., 23, 163, 185
technology, viii, 43, 53–67, 74–6, 92,
    103–4, 215–23, 228
Telford, 230

Thomas, R., 32–3
Touraine, A., 53–6, 61, 99, 214, 218, 220;
    and Ragazzi, O., 45
Town and Country Planning Association,
    7, 35
Townsend, P., 19
trade unions, 58, 219; at Birds, 77–84, 90,
    101, 103–4, 106, 109–10, 114, 119,
    120–7, 193, 222, 232
Trotman-Dickens, D. I., 6
Turner, A. N. and Laurence, P. R., 45
Turner, H. A. L. *et al.*, 45, 56, 141, 214,
    231

unemployment, 42, 59, 111, 202, 210–12;
    among Birds employees, 203–12

wages, 10, 41–9, 57–62, 216; at Birds, 70,
    78–81, 85–9, 91–2, 111, 121, 189–90,
    205, 208, 228
Walker, C. R. and Guest, R. H., 44
Watson, W., 10–12
Weber, A. R., 36, 52
Wedderburn, D., 26, 37–8, 53, 62, 88,
    206–7, 211–12, 216, 260; and
    Crompton, R., 60
Welford, A. T., 53
Wellingborough, 105
Westergaard, J. H., 5
West Midlands: conurbation, see
    Birmingham; Economic Planning
    Council, 4, 7, 238, 260; Planning
    Authorities, 4, 7, 240, 261
Weston-super-Mare, 105
Whitman, E. S. and Schmidt, W. J.,
    108
Whyte, W. F. *et al.*, 47
Whyte, W. H., 11
Wilensky, H. L., 46–7, 65–6, 160, 219,
    232
Williams, G., 57
Willmott, P., 31, 161, 176; and Young,
    M., 12–13
women workers, 35–6; at Birds, 70, 78,
    114, 127–8, 129, 131–2, 145, 150–1,
    158, 166, 180, 202–9, 244–5, 247
Woodford, 12–13, 17, 160–1
Woodward, J., 53–6, 99, 223
Worsley, 21–5

Young, M., and Willmott, P., 19–23, 161,
    182, 184–6

For EU product safety concerns, contact us at Calle de José Abascal, 56–1°,
28003 Madrid, Spain or eugpsr@cambridge.org.